What, exactly, do children understand about the mind? And when does that understanding first emerge? In this ground-breaking book, Karen Bartsch and Henry Wellman answer these questions and much more by taking a probing look at what children themselves have to tell us about their evolving conceptions of people and their mental lives. By examining more than 200,000 everyday conversations (sampled from ten children between the ages of two and five years), the authors advance a comprehensive "naive theory of mind" that incorporates both early desire and belief-desire theories to trace childhood development through its several stages. Throughout, the book offers a splendidly written account of extensive original findings and critical new insights that will be eagerly read by students and researchers in developmental psychology, cognitive psychology, philosophy, and psycholinguistics.

D0208169

CHILDREN TALK ABOUT THE MIND

CHILDREN TALK
ABOUT THE MIND

✳

KAREN BARTSCH
and HENRY M. WELLMAN

New York   Oxford
OXFORD UNIVERSITY PRESS
1995

Oxford University Press

Oxford   New York   Toronto
Delhi   Bombay   Calcutta   Madras   Karachi
Kuala Lumpur   Singapore   Hong Kong   Tokyo
Nairobi   Dar es Salaam   Cape Town
Melbourne   Auckland   Madrid

and associated companies in
Berlin   Ibadan

Copyright © 1995 by Oxford University Press, Inc.

Published by Oxford University Press, Inc.,
200 Madison Avenue, New York, New York 10016

Oxford is a registered trademark of Oxford University Press

Library of Congress Cataloging-in-Publication Data
Bartsch, Karen.
Children talk about the mind / Karen Bartsch and Henry M. Wellman.
p. cm.   Includes bibliographical references and index.
ISBN 0-19-508005-X
1. Knowledge, Theory of, in children.   I. Wellman, Henry M.
II. Title.
BF723.C5B27   1995
150'.83—dc20   94–8235

1 3 5 7 9 8 6 4 2

Printed in the United States of America
on acid-free paper

*To David, Daniel,
Daniel, and Ned*

ACKNOWLEDGMENTS

This book represents part of a continuing effort by a growing number of investigators to understand the basic nature of our everyday understanding of persons. How do we ordinarily conceive of each others' actions, thoughts, and lives? Our concern is not primarily how adults understand people, but how children develop such understandings in the first place. As adults, our understanding of persons seems to be fundamentally mentalistic. We construe people essentially in terms of the mental, psychological states that lie behind overt behavior and appearances, that is, in terms of the person's beliefs, desires, emotions, intentions. But what about children? When do they understand this basic mentalism? How do they conceive of persons' minds?

In this book we aim to answer these questions by carefully scrutinizing young children's everyday talk about persons and minds. The research began in 1988. Consequently, we have reported preliminary findings from the project in several prior presentations: Bartsch and Wellman (1989a, 1993), Bartsch (1990), Wellman (1991), and Wellman and Kalish (1991). The current volume extends these initial reports, provides a comprehensive picture of the entire project, and corrects any errors that may have appeared earlier.

Our research, and the book that has resulted from it, has been a fully collaborative project from initial inception to final writing and editing. Authorship, credit, and responsibilities have been equal; either of us could have been first author; the ordering of our names on the title page is alphabetical. Each of us wishes to begin, therefore, by thanking the other for the help, collegiality, insights, and patience that have been tendered and received.

Many other persons and institutions have contributed to this endeavor. We are especially grateful to Catherine Givens, Bill Bacon, and Mita Banerjee for their help with coding and organization in the early phases of the project. More recently Anne Hickling, Sheba Shakir, Michelle Hollander, Mary Reid Stanley, and Geoff Turner have provided invaluable assistance. The research has been continuously funded by grant HD-22149 to Henry Wellman from the National Institute of Child Health and Human Development, and it also received support from the Center for Study of Child and Adolescent Development at Pennsylvania State University to Karen Bartsch. We gratefully acknowledge the help of these institutions. Writing of the manuscript began when Henry Wellman was a fellow at the Center for Advanced Study in the Behavioral Sciences, receiving support from the center and from the MacArthur Foundation. The opportunity for a fellowship year at the center was critical to completion of the project.

Completion of the project has taken several years. Our home departments and universities have provided continuing support and encouragement during this time:

the Departments of Psychology at the University of Wyoming and at Pennsylvania State University for Bartsch, and the Department of Psychology as well as the Center for Human Growth and Development of the University of Michigan for Wellman. We are grateful, moreover, to the colleagues who have read and helpfully commented on earlier versions of the book and who have discussed these ideas and issues with us—Alison Gopnik, Paul Harris, John Flavell, Lou Moses, Simon Baron-Cohen, Chris Moore, Pat Smiley, Marilyn Shatz, Josef Perner, David Estes, and Michael Chandler, among others.

Finally, but foremost, this research would have been impossible in conception and execution without the existence of the Child Language Data Exchange System (CHILDES) organized by Brian MacWhinney and Catherine Snow and supervised by Brian MacWhinney at Carnegie Mellon University. The CHILDES is a unique data base that represents a collaborative pooling of child language transcripts from a great many selfless investigators world wide. We are particularly indebted to Brian MacWhinney for all his help and energy, and to the investigators who contributed the original transcripts we have exploited in our analyses: Roger Brown, Stan Kuczaj, Jacqui Sachs, Lois Bloom, Brian MacWhinney, and Catherine Snow. And, although we have not even met most of them, we are grateful to the children and families who participated in the research.

Laramie, Wyo.   K. B.
Ann Arbor, Mich.   H. M. W.
April 1994

CONTENTS

CHILDREN TALK ABOUT THE MIND

1

Children, Mind, and Language: An Introduction

Mark at 3 years, 10 months

MARK: When I was going outside, I thought there was a snake on the ground. But there was . . . there wasn't really a snake.

FATHER: No. It was just fake.

MARK: I thought there was a real snake.

FATHER: Just a toy snake.

MARK: Nah-uh. I just thought there was a snake. There was no . . . snake, real snake. There was no toy snake.

FATHER: No snake at all.

MARK: Uh-uh.

FATHER: Oh well. That's too bad isn't it?

MARK: Too bad a snake?!

FATHER: Too bad no snake. Because we like snakes, right? Do you like snakes?

MARK: Yeah. I thought there was a snake.

Adults often talk about the mind. Sometimes we talk about the mind directly: "It slipped my mind." "He must have lost his mind." More often we talk about the contents of our minds, that is, about someone's mental states and activities: "He thinks that there is life on Mars." "I just imagined it." "She was daydreaming." This sort of talk is shaped by and reveals our understanding of persons' internal mental lives. Not only do adults talk about the mind, so do children. The conversation that begins this chapter provides one example. Children's talk about the mind reveals their thoughts about this intriguing subject, just as adult talk reveals adult thinking. But what, exactly, do children understand about the mind, and when does an understanding of mind first emerge? In this volume we attempt to answer this question. In constructing our answer, we advance three arguments and provide extensive new findings to use in forging a comprehensive account of children's developing theories of mind.

The first argument is that children's understanding of the mind is important. This is a conviction we share with a growing number of scholars. The second is that despite mounting empirical studies, we are still far from understanding when children know what about the mind. There is a need, therefore, for new data and a comprehensive account. Our third argument is that these needs can be addressed by turning to a little-explored source of information on children's understanding of mind—their everyday talk about the mind. In this chapter, we outline these arguments by way of setting the stage for the rest of the book.

The Importance and Nature of an Everyday Understanding of Mind

Interest in what children think and say about the mind is spreading among a growing number of researchers who address what has come to be called the "child's theory of mind" (see Astington, Harris, & Olson, 1988; Baron-Cohen, Tager-Flusberg, & Cohen, 1993; Lewis & Mitchell, in press; Perner, 1991; Wellman, 1990). Why is this topic receiving such increased scrutiny? The importance of "theory of mind" stems, essentially, from its role in our ordinary understanding of people. This understanding can be called our everyday, commonsense, or lay psychology. Research on everyday psychology attempts to characterize how people understand each other's actions, thoughts, and lives—understanding our understanding of ourselves. The realm of everyday psychology constitutes, we believe, a foundational domain of human understanding; it is one of the three or four most basic topics that humans think and learn about (Wellman & Gelman, 1992).

The phrase "theory of mind" nicely emphasizes that our ordinary understanding of people is mentalistic. Adults, in our society at least, assume that people possess minds; that is, we assume that behind the public world of physical bodies and manifest action there is for each individual a unique mental world of thoughts, hopes, ideas, intentions, and emotions. Here is an elegant example from Gabriel Garcia Marquez's novel, *Love in the Time of Cholera*:

> In Paris, strolling arm in arm with a casual sweetheart through a late autumn, it seemed impossible to *imagine* a purer happiness than those golden afternoons, with the woody odor of chestnuts on the braziers, the languid accordions, the insatiable lovers kissing on the open terraces, and still he had told himself with his hand on his heart that he was not prepared to exchange all that for a single instant of his Caribbean in April. He was still too young to *know* that the heart's *memory* eliminates the bad and magnifies the good, and that thanks to this artifice we manage to endure the burden of the past. But when he stood at the railing of the ship (upon his return to the Caribbean) and saw the white promontory of the colonial district again, the motionless buzzards on the roofs, the washing of the poor hung out to dry on the balconies, only then did he *understand* to what extent he had been an easy victim to the charitable *deceptions* of nostalgia. (1988, p. 105-6, emphases ours)

In this passage we are given an explanation for why one of the protagonists, Dr. Urbino, has returned home to the Caribbean from Paris, and his reaction upon returning. Because he has nostalgically misremembered the charms of his homeland, he returns. But upon returning, Urbino finds something quite different from what he expected. He has fooled himself—a disappointed "victim to the charitable deceptions of nostalgia." This text illustrates a construal of persons as having imaginations, memories, misunderstandings, and the capacity to be deceived. This construal is basic to our everyday psychology, our social communications, our abilities to make sense of ourselves and others.

As this passage also shows, people's thoughts, memories, intentions, and emotions are intimately interrelated; they cohere in certain ways, accounting for and determining one another. Because an actor has certain beliefs, false or true, he or she attempts to engage in certain actions, the success or failure of which result in various emotional reactions. Urbino's false memories cause him to return to the Caribbean, leading to disappointment. The phrase "theory of mind" emphasizes the coherence of our everyday mentalistic construal of people and action by likening it to a theory.

This ordinary theory, however, is not theoretical in the sense of being removed from practical application in our lives. To the contrary, here are a few applications of our everyday psychology: you want to make someone happy, so you give her something she wants; you want to keep something that someone else also wants, so you deceive him into falsely believing you no longer have it; you know something that someone else does not, so you tell her. As in these examples, our everyday interactions are founded on consideration of people's wants, beliefs, knowledge, and emotions. As a contrast, consider how differently we would interact with one another if we were behaviorists instead of mentalists, attempting to classically or operantly condition one another's behavior, manipulating and arranging stimuli and responses rather than manipulating and assessing beliefs and desires. The expression "theory of mind" endeavors to characterize the understanding of people that frames and determines our everyday social world and our social acts.

An assumption of mind so saturates our everyday thinking that its importance can often be overlooked, like the proverbial importance of water to fish. So it is helpful to have an initial outline of the theory, to highlight the nature of our basic mentalism against the backdrop of our many thoughts and statements about people. In fact, it can be argued that beyond its general mentalistic character, everyday psychological reasoning has a discernible structure or form. How to characterize that form is debatable, but a useful and often adopted approach is to characterize our everyday psychology as largely a "belief-desire" understanding of mind and action. In describing our everyday mentalism in terms of beliefs and desires, beliefs are meant to refer to a general category of thoughts encompassing knowledge, opinions, guesses, convictions, and hunches, that is, all mental states that attempt to reflect something true about the world. More broadly, thoughts include not only serious beliefs but also fanciful ideas, states of imagination, and dreams—mental states that represent fictional worlds. Desires are also to be understood as a general category including wants, urges, and states of caring about something; that is, a whole range of "pro-attitudes" toward or about something (Davidson, 1963).

The underlying structure of our commonsense conception of mind requires consideration of both desires and beliefs. People do things because they *desire* something and *believe* some act will achieve it. Urbino desired a certain sort of life, one that he believed was available in and characteristic of his homeland. So he tried to recapture it. Such a belief-desire explanation of Urbino's action is more than a mere convention or re-description; it is satisfactory. When we learn about Urbino's ideas and feelings in this fashion, we feel we have gained a genuine understanding of his behavior and of his psyche.

According to this sort of analysis, then, at the center of a theory of mind is a conceptual triad of constructs: actions, beliefs, and desires. But beyond this triad, belief-desire reasoning can be quite complicated and can include a host of auxiliary notions. Consider the following example: Why did Jill go to the basement at her uncle's cabin? Well, she was tired and wanted to nap. And she thought she'd seen a nice quiet couch in the basement. Boy, is she going to be disappointed. Belief-desire psychology incorporates a network of related constructs such as physiological states (she was tired), perceptions (she'd seen a couch in the basement), and emotional reactions (she'll be disappointed). A scheme for depicting some of the links between these related elements and the core constructs is shown in Figure 1.1.

According to this figure, and according to our everyday psychology, physiological states and emotions can be said to ground one's desires. Beliefs, however, are often grounded in perceptual experience. Thus physiological states, emotions, and perceptions shape one's actions; they do so indirectly by molding one's desires and framing one's beliefs. Actions, of course, lead to discernible outcomes in the world, and these outcomes in turn can provoke reactions of predictable sorts. At least two basic sorts of reactions are encompassed by the theory: reactions dependent on desires, and reactions dependent on beliefs. As an example of the former, the outcome of an action can satisfy or fail to satisfy the actor's desires. If you want something and you get it, you are happy; if you want it and don't get it, you are sad or angry. Recall Urbino's disappointment on returning to the Caribean. But the outcome of an action can also match or fail to match an actor's beliefs (or expectations). If the actor thinks something will happen and it does not, he or she is surprised or puzzled. Urbino is surprised about how things look to him, or perhaps more correctly, surprised that he could have misremembered so egregiously.

The peripheral constructs in this scheme—perceptions, emotions, physiological states, and more—are part of the web of psychological constructs used to understand and explain action and mind. According to this analysis, however, they are centrally organized by consideration of the actor's thoughts and desires. These two sorts of generic mental states are, of course, internal and unobservable. But unobservable mental states can often be inferred from the actor's perceptual experiences (e.g., what he or she sees), from physiological history (e.g., how long it has been since the actor has slept or eaten), and from emotional expressions and reactions (e.g., a smile or a yelp of surprise), as well as from what the actor does (his or her actions). Thus, another example of the coherence of our everyday mentalism is that the presence and nature of various states are discernible in part because of their role in a coherent array of other states and events.

This brief description of our theory of mind, our everyday belief-desire psychology, is amplified in several more comprehensive accounts (e.g. Bratman, 1987; D'Andrade, 1987; Wellman, 1990) and we will add to it at several places later in this book. For the moment, however, this theory sketch is sufficient to begin to question when and how children adopt this everyday mentalism.

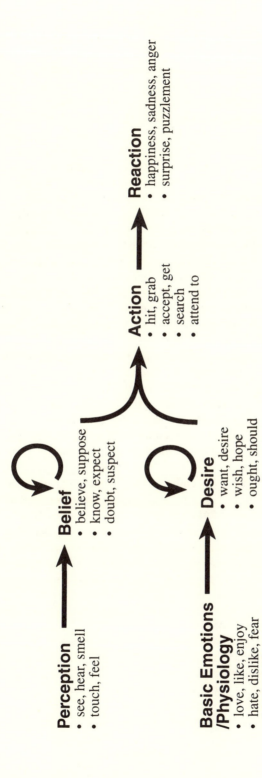

Figure 1.1. A scheme for depicting belief-desire psychological reasoning.

7

Children's Developing Theories of Mind

Even before examining children's conceptions, we can outline several possible answers to the question of when children acquire a theory of mind. One possibility is that children share our adult perspective, construing human action in terms of underlying mental states, such as beliefs and desires, from infancy. Alternatively, perhaps infants and children do not see the world of human action and interaction in mentalistic terms at all, and such mentalism must be acquired in the course of childhood development. If so, two further possibilities emerge with regard to children's understanding about the mind before they adopt an adult perspective.

One possibility here is that young children are at first simply ignorant about the mind, blank slates that become filled with an understanding of beliefs, thoughts, desires, and actions, as they grow older. The other possibility is that even very young children possess their own definite conception of human behavior, but a conception that is distinctly different from our adult mentalistic one, and one that must be replaced or substantially revised in the course of development. From the point of view of our pervasive adult theory of mind, it is difficult to imagine a conception of human action and life that is not mentalistic. However, consider classical behaviorism again. From the perspective of behaviorism, human action can be understood solely in terms of the overt properties of observable behaviors, the external features of environmental stimuli, and functional relations between the two, such as the temporal pattern of contingencies between behavior and stimuli in the prior history of the organism. Notions of internal mental states are carefully excluded from such psychologizing. Behaviorism, then, exemplifies one way in which human action might be interpreted without recourse to notions like beliefs and desires. Perhaps young children are first behaviorists, focusing on the overt aspects of behavior and environment, and only develop into mentalists later in life.

These abstract possibilities are embodied in several competing accounts of development in this domain. The first possibility, that children adopt a belief-desire conception from the start, is endorsed in certain nativist proposals about acquisition of a theory of mind. "Here is what I would have done if I had been faced with this problem in designing Homo sapiens. I would have made a knowledge of commonsense Homo sapiens psychology innate. And I would have made this innately apprehended commonsense psychology (at least approximately) true" (Fodor, 1987, p. 132).

Alternatively, perhaps theory of mind must be learned and constructed by the child, based on observation of self and others as well as on direct or indirect instruction in what to look at or in how to interpret human acts. Jean Piaget (1929) advocated a general constructivist position and, moreover, believed that acquisition of a mentalistic understanding of human action occurred quite late in development, only beginning to appear at about 6 or 7 years of age. Other accounts have been advanced more recently (e.g., Leslie, 1987; Perner, 1991; Wellman, 1990); we will consider several of these in detail in later chapters, as well as presenting an account of our own.

Any of these possibilities, however, generates interest in studying more precisely just what children do understand about the mind and when. Even if innate, theory of mind may undergo development; there may be an early age when this sort of thinking about people is absent, followed by a time when it is triggered and emerges. Whether young children are innately belief-desire mentalists, are ignorant, or are subscribers to an alternative naive psychology, it is important to chart the developmental steps in children's understanding of the mind.

The Need for Further Research

If this topic is so important, and the questions so fascinating, then it would seem that someone must have studied them, and answered them, before now. Indeed, as long ago as Piaget's earliest research (1929), children's understanding of the mind has been studied empirically. And much recent research has readdressed the questions of when children know what about our everyday mentalism. Despite mounting empirical studies, however, we are still far from understanding children's developing knowledge about the mind. There are gaps, contradictions, and significant shortcomings in our understanding. What researchers now agree on is that the development of a comprehensive view of conceptions and developments within a child's life is an important goal.

Briefly, here are some of the current problems to be overcome. Most of the research on the developing understanding of mind has focused on children's understanding of a narrow range of mental states, essentially beliefs (see, e.g., Astington et al., 1988; Butterworth et al., 1991; Frye & Moore, 1991). Why so? One reason is that an adequate understanding of beliefs manifests two very important features of mind in our everyday understanding: the mind represents the world, and the mind influences action. Urbino's beliefs about his Caribbean homeland encompass his internalized representations of this part of the world; beliefs are attempts to reflect the real world. Moreover, because Urbino believes (rather than imagines or pretends) that his homeland is an especially delightful place, he returns. Understanding the relationships between beliefs and the real world requires a conception of mind as representational; children must come to understand that people act with regard to their beliefs about the world, not with regard to the world directly. These properties of mind are nicely manifest in the case of false beliefs (Urbino's belief contrasts with the fact that his homeland is squalid and unappealing). In the case of false beliefs, it is clear that a person's action is determined by his or her representation of the world rather than by reality itself. For this reason, considerable attention, empirical and theoretical, has been paid to children's understanding of belief generally and false belief more specifically.

However, existing studies lead to conflicting conclusions as to when and how children understand beliefs. Utilizing different experimental methods (and perhaps different definitions of "understanding" the concept), researchers have variously concluded that children acquire the concept of belief by 2 years of age (e.g., Chandler, Fritz, & Hala, 1989), at 3 years (e.g., Bartsch & Wellman, 1989b; Mitchell & Lacohee, 1991; Moses, 1993; Siegal & Beattie, 1991; Wellman & Bartsch, 1988), and not until at least 4 years (e.g., Gopnik & Astington, 1988; Moses &

Flavell, 1990; Perner, Leekam, & Wimmer, 1987; Sodian, Taylor, Harris, & Perner, 1991; Wimmer & Perner, 1983).

What are we to make of these different results? Making sense of them is hard in part because the findings come from very different experimental tasks. Do the seemingly discrepant findings reflect method differences, or do they signal developments in children's understanding of belief? For the moment, this question is unanswered because there is little if any extant research that examines a sequence of developments with a method that can be used across the entire sequence.

However, even if the story about children's understanding of beliefs were clear, it would be incomplete. What about desires? What the actor believes (Urbino's thoughts about his homeland) frames action, but what the actor desires (Urbino wants to recapture prior glories) motivates action. Both beliefs and desires figure centrally in our ordinary understanding of actions and states of mind. For this reason, the study of children's understanding of desires, along with beliefs, is necessary. But unlike research into children's grasp of belief, research into children's understanding of desire has only recently begun (e.g., Astington & Gopnik, 1991; Wellman & Woolley, 1990). From even these initial studies the possibility has emerged that children may achieve a useful and sensible understanding of desire well before any comparable understanding of belief. This remains a tantalizing hypothesis, however, because devising comparable methods to study early understandings of desire along with belief poses at least as many problems as devising methods to study belief alone.

In addition to being riddled with contradictory claims and missing data, extant research on children's understanding of belief and desire is limited in other troubling ways. One concern is the almost exclusive reliance on experimental tasks in which various actions are presented to children and they are asked to reason about the actor (How will the actor act? What does he want? What does he think?). Converging data from alternative methods and analyses are needed to corroborate or revise the current picture. Another concern is ecological validity: Do children normally predict or explain human action in terms of desires and beliefs? Research based on experimental tasks that require children to reason in terms of these constructs does not tell us much about a child's everyday conceptions—how often and in what ways children use concepts of belief and desire in their reasoning. A final concern is that much of our knowledge is patched together from bits and pieces of data representing a great number of children of different ages. Does the admittedly sketchy picture of development that emerges from experimental studies of groups of different-aged children reflect the changes that any one child might undergo? Longitudinal data are clearly desirable.

A New Look at Children's Conceptions of Mind

Each of these concerns can be addressed by turning to another source of information on children's conceptual development: their everyday talk. We know from a few preliminary studies that children appear to talk about beliefs and desires in their everyday conversations, beginning at an early age. Use of words like *want,* which adults use to talk about desires, is evident in children's speech by age 2 (Bretherton & Beeghly, 1982). Words like *think, know,* and *guess,* which adults use to talk about beliefs, appear before age 3 (Shatz, Wellman, & Silber, 1983). However, children's understanding of and reasoning about both beliefs and desires has never, to our knowledge, been the focus of a comprehensive natural language investigation. Yet there are reasons to view this line of inquiry as a fruitful and practical alternative approach. First, it seems fruitful because the activities and states of people are frequent topics of young children's conversation. For example, Hood and Bloom (1979) report that in their everyday conversations even 2-year-olds often attempt to explain why people do things. Similarly, Dunn, Bretherton, and Munn (1987) found that by 2 years of age, a majority of children referred to a range of internal states in themselves and others, and discussed the cause of such states in a variety of everyday contexts. People's actions and reactions figure substantially in young children's talk.

A comprehensive natural language investigation also seems quite feasible because longitudinal samples of children's everyday conversations exist, perhaps offering just the right sort of data. A dense and plentiful sample of the everyday talk from children could provide the needed naturally occurring, longitudinal information. Moreover, informative methods exist for the analysis of everyday speech, methods that can be applied in a comparable and systematic fashion to children of younger and older ages, and to talk about desire as well as belief. We describe these methods and our extensions to them in the next chapter.

In the chapters following Chapter 2, we pursue a comprehensive investigation of children's talk about the mind in order to address questions about children's developing understanding of mind. As follows from a characterization of ordinary mentalism as a belief-desire psychology, we have concentrated on children's talk about beliefs, thoughts, and desires. Our database is more than 200,000 child utterances that yield almost 12,000 child conversations about the mind using such everyday terms as *think, know,* and *want* to talk about beliefs and desires. The data come from 10 children studied longitudinally from about 1½ to 6 years of age. The data are not only methodologically useful, they are fascinating; they provide a revealing window onto the everyday but often opaque world of early childhood, and into young children's understanding of persons and minds.

Themes That Organize Our Investigations

When we consider current research and thinking about children's theories of mind, in addition to the general arguments outlined thus far, several more specific questions about children's understandings and misunderstandings emerge. These questions have guided our investigation and therefore deserve some advance mention. The major questions can be organized around five distinctions encompassed in our everyday understanding of mind:

> Objective versus subjective states
>
> Connections versus representations

Fictional versus epistemic mental states

Beliefs versus desires

One's own mental states versus those of others

Subjective versus Objective

First, there is an important and somewhat obvious distinction between internal subjective states and external objective phenomena. When, as adults, we talk about mental states such as beliefs and desires, we are talking about internal subjective experiences of the person, not objective aspects of the world. Take desires as an example: "John wants an apple." When we say this, we mean that John is in the grips of wanting the apple, longing for it, preferring it, desiring it. We see the wanting as in the subject, John, not somehow a property of the object, the apple. Nor do we mean that the "wanting" is objective in the sense of being equated with John's acting to get the apple. We know that John may want the apple but may not, for whatever reason, act to get it. Desires, we ordinarily believe, are subjective states. A corollary of this everyday conception is that desires are specific to individuals. Another fellow, Bill, may not want the apple; he may even wish to avoid it. Specific desires are subjective experiences, as depicted in Figure 1.2A. That sort of subjective conception can be contrasted with a parallel objective construal. An objective misconstrual of desires might depict, for example, that wanting inheres somehow in the object. Some objects are simply attractive and some are not. We will call this sort of misconception about desires "object magnetism"

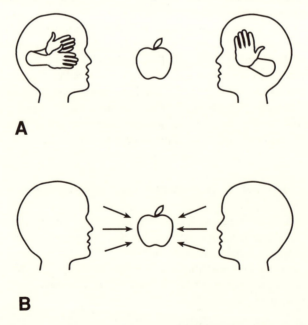

Figure 1.2. Depiction of subjective mental states (A) and an objective misconstrual of mental states, object magnetism (B).

(Fig. 1.2B). This view would hold that apples are attractive objects; they exert that attraction, objectively, on whoever is around.

One possibility regarding children's developing conceptions is that children might move from an objective understanding of behavior—a view that the world affects all persons uniformly—to a more subjective account. Something like this hypothesis is apparent in Piaget's writings (1929) and in more recent proposals that children's first understanding of desires specifically, and mental states more generally, is objective rather than subjective (Astington & Gopnik, 1991; Perner, 1991). Thus, the question arises of whether young children's understanding of human behavior proceeds from an objective to a subjective character, and whether there is some young age when children's understanding of persons is wholly (mistakenly) objective.

Subjective Connections versus Representations

Understanding the subjective, as opposed to objective, nature of mental states does not exhaust an adult conception. A subjective understanding can be contrasted with an understanding of mental states as representations. One way to capture this contrast is by depicting a difference between simple desires and ordinary beliefs, as seen in Figure 1.3.

Our ordinary conception of beliefs is that beliefs are representational in a vague but important sense. Attributing to someone the thought, "That object is an apple," involves construing that person as representing an apple in his mind, something like in Figure 1.3. We do not conceive of beliefs as literally pictures in the head, but nonetheless we do see them as encompassing representational mental content of some kind. But note how that construal contrasts with at least a very crude or simple concept of desire. Simple desires, in the sense we are depicting them here, could require no attribution to the target person of a representation. According to this simple conception, to understand that "he wants an apple" is to attribute to the other a subjective connection to an external object, but not necessarily to attribute to the other anything like an internal cognitive representation of the object. One can imagine, therefore, a distinction between certain mental states that can be construed as providing a subjective connection (to borrow John Flavell's terminology) between a person and an objective state

A   **B**

Figure 1.3. Depiction of a person's (A) desire and (B) belief. Desire is portrayed in simple connection terms, and belief is portrayed as a representation.

of affairs, and other mental states that are construed as a person representing an external state of affairs.

Another possibility regarding conceptual development, therefore, is that children go from understanding subjective connections to a later understanding of representational mental states. Indeed, several researchers (Flavell, 1988; Perner, 1988, 1991; Wellman, 1990) have suggested that children's first understanding of mental states is nonrepresentational in some form or another. One question, then, concerns when young children begin to conceive of mental states as representations.

Fictional versus Epistemic Mental States

It is possible to conceive of representational mental states—fictional imaginings, say (Fig. 1.4A)—that have no connection to states of the world at all; they are fictional or hypothetical, not intended to represent the world, although they are representational in the sense that they encompass internal mental content that depicts an imaginary, not-real state of affairs. Such hypothetical or fictional representational mental states contrast with our ordinary representational understanding of belief. As depicted in Figure 1.4B, beliefs attempt to truthfully represent the world. It is not that beliefs always do correctly represent the world, because they may misrepresent, but beliefs *intend* to reflect the world. Put another way, they are mental state descriptions designed to describe construals reflecting the world.

The epistemic quality of some mental states, like ordinary beliefs, serves to make such states causally influential in the world in two different but interwoven fashions. First, mental states such as belief often causally originate from interaction with the world, specifically from perception. Because John sees the apple, he believes it is there. In contrast, mental states with hypothetical or fictional content do not originate directly from perceptions; they are made up or invented. Second, mental states such as beliefs are supposed to refer to or be reflections of the world. They may fail in the task (e.g., be false beliefs), but they purport to and attempt to reflect the world. Fictional mental states have no such aim. Thus, mental states differ in being epistemic and serious versus fictional and fanciful.

One possibility regarding conceptual development, therefore, is that children might first understand imaginary mental representations and only later understand epistemic representations, or vice versa. Leslie (1988) and Olson, Astington, and

A   **B**

Figure 1.4. Depiction of fictional mental representations (A), and epistemic mental representations (B).

Harris (1988) hypothesize that children first conceive of all representational mental states as being hypothetical or fictional but not epistemic or causal.

Beliefs versus Desires

Of obvious import is the distinction between beliefs and desires themselves. Our belief-desire psychology rests on an understanding of two very different sorts of mental states. Beliefs can explain, for example, why two people with identical desires—both want an apple—might do different things: one thinks that there is an apple in the refrigerator and one does not, so one goes to the refrigerator, the other to the store. Desires can account for why two people with the same belief— that an apple is in the refrigerator—might do different things: one wants an apple and one does not, so one goes to the refrigerator and the other does not.

One important way in which beliefs and desires contrast concerns what Searle (1983) has termed their "direction of fit." If I have a desire (to watch TV) that proves discrepant from reality (the TV is off), I typically attempt to change the world to fit my desire (e.g., I turn on the TV). The direction of fit is from mind to world. In contrast, if I have a belief (e.g., the TV is on) that proves discrepant from reality (e.g., that the TV is off), I change my belief (e.g., I now think the TV is off). The direction of fit is from world to mind. One consequence of this difference is that descriptions of desires often seem to focus more on a person's internal mental states—my desire (for TV)—while descriptions of beliefs may often focus more systematically on the world—(my belief that) the TV is on.

Our commonsense psychology tells us (in this culture, at least) that beliefs and desires are different sorts of things, and even this quick discussion suggests that those differences might at times be profound. It is possible, therefore, that children might understand either desires before beliefs, or beliefs before desires. In fact, several recent investigations (Astington & Gopnik, 1991; Flavell, Green, & Moses 1990; Wellman, 1990) have suggested that children understand desires before beliefs.

Own versus Other Minds

As adults, we think and talk about our own mental states and those of others as well. As subjective states, mental states are specific to different individuals (he wants an apple and she doesn't) but we attribute the same general sort of states, beliefs and desires, to everyone. At the same time, we claim to have a unique first-person vantage point on our own states. We experience directly something about our states, whereas we must deal more indirectly with those of others.

It is possible that children first conceive of and talk exclusively about their own mental states, those they experience first-hand. If so, children's first conceptualizations of other persons may be solely in terms of their external, observable behaviors or characteristics. Huttenlocher, Smiley, and Charney (1983) advance such a hypothesis. Piaget's description of young children's egocentricism, as well as more recent claims about the primacy of first-person experience for children's understanding of the mind (Harris, 1989, 1991; Johnson, 1988), suggest that children

might move from an early conception of their own mental states to a later understanding of the minds of others. Alternatively, perhaps children acquire generic
conceptions of mental states applicable to all persons. If so, children's understanding of and talk about mental states might proceed similarly for themselves and for
others. Describing our everyday mentalistic construals of persons as a *theory* of
mind implies the existence of a system of terms and concepts used to understand
and to explain anyone's states of mind.

Summary

The several distinctions and possibilities just outlined have some interesting com-
plications and overlaps. For example, children might first understand desires as
being subjective, while still misunderstanding beliefs as objective. Yet a bit later,
children might come to understand beliefs as representational first, while adhering
to a nonrepresentational understanding of desire. Children might understand their
own thoughts as representations, but construe other persons' thoughts as being more
directly connected to the real world. Several theories, debates, and confusions currently revolve around these distinctions and children's developing abilities to han-
dle them. In presenting our findings, we consider children's understanding in
respect to these distinctions. This perspective allows us to assemble appropriate
evidence, provide an overview, and comprehensively and precisely portray children's understanding of mental life.

2

Language and Mind: Methods

Mark at 3 years, 11 months and Ross at 5 years, 9 months

> · MARK: Why did the chicken cross the road?
> ROSS: I don't know.
> MARK: Well, because his house always . . . always got . . . haunted.
> FATHER: Haunted? And he didn't like it?
> MARK: Yeah, he, he think . . . he thought there were haunted things in his house.

Our basic assumption is that children's talk about the mind can reveal their conceptions of the mind. Specifically, we assume that at least some uses of terms such as *think*, *know*, and *want* can reveal the speaker's understanding of beliefs and desires, core concepts in an everyday theory of mind. An example might be Mark's statement above that "he thought there were haunted things in his house." Of course, charting children's concepts by examining their everyday language is not simple. On the one hand, children (and adults) may use terms like *think*, *know*, or *want* without any conception of, or reference to, beliefs and desires. For example, they might learn to say "Know what?" to gain a listener's attention without any deeper understanding of notions such as knowledge or knowing. Or they might say "I don't know" in a ritualistic way, as perhaps Ross does above. On the other hand, children might understand something of beliefs and desires but never talk about them. Or they might talk about such mental states but never use conventional terms like *think* and *want*. In these ways, among others, children's language might underestimate or overestimate their understanding.

Even though language development does not map onto conceptual development in any strict sense, an analysis of discourse can nonetheless provide an important window onto conception. We intend to show that systematic examination of children's language provides considerable insight into children's understanding of beliefs and desires. At least it does so if appropriate data are available and careful methods of analysis are employed. This chapter, therefore, describes the dataset we have used and provides the rationale for and a general outline of our methods.

Verbal Methods

Most techniques that cognitive psychologists use to assess persons' knowledge, conceptions, and ability require language competence in some form or other: to

17

instruct the subject, to present the task or experimental materials, to signal the subject to respond, or to be the medium for response. In research on cognitive development, this dependence on language is often regarded as a flaw to be circumvented in some future ideal methodology. Legitimate concerns foster this view. Studies using Piagetian verbal interviews have been found repeatedly to underestimate young children's understanding (e.g., Donaldson, 1978; Gelman, Spelke, & Meck, 1983; Wellman & Estes, 1986). Moreover, recent critiques (e.g., Siegal, 1991) show that similar problems can confound even newer, improved experimental tasks with young children. And of course the study of infant cognition demands nonverbal methods.

But these concerns do not mean that it is possible, or desirable, to entirely eliminate verbal methods in favor of nonverbal ones. Humans acquire language and express themselves through it; this ability provides an important resource for investigating their minds. The crucial goal, therefore, is not the elimination of verbal methods, but the creation of insightful, carefully controlled methods of whatever sort possible. Cooking up insightful methods has no single recipe (such as reducing the verbal aspects of a task); it requires creative problem solving. Children's emerging ability to talk provides research opportunities and obstacles for methodological problem solving.

Observational Methods

In order to investigate children's understanding of the mind, we need access to their thoughts on the subject. In experimental tasks, this is typically achieved by focusing a child's attention on some mental phenomenon or other (e.g., dreams), and then eliciting her judgments, explanations, and understanding of that phenomenon. Especially with a young child, this general experimental approach can prove problematic, because the child is asked to think about a topic at a time and in ways that may not interest her, and to do so with an unfamiliar person (the experimenter). The experimenter is, in turn, unfamiliar with the child's typical way of talking and with her prior experiences, experiences that the child may well cite in order to respond to the experimental task and questions.

Everyday conversations between children and parents are often strikingly different in these regards. With her mother or father, a child may talk about things that interest or puzzle her at that time. In doing so, she is communicating with a partner who is familiar and inviting, who shares relevant past experiences, and who has extensive knowledge of the child's occasionally idiosyncratic pronunciations and discourse habits. The analysis of everyday conversation with parents thus seems a promising vehicle for capturing the child's earliest ideas. It was this general rationale that inspired traditional diary studies (e.g., Leopold, 1949; Stern & Stern, 1931).

But diary studies are prey to serious shortcomings. Diary samples are often haphazard, unrepresentative. The diarist is the child's parent, but also a person interested in a specific sort of phenomena and who, therefore, records only a limited, preselected set of events or speech. For these reasons, language acquisition researchers historically turned to the analysis of complete child speech samples collected systematically at regular intervals. For example, Brown (1973) and his colleagues collected language transcripts for several children, sampling a half to one hour of speech for each child approximately every two weeks for several years.

For the purpose of examining the content of children's ideas as opposed to the form of the child's language, standard language samples have their own limitations. One significant limitation is that talk about any one topic is likely to be infrequent. Whenever children talk, they reveal something of their syntactic competence, but they may seldom talk about any single subject, such as the mind. Past research, for example, shows that for children aged 2 to 4 years or so, speech containing common mental terms such as *think* and *know* occurs only about once in every 20 to 30 utterances (Shatz et al., 1983) and, of course, many such utterances are fragmented or uninterpretable. One purpose of experiments is to tackle this problem, that is, to make naturally infrequent phenomena more frequent (as well as more precisely interpretable) for refined analysis.

However, there is an alternative strategy. The problem of infrequent mention can also be solved by collecting very large samples of speech so that relatively infrequent occurrences are nonetheless abundantly represented. Collecting such extensive samples from an individual child provides the added advantage of a longitudinal record of change and sequence. Of course, considerable effort is required to collect sizable, systematic, longitudinal speech samples. Thus traditional language acquisition samples have been typically restricted to one (e.g., Kuczaj & Maratsos, 1975), two (e.g., Bowerman, 1978), or three (e.g., Brown, 1973) children. Information from so few children is not necessarily representative; the child may be precocious or otherwise atypical in what he chooses to talk about or how he chooses to say it.

With the establishment of the Child Language Data Exchange System (the CHILDES), researchers now have access to extensive, naturally occurring samples of speech from a sizable number of children (MacWhinney & Snow, 1985). In our project, we have taken advantage of this database to analyze the mental-term talk of 10 English-speaking children. Regular longitudinal transcripts were recorded for these children in the age period from 1½ to 6 years, yielding more than 200,000 systematically sampled child utterances. In the future, as this database increases, even larger samples will be available.

Exploiting this large database for our purposes posed certain problems in its own right, however. For example, if talk about the mind is consistent but infrequent, how were we to find it among all this discourse? We could have begun by reading every utterance, but this would have been an overwhelming task given the size of the initial speech samples. Nevertheless, we needed these large speech samples to capture sufficient numbers of mental term utterances. Fortunately, the CHILDES transcripts are computerized and so can be searched mechanically in various fashions. For example, it is possible to search for those utterances containing certain specified words or phrases which is the approach we have taken in the present investigation—identifying, as an initial entry into the data, conversations in which children use certain mental terms such as *think* or *want*.

If talk about a domain of conception typically occurs via certain words or phrases, then those terms provide natural markers for many (though of course not all) of the conversations of interest. For adults at least, talk about the mind, and especially about belief-desire mental states, often takes place through the use of a modest set of mental verbs such as *think*, *want*, and *know*. Obviously, we can also talk about mental states without using such terms; for example, one can inquire about someone's desires by saying, "What's she after?" Talk involving mental verbs does not exhaust references to beliefs and desires, but such words constitute our typical mode of communicating about the mind.

What about children? We know from preliminary research (e.g., Bretherton & Beeghly, 1982; Limber, 1973) that even very young children use mental verbs in their everyday conversation. Starting at about the second birthday or just before, words like *want* and *think* appear in the speech of normal children. To the extent that such early speech reflects talk about the mind, it can be examined in order to study children's conceptions. Does young children's use of such verbs represent early talk about the mind? Prior research by Shatz et al. (1983) suggests that it does. Moreover, Shatz's research outlines a set of general methods that permit careful analyses of children's conceptions. Our project began by employing and extending those methods.

Shatz, Wellman, and Silber's Research

Shatz and her colleagues (1983) examined children's use and comprehension of cognitive mental state terms such as *think*, *know,* and *remember*. Primarily, they examined the use of such cognitive terms by one child, sampled from the ages of 2½ to 4 years, using a two-pronged method. First, out of all utterances using such mental terms, they attempted to identify those in which the child was genuinely referring to internal mental states. This identification was necessary because, as we mentioned earlier, if adults often use terms such as *know* and *think* and *remember* without referring to mental states, then young children may do so exclusively. One such possibility concerns conversational uses. Initiating a conversation by saying, "*Know* what?" does not necessarily reflect an awareness of or reference to a person's state of knowledge; it may simply be a device to introduce a topic into the conversation. Another possibility concerns behavioral references. Children might use mental terms to refer only to observable behaviors, rather than to mental states. For example, a child might use the term *remember* to refer merely to acts of successful retrieval; "I remembered my gloves" might be equated simply with retrieving the gloves from the drawer. Another possibility concerns simple repetition of someone else's speech, mimicking an adult's terminology without really understanding its meaning. Shatz et al., therefore, weeded out conversational uses of mental terms, excluding possible behavioral uses of the terms or simple repetitions, and then identified uses that more convincingly seemed to refer to a mental state or activity.

Of course, even such carefully screened utterances may overattribute knowledge of mental states to young children. However, Shatz et al. (1983) additionally found that their focal child occasionally made very explicit remarks about mental states, in which he compared a person's mental state with some real world alternative. In such "contrastives," as Shatz et al. defined them, the child contrasted, for example, a mental process with physical objects or actions (e.g., "I'm not doing nothing, just thinking"), or a mental content with a real-world content (e.g., "I thought it was an alligator; now I know it was a crocodile"). These contrastives, Shatz et al. (p. 308) argue, are

> especially informative cases because the recognition that mental events can be at variance with observable events seems to be a core element in understanding the internal world. Indeed, making the difference explicit seems to be a prime motivation for expressing mental states among adults. These sorts of contrastive utterances, then, constitute a paradigm case of mental state expression, and they would be good evidence that the young child's conception of the internal world is similar at least in one way to the adult's.

The presence of explicit contrastives in young children's speech convincingly corroborates the presence of mental-state reference. Moreover, such contrastives provide a database in which to search for evidence of children's grasp of various critical conceptual distinctions, for example, the distinction between thought and reality, or between one person's thought and another's.

Like previous researchers (Bretherton, McNew, & Beeghly-Smith, 1981; Limber, 1973), Shatz et al. (1983) found that cognitive mental verbs appeared in children's speech in the third year. However, they discovered that such terms were first used not in reference to internal mental states but instead for pragmatic conversational functions. In their study of one child, Shatz et al. found that while cognitive verbs appeared as early as 2;4,[1] true mental-state references with those verbs appeared at 2;8. Corroborating this finding, contrastives appeared at about 2;9.

Shatz et al.'s (1983) findings were themselves limited in several fashions. First, the data were largely restricted to the language of a single child. Some investigators have argued that this was an atypical and unusually precocious individual (e.g., Perner, 1991). Second, although the contrastives identified by Shatz et al. were sufficiently numerous that they provided corroboration for the more general codings, they were sufficiently few that it was virtually impossible to analyze them further. Thus, it was not possible to distinguish and examine different sorts of conceptual distinctions and to chart when they appeared. For example, what if children's earliest contrastives were typically of the sort, "I think it's nice, but he thinks it's yucky"? Such contrastives might indicate that children have a correctly subjective understanding of belief but not a representational understanding (as these distinctions were outlined in Chapter 1).

Third, the scope of Shatz et al.'s (1983) project was limited, from our perspective, in that it focused only on belief terms like *think* and *know*. Important substantive and methodological advantages would be achieved by including terms referring to desires, such as *want* and *wish*. Substantively, a focus on children's understanding of desire complements a focus on belief in affording a more comprehensive picture of belief-desire reasoning. Methodologically, it is useful to be able to compare and contrast children's talk about beliefs with their talk about some different but related mental states. An examination of children's talk about desires serves this purpose admirably, as we will demonstrate.

Overview of the Methods

The Database

The CHILDES database is a growing collection of computerized child language corpora contributed by different researchers (MacWhinney & Snow, 1985, 1990). Available for our project were data from 10 children: Adam, Eve, and Sarah (Brown, 1973); Abe (Kuczaj & Maratsos, 1975); Ross and Mark (contributed by Brian MacWhinney); Allison (Bloom, 1973); Peter (Bloom, 1970); Nathaniel (contributed by Catherine Snow); and Naomi (Sachs, 1983). Most of these data have been analyzed elsewhere for other purposes, typically descriptions of initial language acquisition. In addition, Abe was the focal child in the Shatz et al. (1983) study.

Because data were contributed by different researchers, collection procedures varied across the children. Table 2.1 shows this information, along with demographic information about the children's families, indicates the ages of each child for which data were available, and the number of transcripts collected. The number of samples taken for each child differed, ranging from 6 to 210 samples, each sample typically representing a half hour or more of recording. Table 2.2 gives further information about the data collected, including total number of utterances and the mean length of utterance (MLU) for each child at the various ages sampled. That table shows the data blocked into four-month time periods, three to a year. For many analyses, we will use these time periods in presenting our findings. In other analyses, focusing on smaller subsets of the data, we format the data into six-month or one-year time periods. These formats provide a good balance between depicting the developmental trends yet aggregating the data sufficiently to avoid misrepresentations based on very small numbers of instances.

It is important to consider the sort of population that these children represent. On the one hand, we certainly do not claim to have a representative sample of English-speaking children. This is a sample of convenience, for the most part consisting of children raised in intact nuclear families, often chosen for study because their first language was clearly articulated and understandable. On the other hand, this sample offers useful and reasonable variation in subject characteristics. Six children are boys and four are girls. One child (Adam) is African-American; the others are white. Socioeconomic information on the children's families is meager; most of the children come from a mix of middle-class homes, but one child is from a working-class family (Sarah). Six of the children (Abe, Allison, Ross, Mark, Nathaniel, and Naomi) are children of language investigators, but four are not.

The children's language development itself provides further evidence of variation. For example, the children's MLU at equivalent ages varies substantially across this sample. Table 2.2 shows that at the time of the third birthday (36 months), MLUs ranged from 2.3 to 6.0 words per child. This measure of average

Table 2.1. Subject and Sample Descriptions

Child	Contributor[a]	Number of Samples	Age Range	When Collected	Collection Procedure	Demographic/Parent Information
Adam	Brown (1973)	55	2;3–4;10	1962–65	1 or 2 hrs every 2 wks	First-born African-American male; middle-class
Abe	Kuczaj & Maratsos (1975)	210	2;4–5;0	1973–75	1 hr a wk from 2;4–4;0, ½ hr a wk from 4;1–5;0	First-born white male; graduate student family
Sarah	Brown (1973)	139	2;3–5;1	1963–66	½ hr once or twice a wk	First-born white female; working-class
Ross	MacWhinney	67	2;6–7;10	1980–85	Multiple short episodes every 2–3 wks	First-born white male; college professor family
Naomi	Sachs (1983)	93	1;2–4;9	1969–73	1 hr every two weeks from 1;8–3;0 (less systematically before and after, and more intensively at 1;10–2;0)	First-born white female; college professor family
Allison	Bloom (1973)	6	1;4–2;10	late 60s	40 min every 2–4 mos	First-born white female; college professor family
Eve	Brown (1973)	20	1;6–2;3	1962–63	1 hr every 2 wks	First-born white female; middle-class
Nathaniel	Snow	31	2;5–3;9	1979–80	approximately 1 hr a wk	First-born white male; college professor family
Peter	Bloom (1970)	20	1;9–3;1	1971–73	4 hrs every 3 wks	First-born white male; upper middle-class
Mark	MacWhinney	56	0;7–5;11	1980–85	Multiple short episodes every 2–3 wks	Second-born white male; college professor family

[a]Most contributors to the CHILDES collection ask that users cite a particular reference. MacWhinney and Snow are exceptions.

Table 2.2. Total Utterances Available from Each Child by Age in Months

Child	18–24	25–28	29–32	33–36	37–40	41–44	45–48	49–52	53–56	57–60	61–64	65–78	69–72	Total
Adam	—	4,194	6,700	7,412 (2.8)	7,529	6,476	3,480 (4.2)	4,075	3,076	2,430	1,106	—	—	46,478
Abe	—	50	3,517	4,579 (6.0)	4,438	3,343	2,486 (8.0)	1,630	1,290	1,204	—	—	—	22,537
Sarah	—	3,172	4,479	4,710 (2.3)	4,572	2,953	3,186 (3.2)	4,818	4,282	3,707	200	—	—	36,079
Ross	—	—	1,079	3,570 (4.3)	3,432	4,060	1,204 (5.2)	2,300	1,563	—	1,186	394	2,241	21,029
Naomi	8,671	2,337	1,112	914 (5.2)	596	498	—	—	540	—	—	—	—	14,668
Allison	1,170	305	—	419 (4.0)	—	—	—	—	—	—	—	—	—	1,894
Eve	8,380	4,104	—	—	—	—	—	—	—	—	—	—	—	12,484
Nathaniel	—	—	5,914	1,097 (4.1)	3,490	136	256 (3.5)	—	—	—	—	—	—	10,893
Peter	5,931	9,003	10,217	3,856 (3.9)	2,088	—	—	—	—	—	—	—	—	31,095
Mark	112	113	102	53 (4.0)	—	666	1,996 (4.5)	295	—	—	—	—	—	3,337
													Total:	200,494

Note: Utterances are grouped in 4-month blocks except in the earliest (18–24 months) and latest (69–72 months) periods. MLU at 3 and 4 years of age in parenthesis.

sentence length roughly indexes age-related verbal ability. Indeed, average length of utterance provides a means of comparing these children with other samples. For example, Miller and Chapman (1981) summarize data from five classic language development studies (e.g., McCarthy 1930, 1954) with regard to mean length of utterances (in words) at various ages. They report average utterance lengths of from three to four words for 36-month-olds and from four to five words for 48-month-olds in those studies. Moreover, they offer data relating MLU and age for a sample of 123 middle- to upper-middle-class midwestern children. Based on a regression analysis of the entire sample, they report predicted MLU at age 36 months to be 3.2 and at age 48 months to be 4.4. A 95% confidence interval around these means yields a range of 1.6 to 4.7 for 36 months and 3.2 to 5.7 for 48 months. The children in Table 2.2 fall within this range with the exception of Abe and Naomi at 36 months and Abe at 48 months.[2]

Miller and Chapman's data underwrite the concern about conclusions based on Abe's data alone (as in Shatz et al., 1983); Abe is a linguistically precocious child, as is Eve, according to Brown (1973). However, Miller and Chapman's data also suggest that, excluding Abe and Eve, the children in our study are quite similar to other middle-class samples and, by including Abe and Eve, our sample encompasses substantial variation. At the least, the variation is substantial enough to rule out some possible confounds. For example, if all these children and not just Abe exhibit some competency at a young age, it is unlikely to be simply an artifact of precocity or language fluency. Or, if all exhibit the same sequence of developments, it seems unlikely that it constitutes an artifact due to some peculiar individual circumstance.

One related point deserves special emphasis. The data from these children were collected at very different points in time (spanning 20 years or so), in different parts of the country, and by different investigators. Each investigator had unique research goals, none of which involved examining talk about mental states (at least, not when the data were collected). It is therefore unlikely that the children were especially primed to talk about the mind, or were exposed to parents or investigators unusually likely to encourage, model, instruct, or sample such talk. For our purposes, the data were collected "blind" from haphazardly sampled children, providing us with a group that represents an informative range of young American children.

Terms

In order to cull this large dataset for evidence relevant to children's understanding of desires and beliefs, we searched for all instances of preselected desire, thought, and belief terms. The terms we selected initially are shown in Table 2.3. In part, our selection of terms was justified by previous findings. For example, one reason for including *know* and *think* was Shatz et al.'s (1983) finding that these terms were by far the most common cognitive terms used by 2-year-olds. Similarly, because Shatz et al. (1983) reported that 95% of the mental terms in their study were verbs, not nouns or adjectives, we examined mental verbs.

More fundamentally, our selection of terms resulted from an analysis of the

Table 2.3. List of Belief and Desire Terms Sought

Desire	Thought and Belief
Want	Think
Hope	Know
Wish	Believe
Care (about)	Expect
Afraid (that)	Wonder
	Dream

Note: All possible variants of a term were included. Thus *want* includes want, wan'; wants, wanna, wanted; *think* includes think, thinks, thought, thinked; *believe* includes believe and believed as well as make believe; and so on.

type of reasoning we were investigating. In English, as in most languages, a whole set of verbs enable us to talk about various aspects of belief-desire mentalism. These different verbs are partly defined by their contrasts with and similarity to other mental verbs. In a parallel fashion, mental constructs, as concepts, are defined in part by their roles and relations to other mental constructs. An understanding of belief, for example, is intimately related to an understanding of thoughts and thinking, to issues of certainty and conviction, to differences between serious and playful mental states, and to how belief and desire interact in explaining intentional action. Compare the statement ''I believe that,'' for example, with ''I am thinking that,'' ''I wonder if,'' ''I imagine that,'' or ''I want that.''

The interdependencies evident in both mental concepts and mental terms must figure somehow into any investigation of children's mental talk and reasoning. That is why we are so interested in studying belief and desire together, in addition to studying a coherent package of verbs.

We did not attempt to comprehensively sample all mental verbs. For purposes of analysis, we wanted a more tractable task and we wanted to focus on verbs used by young children. But we also chose the verbs in Table 2.3 with a view to how each might represent different aspects of beliefs or desires when these are considered as a system of constructs. The following partial analysis provides one example of our concerns. Consider two crude dimensions, one related to thought and belief which could be called certainty or conviction, and one related to desire and which could be termed desirability. Verbs such as *wish*, *hope*, and *believe* can be seen as occupying different places vis à vis these two dimensions. With regard to conviction, if I say ''I know that x,'' I am expressing more confidence or conviction in my belief than if I say ''I think that x.'' With regard to desirability, if I say ''I hope that x,'' I am indicating that I desire it more than if I say ''I fear that x.'' The location of our selected mental verbs on these dimensions is illustrated in Table 2.4.

Most verbs do not purely express some generic concept of desire alone or thought and belief alone, but a package of verbs together can elucidate the basic belief-desire ''space.'' The verbs in Table 2.4 do not exhaust English-language ways of filling and defining this space, but they do illuminate most of the space and, significantly, occur early in development.

Note that children can reveal an understanding of the basic belief-desire framework by using only a very few terms in the matrix. For example, use of *want* and

Table 2.4. Some Interdependencies Between the Targeted Mental Verbs

		Conviction		
		More conviction	*Less conviction*	*Neutral*
	Want	Expect	Hope Wish	Want
Desirability	*Don't want*	Afraid (that)		Don't want
	Neutral	Believe Know	Think	Dream Make believe Don't care Wonder

don't want can be sufficient to express differences of desire, and use of *think* and *don't think* (or *know* and *don't know*) can express differences of belief. Thus, our analyses of these expressions were designed to be sensitive to chidren's very early understanding of belief-desire reasoning.

Mere production of mental terms is of little interest in contrast to analyses of children's conceptions as expressed with these terms. Nevertheless, general information concerning the frequencies with which children used the focal terms provides both a needed backdrop for later substantive analyses and an initial introduction to the data. Table 2.5, therefore, shows the occurrence of utterances containing the verbs listed in Table 2.3 for each child at ages ranging from 1½ to 6 years.

Shown at the bottom of Table 2.5 are the number of children producing any such utterances and the total number of utterances produced. These data indicate that for all practical purposes our analyses span the period from 2 to 5 years (25 to 60 months). In each of these months, on average, about 7 of the 10 children contributed data. Over this range, 11,169 of the total 11,859 "belief-desire" verb utterances (94%) were produced. The period from 25 to 60 months was also rich in terms of when data were available from children at all, with most children contributing samples in this range. As the totals on the far right of Table 2.5 show, total desire verb utterances consistently exceeded total belief verb utterances for all the children and for each child individually. An overwhelming use of desire verbs, often found in conjunction with no belief verb uses at all, is characteristic before about 2½ years of age. After that time, the amount of belief verb production increases, with verbs of belief and desire becoming equal, and then with belief talk often exceeding desire talk from about the fourth birthday on.

The varying nature of the transcripts available to us—how the data were collected from each child, how long and at what ages language was sampled—constrained our analyses. Note in this regard that while 10 children appear consistently in the transcripts, and we will at times make use of that by reporting data for each of the 10 separately, 4 children provided the bulk of the data. As shown in Table 2.1, Adam, Abe, Sarah, and Ross provided 471 (68%) of the total 697 speech samples encompassed in our database. Because samples varied in size from a half hour to two hours in length, number of samples is an imperfect measure of each child's contribution. Table 2.2 shows, however, that in terms of total utter-

Table 2.5. Total Utterances Using the Terms for Desire and for Thoughts and Beliefs by Age in Months

Child		18–24	25–28	29–32	33–36	37–40	41–44	45–48	49–52	53–56	57–60	61–72	Total
Adam	Desire	—	5	146	326	393	129	135	142	157	100	67	1,600
	Belief	—	5	19	68	93	103	201	161	109	111	39	909
Abe	Desire	—	8	394	581	225	293	152	83	75	88	—	1,899
	Belief	—	1	50	176	370	230	276	184	163	108	—	1,558
Sarah	Desire	—	21	14	282	169	116	113	108	143	62	7	1,035
	Belief	—	0	15	31	37	122	51	102	156	136	21	671
Ross	Desire	—	—	86	215	154	159	64	96	62	—	129	965
	Belief	—	—	6	38	64	100	58	118	97	—	207	688
Naomi	Desire	131	'139	54	77	88	46	—	—	47	—	—	582
	Belief	0	1	29	19	31	29	—	—	25	—	—	134
Allison	Desire	0	49	—	22	—	—	—	—	—	—	—	71
	Belief	0	0	—	14	—	—	—	—	—	—	—	14
Eve	Desire	67	161	—	—	—	—	—	—	—	—	—	228
	Belief	14	6	—	—	—	—	—	—	—	—	—	20
Nathaniel	Desire	—	—	146	10	71	12	4	—	—	—	—	243
	Belief	—	—	27	21	29	10	1	—	—	—	—	88
Peter	Desire	6	86	423	200	42	—	—	—	—	—	—	757
	Belief	1	20	43	59	49	—	—	—	—	—	—	172
Mark	Desire	1	1	11	6	—	46	41	21	—	—	—	127
	Belief	0	0	2	1	—	30	63	2	—	—	—	98
Subtotal	Desire	205	470	1,274	1,719	1,142	801	509	450	484	250	203	7,507
	Belief/Thought	15	33	191	427	673	624	650	567	550	355	267	4,352
Total utterances		220	503	1,465	2,146	1,815	1,425	1,159	1,017	1,034	605	470	11,859
Number of children represented		5	8	8	9	7	7	6	5	5	3	3	10

Note: A — indicates that no transcripts were available. A 0 indicates that transcripts were available but no desire or belief term uses were found.

28

ances these 4 children were indeed sampled more extensively than the rest,[3] and Table 2.5 shows that in consequence these same 4 children contributed 9,325 (79%) of the 11,859 mentions of belief-desire verbs in the dataset. For the most part, therefore, when we want to consider individual patterns of development, we will examine these 4 children; they provide sufficient data across sufficient time periods for informative individual analyses.

Fortunately, these 4 children largely represent the same range of variation in subject and family characteristics found across all 10 children. These 4 children include 1 female and 3 males, 1 African-American and 3 Caucasians, 1 child of a working-class family, 1 of a middle-class family, and 2 children of language investigators. As shown in Table 2.2, these children encompass a wide range of MLUs; at the third birthday, MLUs for these 4 individuals range from 2.3 to 6.0.

Our data are dominated not only by four children but also by three verbs: *want* accounts for 97% of the utterances that used any of the desire verbs listed in Table 2.3, and *think* (26%) and *know* (70%) account for 96% of the utterances that were produced using any of the belief verbs listed in Table 2.3. Because the dataset is large, it contains hundreds of useful utterances of the other belief and desire verbs as well, but much of what we have to say could be based on the children's use of the terms *think*, *know*, and *want*. Indeed, while several advantages were gained by casting a wider net, it is worth noting for future investigations that many of our conclusions would have been apparent had we confined our analyses exclusively to the uses of *think*, *know*, and *want* from Adam, Sarah, Abe, and Ross.

In the following analyses of how children use the belief-desire terms that they produce, we faced an important question: what baseline to use in order to quantify our findings. One possibility, which we used at times, was to express children's utterances of any one sort (say, their utterances judged to be genuine references to belief) as a proportion of their total utterances. If we had used that procedure exclusively, however, our results would have consisted of a cluster of very small numbers, at times fractions of percents; children's uses of belief-desire verbs at all are relatively infrequent, and their interpretable uses of some one kind even more rare. For our purposes, we were not often interested in the absolute frequencies of uses of these verbs. Table 2.5 depicts much of what we have to say about that, namely, that verbs of desire and later verbs of thought and belief are produced from about age 20 months on, and that they increase in frequency but always remain somewhat infrequent throughout the preschool years.

We were interested instead in the advent of uses of these verbs to refer genuinely to mental states and in the development of various kinds of reference to, and conceptions of, desires and beliefs. For these kinds of questions, it was more informative to consider children's use of various terms as a percent of their total belief-desire language. Thus, the totals at the bottom of Table 2.5 provide the denominators in most of our analyses, and we report children's genuine references to thoughts and beliefs, for example, as a percent of utterances that included any belief-desire verb.

In several analyses we explored when children first evidenced certain usages, for example, when they first began to genuinely refer to people's thoughts and beliefs. A straightforward measure to use for these analyses was the children's ages at their first observed utterance of the focal sort; we often report our data in this fashion. Like any measure, this one is susceptible to false positives and negatives. On the one hand, we obviously do not claim that first occurrence in these transcripts necessarily represents first occurrence in the children's speech; the transcripts sample their utterances periodically rather than provide a running record of all of a their speech. The samples are reasonably frequent, however, typically every one or two weeks, and thus likely to track changes in children's productions fairly closely. On the other hand, even given our generally stringent coding criteria, any single instance could be misclassified (e.g., a child's first recorded genuine belief utterance could represent a stray, unusual, or miscoded utterance instead). To offset this possibility, when we report first occurrences we also cite the children's ages at their third recorded instance of a type. Using three instances as an index is also arbitrary; the number could be larger (but at risk of misrepresenting relatively infrequent productions) or smaller. Other natural language research has often used from three to five productions to provide this sort of information (e.g., the various studies in Bloom, 1991).

Overview of Coding Categories and Procedures

What do children mean when they use various terms of belief and desire, terms that adults would use to talk about mental states? The essence of our method is to provide codings of children's utterances, considering their contexts, that allow us to answer that question. Our goal was to identify and characterize talk about beliefs and desires, and to examine various distinctions and conceptions within children's belief-desire understanding.

The transcripts were searched, via computer, for all child utterances using the belief-desire terms listed in Table 2.3. For each child, a record of all of his or her utterances that contained the target terms was obtained. Each such utterance was printed together with a conversational window including the four preceding and three succeeding utterances. For example:

> MOTHER: No, don't pick it out, you'll make it worse and you'll make it bleed. We'll put something on it, so don't touch it.
> NATHANIEL (2;6): Touch it.
> MOTHER: No, leave it alone.
> NATHANIEL: *Wanna* touch it.
> MOTHER: I know you want to touch it, but you mustn't. Here, let's put some cream under your chin.
> NATHANIEL: Make all better.

This window gave a partial context to aid in understanding and coding the target utterances. Coders could also, and often did, refer to the entire extended transcript in order to optimally understand and code any given utterance.

The recorded data for most of the CHILDES transcripts utilized audio rather then video recordings, with only periodic brief description of the environment around which the conversations took place. The contextual information available, therefore, was mostly contained in other utterances. In our analyses we did not attempt to code the contexts of children's utterances into a separate set of categories, but more simply scrutinized such contextual information in order to understand the nature and sense of the children's targeted utterances—a common practice in one form or other in much research on early child language (e.g., Bloom, 1991; Brown, 1973).

Along the lines of Shatz et al. (1983), we coded children's mental verb utterances in several ways, ranging from broad categories designed to characterize the bulk of the data to narrower categorizations to identify special subsets of utterances for more precise analysis. For example, like Shatz et al. we looked for genuine references to mental states, broadly defined, but also identified utterances that more explicitly mentioned various aspects of mental life, such as contrastives. Given the inevitable vagueness of everyday conversation, and the incompleteness of any record of social interaction, a proportion of target utterances remained ambiguous. Our aim was to identify clearly interpretable utterances rather than definitively type each utterance.

Genuine psychological references. Our initial, broadest coding level of children's utterances was designed to identify genuine references to psychological states. Coding utterances as genuine psychological reference thus involved sorting out those uses of belief and desire terms that indicated reasonable understanding of thoughts, beliefs, or desires.

While beliefs and desires refer to two different sorts of states, both beliefs and desires are similar in referring to psychological, mental aspects of persons and not their physical qualities or overt behaviors. Moreover, these mental states are similar in being intentional, in the philosopher's sense. Intentional states are states that are "about" something else. Thus, a desire is about or for something, for example, a desire for an ice cream cone. A belief also is about something, such as the belief that water is wet. Beliefs and desires are hybrid constructs, spanning mind and world in a particular way by describing an internal mental state about, for, or toward the world. This character of mental states is often described by philosophers in terms of propositional attitudes. Talk about beliefs and desires describes both an internal mental attitude (wanting that or thinking that), and some content of that attitude; the object of the attitude, the thing, event, or state of affairs that is wanted or thought about. The content of a propositional attitude can be captured in a proposition, for example, "that the earth is round" or "that I get some dinner." In coding for genuine psychological reference we were looking for evidence that the children were using belief or desire terms to refer to such intentional mental states, the psychological attitudes and contents of their minds. An example is the utterance "he thought there were haunted things," in the conversation that begins this chapter.

Following Shatz et al.'s (1983) general procedures, we carefully excluded any mentions of belief or desire terms that appeared to be conversational uses, that might be referring to merely overt behavioral aspects of a situation rather than mental states, or that were direct repetitions of someone else's use of the term. Specifically, a term was not counted as a genuine belief or desire reference if it served only such conversational functions as getting someone's attention (e.g., "You know what?"), turning over the conversation to someone else (e.g., "Let's go to the park, what do you think?"), or softening a command or request (e.g., "I wonder, Mom, can we have spaghetti?" or "I think it's time to watch Sesame Street"). Also excluded were short, unembellished, or idiomatic phrases, such as "You know," "I think so," "Don't know," and "I wanna."

Mere repetitions of phrases uttered by other persons (such as an adult) were not counted as genuine psychological references, nor were uses explicitly prompted by another person (e.g., the mother says, "Tell him you know where it is," and the child says, "I know where it is"). Even inexact repetitions were regarded with suspicion (e.g., the mother says, "Where's daddy, what do you think?" and the child responds, "I think Daddy's at the office"). If a child repeated exactly his own utterance (e.g., "I want it; I want it"), only the first occurrence could potentially be counted as a genuine psychological reference, unless the repeated phrases were interrupted by someone else's utterance and the coder judged that the child was responding to that new utterance and was not simply parroting himself.

Finally, care was taken to exclude uses of the terms that conceivably referred only to external aspects of behavior. For example, "He remembers his coat," said in the presence of a person putting on his coat, might refer only to the ongoing action. And unadorned statements such as "I want that" might only be behavioral commands similar to "Give me that."

After we ruled out instances judged to be conversational, repetitious, or behavioral, for the remaining instances we judged whether the term was used in a genuine psychological sense. An utterance was classified as a genuine psychological reference only if, with regard to its context, it referred to thoughts, desires, beliefs, or knowledge, or to similar psychological states. The judgments required here varied depending on whether the reference was to beliefs or desires, to thoughts or knowledge, and so on. We discuss these judgements in detail in the chapters that follow.

Contrastives. In addition to coding the data broadly for genuine psychological references, we also coded them at several more precise and conservative levels that provided especially convincing evidence of a genuine understanding of beliefs and desires as intentional psychological states. Some of the most convincing utterances of this sort are contrastives, in which the child indicates a contrast between some essential feature, content, or nature of a mental state versus an informative alternative. One type of contrastive, for example, concerns the distinction between a psychological state and the real world that was the focus of Shatz et al.'s (1983) analysis. For example, Adam at 3;11 said, "It doesn't talk. Does he think it talks?" Here the child contrasts reality (it doesn't talk) with a possible belief (he might think it talks). More broadly, however, there are several informative varieties of contrastives. To begin with, therefore, we identified two very general types of contrastives for all belief and desire term uses: mental state–reality contrastives, and individual contrastives.

Mental state–reality contrastives, as in the Shatz et al. (1983) research, were defined as utterances "which mark an understanding of a difference or discrepancy between some psychological state and present or observable reality''(p. 309). Because of our focus on both belief and desire states, we identified two different but parallel sorts of mental state–reality contrastives: thought–reality contrastives with regard to the terms for thoughts and beliefs, and desire–outcome contrastives for the desire terms. The example cited previously is more specifically an example of a thought–reality contrastive, as is this utterance by Abe (3;9), ''I thought there wasn't any socks, but when I looked, I saw them.'' Here the child draws an explicit contrast between his (prior) belief and reality. Another set of thought–reality contrastives mention lack of specific knowledge about a state of affairs, for example, Sarah (4;4), ''You don't know the pieces go here.'' Such references involve a recognition of both a present known reality and a psychological state that does not accord with that reality.

Desire–outcome contrastives express an understanding that a desire is distinct or independent from reality or from an outcome or action. Generally, we were interested in evidence demonstrating the child understood that desires describe states of mind, not states of the world, so we sought talk about desires that was not simply an alternative terminology for talking about outcomes or actions. We were interested whether children understood that desires do not necessarily bring about the desired outcome, nor do they always lead to actions. An example of a desire–outcome contrastive was Eve (1;11), ''I don't want some soup. I want some cheese sandwich.'' In this case Eve had gotten some soup for lunch and was commenting on the discrepancy between what she wanted and what she had received. Context was essential for judging these distinctions; the coder could only judge a distinction to have been made when it was evident from the context that the child recognized that the outcome or action did not match the desire. Other examples of this type of contrastive include Sarah (3;3), ''Wan' me wash my face?'' said to her mother when Sarah clearly had a dirty face, and Peter (2;3), ''I want my paper: be right back'' when Peter was explaining why he was leaving the room (to find a desired but as yet unfound object).

Individual contrastives are a second general category of utterances, in which one person's psychological state is contrasted with another's. An example involving thoughts and beliefs is Ross (3;7): ''Do you think God is good?'' Father: ''Yes.'' Ross: ''But we think God is mean.'' Abe (3;4) illustrates an individual contrastive concerning desires in his statement ''I wanna do everything you don't wanna do.'' In such contrastives, the child distinguishes two different psychological states, perhaps his own from another person's, or perhaps the states of two other persons.

Mental state–reality contrastives seemed an especially informative source for examining children's conceptions of mind and world, as well as such related distinctions as representations versus connections and fictional states versus epistemic ones. Individual contrastives, in comparison, seemed a good source for examining children's understanding of the individuated, subjective nature of mental states and hence the subjective versus objective distinction.

Other codings. We coded several other aspects of children's belief-desire talk. Here are two illustrative categories.

Potentially, children might at first comment only on their own beliefs and desires, or only those of others, or only their own desires but others' beliefs, and so on; therefore, for each utterance coded as a genuine reference to belief or desire, we coded whose belief or desire was being described. Specifically, was it the child's own mental state (first person) or someone else's (second or third person)?

Talk about beliefs and desires can be potentially quite simple ("I want it") or complex ("I don't believe that you are the person they were talking about"). As an initial measure of this complexity, we coded for each utterance whether it involved one verb, the focal mental verb (as in the first example), or two or more verbs (as in the second example). Because mental states of belief and desire are two-place states, including a mental attitude and a content, there are often two verbs involved: the mental verb (I *think*) and the verb of the related proposition (that it *will rain*).

Reliability

These codings, especially those for genuine psychological references but for others as well, required judgment and inference on the part of coders to appropriately attribute certain meanings or features to the children's utterances. It is important to establish, therefore, that such judgments could be consistently and reliably achieved. In our samples, a total of 11,859 belief and desire term uses were produced by the 10 children. Two coders were trained to use the coding schemes and, between them, coded the entire dataset. One of these coders was the first author, but the other was a paid assistant, blind to advance hypotheses or theoretical positions concerning the project. The ages of the children at the time of each utterance were not evident in the transcripts to be coded, apart from what might be deduced from the content of the transcripts.

At five points during the coding, the coders independently coded some of the same data, which provided various reliability checks. In total, these samples included 723 belief and desire term uses, representing all the children (except Allison, due to her minimal contribution; see Table 2.5); all the different belief and desire terms; and the periods before 3½, from 3½ to 4½, and after 4½ years of age.

All 723 utterances were coded as to who was attributed the mental state: self, other, or indeterminable. Percent agreement between the independent codings of the two coders, the number of agreements divided by the total of agreements plus disagreements, was 100%. For the 334 belief term uses, agreement between the coders on whether the uses were genuine psychological references was 91%. (An alternative statistic for calculating reliability, Cohen's kappa, was .81). For 389 desire term uses, agreement on geniuine psychological references categorizations was 90% (Cohen's kappa = .79). From these same samples, reliability on contrastives was assessed. Of the 334 belief term uses, 208 had been judged to be genuine psychological references. Of these 208, agreement on whether each was or was not a contrastive was 76% (Cohen's kappa = .53). Of the 389 desire term uses, 256 were judged to be genuine psychological references. Of these 256, percent agreement for contrastives categorization was 83% (Cohen's kappa = .66).

Because coding for contrastives was intended to provide a stricter corroboration of children's reference to mental states, identifying relatively incontrovertible instances of mental talk, all other candidate contrastives, in addition to those de-scribed in the preceding paragraph, were coded by two individuals. Utterances for which there was disagreement were, conservatively, excluded as contrastives. Fur-thermore, after the coding was completed, a second check was made on all con-trastives. Any utterance identified as a contrastive was reviewed by a third coder (the second author), and again, any instances on which there was disagreement were excluded. Thus, all term uses finally counted as contrastives were coded to a reliability of 100%.

Omissions and Limitations

The conversations in these transcripts are amenable to a wide variety of analyses, many of which would add to our understanding of the nature and development of children's talk about the mind. One topic of obvious importance concerns the speech to children that shapes and influences their talk about the mind. In Chapters 5 and 7 we provide information about parental input, focusing on data necessary to decide between several alternative interpretations of our core findings. However, this is a limited foray into a large and intriguing topic. Our analyses focus primarily on characterizing children's productions rather than those of the parents. Ultimately, we would like comprehensive data about children and parents, and about the dy-namics of parent–child interactions that shape children's language and understand-ing. Dunn et al. (1991a), Brown and Dunn (1991a), and Furrow, Moore, Davidge, and Chiasson (1992) provide some additional information about parental talk to young children about mental states.

Our knowledge of the social situations that framed the conversations we analyze is similarly sketchy. As described, our codings rely on extended conversational contexts. Moreover, in several places we consider children's uses of language of the mind in precisely coded situations and for specifically identified social purposes. For example, in Chapter 6 we consider situations involving disputes and utterances designed to explain actions. We have not, as yet, undertaken comprehensive anal-yses of the sorts of social partners, social situations, pragmatic purposes, or social dynamics involved in learning or talking about the mind. In part we are limited by our data. For example, these transcripts contain predominantly adult–child conver-sations, with infrequent child–child interactions, obtained in easy-to-record situa-tions. The transcripts include eating, bathing, dressing, storybook reading, and various indoor and outdoor at-home play situations. They do not include preschool, playground, work, the doctor's office, car riding, or shopping situations, among others. As mentioned earlier, the transcripts record spoken language with little or no extended description of gestures, facial expressions, and actions. Brown and Dunn (1991) report several initial categorizations of the pragmatic contexts of chil-dren's internal state utterances. They distinguish, for example, among utterances used to call attention to the child's own immediate needs, utterances attempting to influence another person's behavior or feelings, and reflective utterances about in-ternal states. For the most part, however, informative analyses of the contexts of developing talk about the mind await further research. It is worth reiterating that the context of most research examining children's understanding of the mind is the research laboratory. A straightforward question arises whether children's responses and judgments, made in such situations, are context-dependent; that is, if they are evident only in contrived controlled tasks. Our data emerge in a very different context: natural language conversations in the home with familiar conversational partners.

Finally, we have not extensively analyzed the linguistic forms of children's utterances. We do provide some information of this sort in Chapters 3 and 4, and additional analyses in Chapter 5 when it is needed to evaluate several interpretations of our findings. However, our approach focuses primarily on what children mean in their talk about the mind, their underlying conceptions, rather than on their developing syntactic competencies. Fortunately, Lois Bloom has provided extensive analyses of the forms children use in their utterances with such verbs as *want* (Bloom, Tackeff, & Lahey, 1984) as well as *think* and *know* (Bloom, Rispoli, Gartner, & Hafitz, 1989).

Our limited analyses of parental input, social-pragmatic context, and linguistic forms means neither that we judge such factors to be insignificant, nor that we assume children's talk about the mind to be an asocial, individualistic enterprise that employs language merely as a neutral medium of expression. To the contrary, we assume that children's talk about the mind is social, collaborative, and linguistically shaped as well as linguistically expressed. Our analyses, while not codifying these factors comprehensively, attempt to be sensitive to them in several fashions. Our omissions reflect, quite simply, limits to our energies and time; we focused first on some analyses and questions, and not others, in order to keep the project tractable. We believe that the questions we address are important ones that have not been addressed or resolved in prior research and hence are worthy of concerted effort.

Summary

This chapter gives an outline of our methods and some baseline data for interpreting our later more substantive findings. We are ready to turn, therefore, to an examination of, first, children's talk about beliefs and, second, children's talk about desires.

Notes

1. Throughout this book we will cite ages in years and months, separated by a semicolon. So 2;4 means 2 years and 4 months old.

2. Miller currently is conducting a larger study with a more representative sample of 252 children aged 3 to 13 (1993). From these data he reports mean MLUs at 36 months of 3.5 and at 48 months of 4.2 (Miller, personal communication), very similar to his 1981 data.

3. Peter's transcripts also provide a large number of utterances, but only over little more than one year (see Table 2.1). The transcripts for Adam, Sarah, Ross, and Abe not only provide many utterances but span two and a half years or more for each child.

3

Talk about Thoughts and Beliefs

Abe at 3;7

ABE: I don't wanna go.
FATHER: Why?
ABE: Because.
FATHER: How come?
ABE: They would think I'm not there.
FATHER: What?
ABE: They would think Stan and Ann (the child's parents) had not a kid.
FATHER: Why would they think that if you came?
ABE: No. They would think that if I didn't came.

We examined children's use of the terms *believe, think, know, wonder, expect,* and *dream* in order to chart their early understanding of mental states such as thoughts generally and beliefs more specifically. The concept of belief is central to our everyday understanding of mind—our ordinary belief-desire psychology—as noted in our introductory chapter. Beliefs, as intentional states, involve thinking about something. More specifically, beliefs are thoughts that some potential state of affairs is actually so. Of course, the believer can be mistaken, that is, can believe falsely.

The case of a false belief illustrates several important features of beliefs, and of thoughts in general, that children must come to understand and articulate. First, beliefs have their own contents that are separable from the actual state of the world. Beliefs are mental and potentially completely independent of the world itself. In this potential independence, beliefs are like imaginings, fantasies, and dreams; but second, beliefs purport to be about the world, for their holder, the believer. Beliefs can prove false, and beliefs can be held with little real conviction, but they aim to be true. Talking about someone's beliefs involves talking about certain mental contents and not others; those contents that the person takes to be true, mental contents that are attempts to represent the world. In this regard, beliefs are unlike imaginings and fantasies, because those fictional mental states do not aim to be true at all. Fictional mental contents do not aim to represent the world in this sense. The term *think* can refer to either of these possibilities, epistemic or fictional mental contents, as in "I think that's an apple" to express belief, or "I'm just thinking of an apple" to express imagination. Because beliefs refer more specifically to a person's convictions as to what is so, they can come in different degrees of credulity or conviction. A thought that something is so can vary from certain knowledge (*know*), to a firm belief (*believe*), to mere speculation (*wonder*).

All of these distinctions and conceptions are of interest and justify examining children's understandings at several levels: their most general reference to all thoughts; a more specific understanding of beliefs; and the distinction between serious and fictional thoughts, and between knowing, believing, and wondering. This chapter identifies and tracks these various meanings in children's talk about the mind.

Genuine Reference to Thinking

Our examination of children's utterances using verbs *believe, think, know, wonder, expect*, and *dream* proceeded in several phases. We first identified the use of mental terms that referred to states of thinking at all, regardless of whether the contents of those states were fictional or about the world. Here we were not concerned with whether the child distinguished between "just thinking [imagining] it's raining" and "thinking [believing] it's raining." We deliberately included verbs of belief (*know, believe, expect*) because of our larger interest in belief-desire reasoning, but even in considering these verbs, our initial goal was simply to identify uses of these terms to genuinely refer to any sort of contentful mental state. By "contentful" we mean mental states designated as having content, such as a belief that the world is round or a thought about a unicorn. And of course our inclusion of *think, wonder, dream*, and *make-believe* expanded our focus beyond narrow belief. The verb *think* can be especially ambiguous but also nicely comprehensive in this regard, as illustrated above. In subsequent analyses, we carefully distinguished between fictional and convictional mental states, but our initial search and categorization paralleled that of Shatz et al. (1983) by coding generally for mental references to thoughts, ideas, and mental contents, as distinct from external observable behavior, situations, or facts.

This first coding resulted in a subset of utterances that were categorized, as described in Chapter 2, as genuine psychological references. Specifically, our codings identified genuine reference to thinking, believing, and knowing, considered broadly. Examples are Sarah's statement at 3;7, "I think it disappeared," and Adam's at 2;11, "I don't know his name." The decision that these or any other utterances genuinely make a reference to mental state is, of course, open to dispute because it requires an inference from the child's use of the terms, an inference that could be wrong. For example, Sarah might be politely asserting a fact, "it's gone," rather than referring to a thought with that content. Alternatively, Adam could just be refusing to respond to a request via a socially accepted convention. In making our judgments, however, we carefully scrutinized the larger context of the child's utterance in order to determine whether the child was likely to be referring to a mental state. Thus, a more complete citation of the interchange in the first example was

SARAH: Where's the bed?
MOTHER: Whose bed?
SARAH: Her bed.
MOTHER: I don't know.
SARAH: I think it disappeared. You think it does?

Since Sarah queries what her mother thinks, as well as describing her own thought, it seems unlikely that she is claiming simply that the item is gone, and more likely that she is referring to a mental state, in this case her belief that the bed has disappeared.

For the second example, some of the surrounding context was

ADAM: What dat little boy name?
ADULT: His name?
ADAM: His name. His name, Ursla?
ADULT: I know his name.
ADAM: No . . . I don't know his name. I don't know.

In this example, far from using "I don't know" as a refusal, Adam is struggling to recall or learn a name and seems to genuinely comment on his state of ignorance.

Some utterances considered in context are even more convincing, such as the following made by Abe at 3;3.

ABE: Some people don't like hawks. They think they have . . . they are slimy.
MOTHER: What do you think?
ABE: I think they are good animals.

Especially explicit examples of this sort were captured by our coding for contrastives, to be detailed later. But even when lacking sufficient explicitness to qualify as contrastives, the child's utterances could indicate convincingly that he or she was talking about mental states rather than either referring to facts and behaviors or employing certain conversational conventions.

Our first coding, for genuine psychological reference, identified such instances, carefully culling them from myriad conversational uses of the terms and from unclear instances. The large number of utterances allowed us to be conservative in this coding, rejecting any mental term uses that were not sufficiently clear. Unclear instances occurred, in part, because the transcripts often provided little in the way of independent description of the objects and actions of the parties. The larger context of an utterance had to be identified, to the extent possible, mostly from the speakers' discourse. Often, the surrounding conversation was sufficient, as demonstrated above, but of course unclear instances remained, which we simply excluded from further consideration.

Each utterance using any of the focal verbs was coded in this general fashion, sorting references to thoughts and beliefs from other uses. However, the verbs provided both unique difficulties and unique opportunities for coding. A description follows of the considerations we adopted for coding utterances using the different verbs. As noted in the last chapter, the vast majority of belief term utterances we considered involved the verbs *think* and *know*, so we begin with those. There were also a substantial number of uses of *wonder*, *dream*, and *believe*, but almost none for *expect*.

Think. We were interested in any sort of reference to thoughts and thinking, including at least three separable sorts:

Thought-as-belief—using *think* to refer to a propositional belief state, to attribute a propositional conviction. For example, Adam at 4;5 said of his infant brother, "He thinks dis a monster. He thinks it's a real one, doesn't he?"

Thought-as-imagination—referring to a mental state that is fictional or imaginary. For example, at 2;11 Abe answered his parent's questioning, "Why did you paint your hands?" by saying: "I thought my hands are paper."

Thought-as-activity—referring to mental activity, to a mental process, for example,

> ADAM (2;11): I . . . just thinking?
> ADULT: You're just thinking?
> ADAM: Yes.
> ADULT: What are you thinking about?
> ADAM: Thinking 'bout leaf.

Of course, some utterances did not clearly serve only one or the other of these different functions, but making precise distinctions was not our aim in this initial coding. Our aim was to identify reference to mental-content states at all, as distinct from references to mere facts or physical objects. Note that even in the previous example of thought-as-activity, the child identifies a mental-content state, "thinking 'bout leaf." Other examples are included in Table 3.1.

As noted in the preceding chapter, our interest in the term *think* includes all variations of that term, such as *thought*, *thoughtful*, and *thinked*, terms that we found to vary in their usefulness. Use of the past tense *thought* or *thinked* was especially informative for articulating an implicit or explicit contrast to an acknowledged reality. For example, Abe at 3;9 said, "I thought my socks were in the drawer, but they weren't." In contrast, the term *think* was often used for functions other than mental reference that were excluded from consideration. Examples of these exclusions were any uses of *think* that might potentially be politeness markers ("I think we should go"), simple extensions of yes or no ("I think so," or "I think not" to mean simply yes or no), or devices for turn-taking ("What do you think?").

Know. Adults use *know* to refer to a belief that is felt to be justified, assumed to be true, or that enjoys markedly higher conviction than one described by *think*. At first disregarding whether the child correctly distinguished *know* from *think*, we simply coded instances of use of *know* to refer to contentful mental states, fictional or factual, just as for *think*. Several examples are given in Table 3.1. As with *think*, we also coded variations on the term *know* including *knew* and *knowed*.

Conservatively, we did not include some ambiguous uses of *know* that might

Table 3.1. Example Thought and Belief Verb Utterances Coded as Genuine Reference to Psychological State

Think

ABE (3;3): I didn't get you a surprise.
ADULT: You didn't. I'm sad.
ABE: No, don't be sad. I thought I would 'cept I didn't see one for you.
ADULT: I bet someone else found that rock and took it home.
ABE (3;9): I bet nobody found it because I think it's burned.
ADULT: Huh?
ABE: I think it's burned.

ADAM (3;10): Flawingo, flawingo.
ADULT: No. It's flamingo.
ADAM: I thought I said flawingo.

SARAH (3;10): He's coming back after . . . we have another day.
ADULT: Really?
SARAH: That's when he's going to come back.
ADULT: That's nice.
SARAH: I think he's gonna come back. I think he's gonna come back on Monday.

Wonder

ABE (3;4): I didn't want to be out. I wondered if Jason was out. But he wasn't.

ADAM (3;11): Why he knocked it down?
ADULT: He didn't really knock it down.
ADAM: I wonder why it comes loose, huh?

SARAH (4;8): Does fishy go over here? Nope. I wonder where . . .

Expect

(Ross saw that his couch had been put in the wrong position when it was opened up in the wrong way. He wanted to go watch TV.)

ROSS (6;0): Dad, do you expect me to sit on that?
ADULT: No, of course not.

Know

ROSS (2;10): Mommy can't sing it. She doesn't know it. She doesn't understand.

NAOMI (3;5): I like this. Because this not your game. My game. You don't know what it is, right?

ROSS (3;3): He was trying to rip it up, right?
ADULT: No, he won't rip it.
ROSS: But I know he could rip it.

SARAH (4;4): You put it . . . see? You don't know where the pieces go. I know. An' that goes there, right?

Believe

ABE (4;10): Mom, remember that one dog that was just this big?
ADULT: Uh huh.
ABE: Dad, do you believe a dog could be that big?

ADULT: I told dad you decided you didn't want to go to Texas for Christmas.
ABE (4;10): I did too. Don't believe Mom.

Dream

ADAM (3;3): I dream sometime.
ADULT: Do you dream sometimes?
ADAM: Yeah.
ADULT: What do you dream about?
ADAM: I 'bout. I dream 'bout somebody.

NAOMI (2;11): I'm dreaming flowers and doggies.
ADULT: You think maybe you're asleep already.

have made indirect reference to some sort of mental process, but which alternatively might have referred only to behavioral acts or events. These exclusions included unadorned references to being familiar with someone or something (e.g., "I know Mary," perhaps meaning no more than "I have met Mary") and to know-how (e.g., "I know how to tie my shoes" perhaps meaning no more than "I am able to tie my shoes").

As with *think*, merely conversational uses of *know* were excluded, for example, the conversational openers "Know what?" and "Do you know. . . . " Following the reasoning of Shatz et al. (1983), we also excluded unelaborated uses of the phrase "I don't know." In children's early talk in particular, this expression seemed to be a convention meaning simply "No," or "I can't answer." Of course, use of "I don't know" was coded as a mental reference when there was good contextual evidence that it was a meaningful expression of ignorance, as in the example for Adam (2;11) that we detailed earlier. Uses of *know* were particularly rich in reference to the mental state of ignorance. For example, Naomi (4;7) said, "I didn't know that I couldn't run."

Wonder.   Children used the term *wonder* much less frequently than either *think* or *know*, yet a substantial number of uses occurred. *Wonder* seemed particularly appropriate when it referred to the psychological state of not knowing yet speculating about something. Examples are given in Table 3.1. In some cases, this function was quite explicit: Adam at 3;9 said about a toy snail, "I wonder what that is? Is it a fish?" We initially supposed that *wonder* might also be used to comment on mental activity akin to thought-as-activity. For example, Ross at 4;1 answered his father's question, "What is she doing?" by saying, "She's wondering." However, only two such uses were found.

Believe.   Adults use the term *believe* primarily to talk about states of conviction in, or endorsement of, the factuality of a proposition. In seeking children's uses of *believe* that referred to mental states, we looked for uses that referred to the same sorts of states as did thought-as-belief (see above, and Table 3.1). We also looked for uses of *believe* to talk about imagination or mental states with fictional content, as in *make-believe*, when Sarah at 3;2 said, "Make believe this is a crib." Uses of *believe* to refer to belief in something (e.g., "He believes in witches") were counted as genuine psychological references if, as in this example, they seemed to refer to a propositional belief (i.e., a belief that witches are real).

Dream.   The term *dream* can be used to refer to special contentful mental states while asleep or to wishes ("I'm dreaming of a white Christmas"). In our data, as it turned out, all psychological uses of *dream* seemed to refer to dreaming while asleep (Table 3.1), as when Naomi at 3;11 claimed, "I dreamed about a swimming pool." Use of *dream* was relatively rare in these transcripts.

Expect.   Children's uses of *expect* were examined for references to not knowing for sure, but believing or anticipating something (see Table 3.1). Other uses, such as to indicate pregnancy ("She's expecting a baby") or social prescription ("I expect you to be good"), were not counted as psychological references, and of course neither were merely conversational uses. Only two uses of *expect* were coded as making genuine psychological references.

Children's Reference to Thinking and Knowing

When coded according to the categorization scheme described above, each use of the verbs *think, know, wonder, believe, expect,* and *dream* (and variations on these terms) fell into one of four exhaustive and mutually exclusive categories:

> Genuine psychological references (as described above)
>
> Other substantive uses (including instances of behavioral reference and references like "know-how" or "I don't know")
>
> Conversational uses, including repetitions
>
> A residual set of simply uncodable, unclear utterances

There were a total of 4,352 uses of these verbs: 1,727 (40%), genuine psychological reference; 1,240 (28%), conversational uses; 1,014 (23%), other substantive uses; and the remaining 371 (9%), uncodable. There were approximately 200,000 child utterances in the entire dataset, and genuine references to mental states via verbs of thinking and believing occurred, on average, once in every 120 utterances. Of course, this rate of occurrence changed with age. Figure 3.1 depicts the data developmentally, with the children's genuine psychological reference in the use of thought and belief terms presented (a) as a percentage of all utterances containing belief-desire terms in any fashion, and (b) as a percentage of total utterances.[1] Recall that 96% of all uses of thought and belief terms occurred via some use of *think* or *know*. In Figure 3.1 we see that genuine references to thoughts and beliefs appear at just before the third birthday and steadily gain until about the fourth birthday, leveling off at about 25% of the children's total use of belief-desire terms.[2]

Of course, this graph portrays the grouped data from all 10 children; an examination of individual trajectories was also desirable. As noted in the introductory chapter, we were interested in whether early emergence of talk about contentful mental states such as thoughts and beliefs characterizes only precocious children such as Abe, or is more widespread. Table 2.5 in the previous chapter showed that 2 of the 10 children, Eve and Allison, for whom data were collected only at very young ages, produced very few "belief" verb utterances. Figure 3.2 therefore shows the emergence of genuine psychological reference to thoughts and beliefs for each of the remaining 8 children. For every child, belief references were found by age 3;5, first appearing at an average age of 2;9.

These data suggest that a concept of thinking is available to these children quite early, and that it plays a significant role in their psychological talk from about the third birthday on. As we noted earlier, however, it is important to determine whether this conclusion is corroborated by an examination of children's explicit talk about mental states appearing in contrastives.

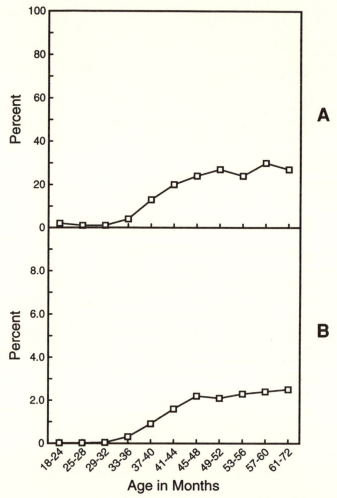

Figure 3.1. Genuine psychological references to thoughts and beliefs, shown as a percent of all utterances using terms of desire, thought, or belief (A), or as a percent of total utterances (B).

Contrastives

Contrastive utterances, which distinguish a person's thoughts and beliefs from other states of affairs, potentially come in several overlapping varieties: those contrasting belief with reality, fiction with belief, one's own mental state at one time with a later changed state, one's own mental state with another's, the contrasting mental states of two other people, and so on. As outlined in Chapter 2, we initially dealt with this variation by coding for two general sorts of contrastives: the child specifically contrasted a belief or thought with the world (thought–reality contrastives); or the child contrasted the thoughts of one person with the thoughts of another

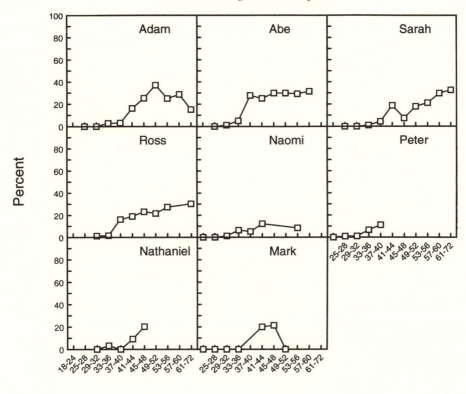

Figure 3.2. Genuine psychological references to thoughts and beliefs for individual children, shown as a percent of all mental-term uses.

(individual contrastives). Thought–reality contrastives include examples such as this one from Adam at 3;11:

> ADAM: No, dat not de right wheels.
> ADULT: Oh, why isn't that the right one?
> ADAM: Dis de right wheel to de bus.
> ADULT: Oh.
> ADAM: You thought that was the wheel to that.

Here Adam contrasts what is so (this is the right wheel) and what the adult mistakenly thought. Some thought–reality contrastives explicitly mentioned both alternatives, the real state of affairs and the contrasting thought, as in the example above. A child could also express a clear contrastive meaning by only mentioning one of the alternatives explicitly. For example, Abe at 3;4 said

ABE: Hey, don't eat it.
ADULT: I'm not.
ABE: I thought you were.

Even though Abe does not say something like "I thought you were, but you're not," he expresses the contrast between thought and reality. Utilizing such criteria, we included both explicit and implicit instances as contrastives.

To convey more fully what these contrastives are like, several thought–reality and individual contrastives are presented in Table 3.2. Because the earliest contrastives are of special interest, the table presents contrastives from children younger than four years.

Figure 3.3 shows the appearance of both types of contrastives in children's speech. These contrastive uses are once again portrayed as a proportion of all mental term uses, but because contrastives are of course less frequent than ordinary uses of the terms, the scale is altered (the top of the scale is 10% of the total data). The important point is that the pattern for contrastives mirrors the previous findings for genuine psychological reference that were depicted in Figure 3.1. Contrastives were apparent at right around the third birthday, as were genuine references to mental state in our broader coding.

Though contrastives occurred consistently, they were relatively rare. There are

Table 3.2. Contrastives for Thoughts and Beliefs

Individual Contrastives	Thought–Reality Contrastives
ADULT: I thought you were downstairs. ROSS (3;3): I thought me was upstairs.	ADULT: I'll get you a small surprise, ok? ABE (3;1): I think it's gum drops . . . Nope.
ADULT: It's kind of orangish red. ABE (3;1): Orangish red? ADULT: Yeah. ABE: I don't think it's orangish red. ADULT: You don't think it is? ABE: Uh huh. I don't think so, because it's orange not red.	ADULT: Adam, you look so tall. ADAM (3;1): Yeah. Is dat a . . . I thought I was a ba . . . a little baby.
	MARK (3;8): Do you know what? When we were going on our walk I thought we were lost. I thinked we were lost. When we were going on a walk and it was dark.
ADULT: Oh I think so. I think it goes in mommy and daddy's room. PETER (3;1): I think it goes right here.	ABE (3;8): I think . . . I thought I could rip the papers off, 'cept it doesn't have any paper.
ABE (3;3): They think they hace . . . they are slimy. ADULT: What do you think? ABE: I think they are good animals. ADULT: You don't think they are very nice? ABE: I think they are, 'cept mean ones.	ADULT: Do you really think it was haunted? By real ghosts? You think those were real ghosts who did it? MARK (3;11): I thought they were . . . that . . . there was a real man.
ROSS (3;7): Do you think God is good? ADULT: Yes. ROSS: But we think God is mean. ADULT: Why? ROSS: Because he spanks me.	

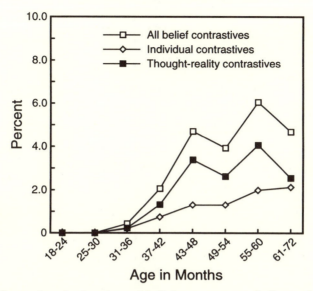

Figure 3.3. Contrastives for thoughts and beliefs, as a percent of all mental-term uses.

two good explanations for this: (1) because of our strict definition, only a subset of even genuine mental-state utterances qualify as contrastives, and (2) in normal conversation even adults rarely need to be so explicit. Indeed, from 3 to 4 years of age (37–48 months), contrastives account for only 17% of genuine psychological reference with verbs of belief and 7% of all use of belief terms. Considering only the eight children for whom we have substantial samples in the ages beyond 36 months (those in Figure 3.2), we find that all eight children contributed contrastives well before age 4. Contrastives first appeared in the talk of these eight children at an average age of 3;0 (ranging from 2;8–3;8).

As noted before, however, four children contributed the most material and were most appropriate for individual analysis, especially when the phenomena of interest were rare, as in the case of contrastives. Adam, Abe, Sarah, and Ross provided 75% of all the ''belief-desire'' term uses in the data, and not surprisingly these four children also provided 85% of all contrastives for thoughts and beliefs. Figure 3.4, therefore, depicts the data for contrastives for Adam, Abe, Sarah, and Ross. For each child, the same trend emerged as in the overall data: contrastives appeared initially at about the third birthday, plus or minus a few months, and steadily increased thereafter. For each child, the first appearance and subsequent use of contrastives closely paralleled that child's data for genuine psychological references, shown earlier in Figure 3.2.

Recall that in some contrastive utterances the child him- or herself explicitly mentioned both alternatives, as when Ross (4;0) said, ''He [Mark] thinks finished is not finished. Marky, not finished is not finished.'' Another example is Abe (3;8), ''I thought I could rip the papers off, 'cept it doesn't have any paper'' (Table 3.2). In the first case Ross states both what Mark thought and (in contrast) what is so. In the second case Abe similarly refers to both his own thought and the state

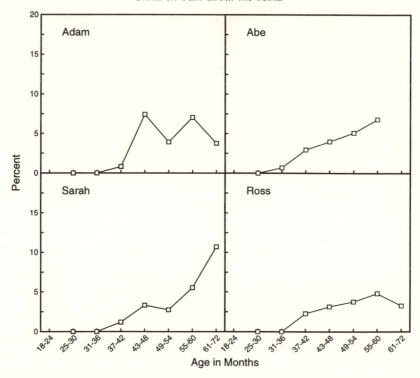

Figure 3.4. Contrastives for thoughts and beliefs (percent of all mental-term uses) for the four primary children.

of the world. Explicit contrastives, as in these two examples, generally had the form "X (but, only, except) Y," as when Adam (3;3) said, "It's a bus; I thought a taxi." A child could also express a clear contrastive meaning by mentioning only one of the alternatives explicitly—an implicit contrastive. For example, in Table 3.2 an adult first says, "I thought you were downstairs," to which Ross reacts with "I thought me was upstairs," definitely contrasting the two thoughts, but only explicitly mentioning one of them.

We did not comprehensively distinguish between explicit and implicit contrastives in our coding, although explicit contrastives could be argued to be more convincing evidence of children's understanding. Perhaps in some implicit contrastives the child was just stating his or her own thought after the adult had spoken and had not processed the adult's statement in any meaningful way. The use of explicitly contrasting connectives such as "but" or "no" argues against this suspicion in many cases (e.g., in the excerpt from Ross at 3;7 in Table 3.2), but such contrasting connectives are not always present. A related suspicion might be that explicit contrastives are actually quite rare, and so the bulk of young children's contrastives would in fact be cases in which adults were doing most of the talking.

To address these concerns, we examined each child's first 10 thought–reality and first 10 individual contrastives. We coded each instance as explicit or implicit as described above. Two independent coders examined 70% of these contrastives, representing 6 of the 10 children. Agreement was 92% (Cohen's kappa = .84). Disagreements were resolved in discussion. Overall, 42% of children's first thought–reality contrastives were explicit, as were 33% of their first individual contrastives. For the 4 children with the most data, the figures ranged from 4 of 10 explicit contrastives (for Adam) to 7 of 10 (for Abe) in the case of thought–reality contrastives, and from 2 of 10 (for Ross) to 4 of 10 (for Sarah) for individual contrastives.

This analysis of contrastives speaks to the methodological concern with whether the initial, broader coding genuinely captured reference to mental states, or whether it misattributed such understandings to young children. The analyses and findings replicate the findings of Shatz et al. (1983), although adding considerably to their generalizability and comprehensiveness. Genuine reference to persons' thoughts and thinking occurs quite early in development, at right about the third birthday. This is evident in comprehensive identification of children's reference to mental states in their use of such terms as *think* and *know* and is corroborated more precisely in their contrastive utterances.

Further Analyses of Contrastives

Beyond simply replicating and generalizing findings of early mental-state reference in young children, our data contain enough contrastives to permit detailed consideration of the nature of these early conceptions of thoughts and beliefs. Our next analyses undertake this task, including consideration of children's understanding of subjective mental states (versus objective states of affairs), of mental representations (versus connections), and of epistemic (versus fictional) mental states.

Objective versus Subjective Understanding

One general possibility, outlined in Chapter 1, is that young children have no conception of subjective mental states that differ across people. There are several ways in which this might be the case. For example, suppose children have no concept of the mind and simply misconstrue talk about the mind to be talk about the world. The world is an objective reality identical for everyone; children may be talking of that objective reality even when using terms like *think* and *know*. Alternatively, suppose children have some first-hand awareness of their own mental experiences, say images or dreams, but treat these as public experiences. That is, perhaps children construe all people as inevitably having those same experiences, not just the same kind of experiences generally, but the same specific images or dreams as they experience. Piaget's (1929) claims that young children's understanding of the mind is both egocentric and physicalistic implies this sort of objective, public, externalized misunderstanding of mind. If children's understanding is either egocentric or physicalistic, they should fail to understand the subjectivity of mental states—that you and I might have quite different internal mental states or contents, indeed might even have different thoughts about the exact same objective state of affairs.

The existence of individual contrastives in the young children's speech we studied, however, argues against such a characterization. In individual contrastives the child distinguishes between two persons' thoughts by noting their difference (see the examples in Table 3.2). Potentially, individual contrastives could have included instances in which the child contrasted someone's mental state toward an object with someone's else different mental state about another different object, perhaps something like, ''I was dreaming about a witch; you were expecting a phone call.'' In actuality, however, all instances of individual contrastives for verbs of thought and belief were of a narrower sort, contrasting two different mental states about the same object or contents, such as the examples in Table 3.2. These contrastives therefore qualify as subjective contrastives more specifically. When children explicitly comment on two contrasting or divergent mental states about the same experience, as they do in these contrastives, they are directly acknowledging the subjective character of mental states, that is, their individuation across persons.

Individual (here, specifically subjective) contrastives were produced well before 4 years of age by all eight of the children who used any belief terms. The average age of first occurrence was 3;3. Table 3.3 presents the data as to the occurrence of these subjective contrastives in the children's conversations. Although rare in frequency, such contrastives were consistently apparent, starting at just about 3 years. In such contrastives, as illustrated in Table 3.2, young children clearly commented on the difference in mental states between two other people, as well as between themselves and others. In these utterances they demonstrated an understanding of mental states that was neither merely egocentric nor physicalistic but, indeed, subjective.

Other contrastives, besides those coded as individual contrastives, also revealed an understanding of the subjective character of thoughts and beliefs. For example, the false-belief contrastives to be described shortly involved a contrast between what the child thought and what someone else thought, but this contrast was embedded in a further one between what someone believed and what was true (as the child saw it). Individual contrastives, as we coded them, included no mention of what was actually true, but simply the child's acknowledgment that two people had different thoughts about the same subject. Hence, individual contrastives provided clear evidence that the child understood the subjective quality of mental states, but they did not exhaust that evidence.

Table 3.3. Total Subjective Contrastives for Thoughts and Beliefs

Child	Age at First Occurrence	2 Years	3 Years	4 Years	5 Years
Adam	3;3	0	7	11	4
Abe	2;8	4	19	10	—
Sarah	3;7	0	2	17	2
Ross	3;2	0	10	4	4
Others	2;9	2	5	0	—
Total		6	43	42	10

Note: Utterances are grouped by age in years, so that 2 years includes 25–36 months, 3 years includes 37–48 months, etc.

Fictional versus Epistemic Mental States

Evidence that young children understand the subjective nature of mental states does not necessarily mean that they understand other aspects of mental states as well. As noted in Chapter 1, it might be that young children grasp something of the subjective nature of thoughts yet incorrectly conceive of such states as solely fictional, like fantasies and pretenses that are not about the world. Even though adults often refer to thoughts in terms of "believing" and "knowing," young children might conceive of thoughts as merely hypothetical or fictional states (similar to the way they might understand pretense), and as being neither about the real world nor causal in the world. Leslie (1988) at one point put forth this hypothesis, as did the editors of the Astington et al. (1988) volume. Perner (1991), in a similar vein, contends that 3-year-olds might understand something about thinking-of (Jack is thinking of a horse), but that they surely do not understand belief in the sense of thinking-that (Jack thinks that that is a horse) until age 4. An independent question, therefore, is at what age children begin to understand the epistemic nature of mental states that claim to be "about" the world and aim to be true about the world.

In Table 3.4 we have listed four different types of thought–reality contrastives, one type that concerns fiction–reality contrasts (i.e., mental states of imagining and fantasy) and three types that make reference to mental states about the world, labeled false belief, ignorance–fact, and advance belief contrastives. Any of the examples from these last three categories show that even 3-year-olds use belief terms to refer to beliefs about the world. For instance, in one ignorance–fact example, Abe (2;9) is talking about his ignorance of a real-world state—the coat's pockets. In this and the other examples in the last three columns, children are talking about real-world occurrences, referring to mental states about those events, and acknowledging that mental states of ignorance and belief can differ from the world.

The existence of fiction–reality contrastives (see Table 3.4) indicates that the children do at times refer to fictional mental states, that is, mental states of imagination and pretense that do not purport to be seriously about the world. Scrutiny of their genuine references to thoughts and beliefs yields other examples of references to fictional thoughts, imaginings, and dreams. However, examination of the other types of thought–reality contrastives makes it clear that the children also refer to epistemic mental states, in other words, mental states directed at the world rather than at fictions. Specifically, before 4 years of age (48 months and earlier), the children produced 103 thought–reality contrastives of the sort illustrated in Tables 3.2 and 3.4; only 6 of these were fiction–reality contrasts, and the remainder fell into one of the other three categories, those referring to mental states about the world (i.e., epistemic). Table 3.5 provides summary data about children's epistemic contrastives for thoughts and beliefs.

The three different sorts of epistemic thought–reality contrastives provide further information as to the children's understanding of thoughts and beliefs. Consider first the contrastives labeled "advance belief," in which children are stating a belief or speculation about the future or about some unknown state of affairs in the world, when it is not yet clear to the child what is or will be the case. For

Table 3.4. Example Thought–Reality Contrastives of the Four Different Types

Fiction–Reality Contrastives (Fictional Mental States)	Mental States about the World		
	Ignorance–Fact	Advance Belief	False Belief
ABE (2;11): I painted on them [his hands]. ADULT: Why did you? ABE: Because I thought my hands are paper.	(Ross was looking for mommy) ROSS (3;5): Well she's not out back, so we don't know where she is.	SARAH (3;5): In here, mommy? ADULT: Maybe. Let me see. SARAH: Maybe see. I think it's in here. ADULT: Let me see. SARAH: I think it's in here, mommy.	ADULT: Let me see if I can use your scissors. They're not too small. ABE (3;1): I thought so 'cept they weren't.
ABE (3;2): This is not a penis? ADULT: Well, what's it? ADULT: Why do you pss, pss all the time for? ABE: Because I thoughted it was a penis. ADULT: You were pretending.	ADAM (3;9): What is it? ADULT: What do you think it is? ADAM: I don't know, mommy. I wonder what it is.	ADULT: Jack is hiding. NAOMI (3;5): Yup. I think he's going to open the door and walk along.	ROSS (3;4): Hi. ADULT: Hi. ROSS: I thought you were at your home. ADULT: I was until a minute ago.
NAOMI (3;5): Because this is not really your game. My game. You don't know what it is. You can't know what it is, right? ADULT: Right. NAOMI: Yeah. So you'll hafta make believe. You're pretending.	ADULT: Do you know where daddy's shoes are? NAOMI (2;11): No. Maybe they're in bathroom. ADULT: In the what? NAOMI: I don't know where they is.	MARK (3;8): He's coming back after ...we ... after we have another day. ADULT: Really? MARK: That's when he's going to come back. ADULT: That's nice. MARK: I think he's gonna come back. I think he's gonna come back on Monday.	ADULT: I thought it was a bus. ADAM (3;3): It's a bus. I thought a taxi.

ADULT: Somebody was laughing. Who was laughing?
ADAM (3;4): A witch, I thought.
ADULT: A witch, you thought. I just kidding you.

ADULT: I thought I was my daddy.
ROSS (3;3): I thought you were a son. And so you're yelling at me.
ROSS: Yeah.
ADULT: Cause you're the daddy.

ABE (2;9): You have... you have pockets to keep your hands warm. I didn't know that.

ADAM (3;9): Open it. Open me. Oh. I wonder where the baby's lamb mother... the lamb mother's went.

ABE (3;8): Where's my plastic canteen?
ADULT: What did you do with it?
ABE: I never played with it outside, so I didn't lose it.
ADULT: It must be inside then.
ABE: I think it's upstairs in my bathroom somewhere.

PETER (2;9): Look... think this is a... think this is... bout to fall apart... bout to fall apart.

(Mark sees a piece of red paper on the top of the Raisin Bran.)
MARK (3;8): Oooo, blood! [Adult takes it off.]
ADULT: It's paper.
MARK: We thought it was yucky stuff.
ADULT: You did?
MARK: Yeah, me and Rossy [his brother] did.

(Paul is doing a puzzle.)
ADULT: Where does this go?
ADAM: He [Paul] thinks it goes there.

SARAH (5;1): Where's Paul? [a child who had visited for a few moments with his mother]
ADULT: Huh...
SARAH: I thought... was gonna leave... him here. I thought he was gonna leave him here.

ABE (3;6): The people thought Dracula was mean. But he was nice.

Table 3.5. Total Thought and Belief Contrastives of an Epistemic Rather than Fictional Nature

Child	Age at First Occurrence	2 Years	3 Years	4 Years	5 Years
Adam	3;3	0	29	31	0
Abe	2;9	2	32	29	—
Sarah	3;3	0	11	12	1
Ross	3;3	0	8	11	11
Others	2;8	4	11	1	—
Total		6	91	84	12

example, in the first advance belief example listed in Table 3.4, neither Sarah (3;5) nor her mother knows if the item they are looking for is really in the container because they cannot see into the container. Sarah states that she has a belief about this situation while at the same time acknowledging that she does not yet know if her belief is true; she has a hypothesis. Such mental hypotheses are different from fictional references that are not about the factual world at all; they are epistemic.

It might be argued, conservatively, that in referring to hypothetical mental states the child is talking about thoughts suspended from known reality. Perhaps, this argument would go, the child is confusing such "hypotheses" with fictional imaginings; perhaps he is talking about fictions, unrelated to reality, and we have overinterpreted this talk to be about hypotheses instead. As the examples in Table 3.4 illustrate, however, the child is often quite concerned with whether his hypothesis is right or wrong. The child wants to see, wants to discover whether his hypothesis relates truthfully or falsely to the world. Fictional mental states, in contrast, are neither true nor false, and children do not show a similar concern about whether the focal mental states are true or not in their fiction–reality contrastives. Moreover, even were we skeptically to discount references to advance belief as merely fictional and not seriously about the world, the categories of ignorance–fact and false belief would remain. These two categories account for the majority of children's thought–reality contrastives, 69 of the 99 such contrastives produced before age 4. In short, these 3-year-olds, from the advent of their sensible use of belief terms to refer to mental states, do more than refer to fictional mental states. They often refer to mental states directed at the real world. This finding seems clear in many of their utterances coded as genuine reference to mental states of belief, but it is especially explicit in their use of contrastives.

Connections versus Representations

A third possibility is that children may understand that mental states such as beliefs are both subjective and "about" the world, yet grasp the latter point in only an incorrect and rudimentary way. Specifically, they may use belief terms to simply talk about connections between the believer and the world, rather than the believer's representations about the world, as discussed in Chapter 1. Knowledge and ignorance provide interesting examples for considering this "connectionist" possibility further. A mere connectionist, in saying "Sam knows it's an apple," could mean only that Sam is associated or connected in some sense with that real external apple. He or she would not mean, under this hypothesis, that Sam has an internal mental state of knowledge about the apple, a representation of the apple. For the connectionist to say that Sam "knows" it is an apple is simply to say that Sam is connected to the apple; if Sam is not connected then Sam does not know, he is ignorant. Knowledge, and ignorance, in this miscontrual, are analogous to a state like tactile-feeling. I feel (with my hand) the apple; Sam does not. Analogously, I know this is an apple; Sam does not.

Note that such a misconstrual allows for the possibility that connections can differ across people, resulting in a simple sort of subjectivity: I'm connected, Sam is not. Furthermore, this mere connectionist misconstrual admits that such mental connections are about the world: I'm connected (or not) to *that* apple. In other words, it is conceivable that young children have a conception of knowledge and belief that is legitimately subjective and also about the world (not merely fictional), but that is nonrepresentational and hence quite unlike our own.

How can these two possibilities—that children might understand beliefs as mere connections to real-world states of affairs, versus (more appropriately) as representations of real-world states of affairs—be empirically distinguished? Figure 1.3 shows the critical difference. In the connections construal (Fig. 1.3A) there is only one sort of contents, the apple in the world, and people may be connected to this real world or not. But in the representational construal (Fig. 1.3B) there are real-world contents and there are mental contents, the apple in the world and the representation of an apple in the mind. Of course, the dualism between mental representational contents and real-world physical contents collapses somewhat in this figure, because what we have portrayed is a case of true belief, in which the mental contents and the real-world contents correspond or match. The dualism is easier to see where there is mismatch or noncorrespondence, such as in the case of a false belief. Still the critical point is clear: When children understand that mental contents exist as distinct from real-world contents and appropriately consider both, then they have moved beyond a simple connections construal of a mental state to a representational one.

Adults are able to demonstrate their understanding of both sets of contents by referring to false beliefs—acknowledging that the world is one way while a belief about the world has a different content. The possibility of such a demonstration is what accounts for the attention now paid to children's understanding of false beliefs in experimental studies. To appropriately attribute to someone a false belief, one must understand that the content of the world is one thing (say, an apple), but the content of the corresponding belief about the world is something else (say, grapes).

If children at some young age are mere connectionists, construing mental life as nothing more than a rudimentary connection between persons and the world, then although they could comprehend knowledge versus ignorance in the simple sense already described, they should not be able to conceive of a false belief. More generally, they should not be able to conceive of and comment on mental contents separate from, or contradictory to, real-world states of affairs.

An obvious possibility, therefore, is that young children misinterpret (and misproduce) talk about thoughts and beliefs as talk about the world, or about a direct connection of some sort to the world. The occurrence of ignorance–fact contrastives sheds no light on this possibility because, as argued above, ignorance could be talked about passably well from a connectionist conception alone. However, false belief contrastives, when they occur, speak directly against a simple connectionist conception.

Consider the first false-belief example in Table 3.4. In that contrastive, Abe (3;1) speaks of two different realms of content, the real world (the scissors are big enough) and his thoughts about the world (that the scissors were too small), and contrasts the two. A child who assumes mental talk is talk about the world could not make such a distinction; a child who makes such a distinction reveals his or her understanding of mental contents distinct from world contents, his or her rudimentary understanding of mental states that represent and misrepresent the world.

Even Perner (1991), who is particularly cautious about what might qualify as evidence of a representational understanding of mind, acknowledges that contrastives such as, "I thought this was a crocodile; now I know it's an alligator," or "the people thought Dracula was mean, but he was nice," which were uncovered in earlier analyses of Abe (Shatz et al., 1983; Wellman, 1985), are "rather convincing cases" (p. 307). But he suspects that "Abe's statements are due to his precocity." Table 3.6 presents the empirical data as to the occurrence of false belief contrastives. In order to convey more comprehensively the nature of these contrastives as they appear early in children's talk, all of the thought–reality contrastives in Table 3.2 as well as the false belief contrastives in Table 3.4 are in fact false belief contrastives produced by the children before the age of 4.

It is clear in Table 3.6 that Abe is indeed the first child among our subjects to refer to false beliefs, partly justifying Perner's concern about him. However, Abe is not unique. The four primary individuals, Adam, Abe, Sarah, and Ross, provide 80 false belief contrastives, and three of the four do so as young 3-year-olds. More to the point, there is no evidence in these data that false belief contrastives appear later than other thought–reality contrastives. Adam, Abe, and Ross all begin producing false belief contrastives in the same month in which they first produce thought–reality contrastives of any sort. Sarah produces only one sort of thought–reality contrastive at all, advanced belief contrastives, until she is 4.

In addition, we believe that it makes sense also to regard children's reference to speculative beliefs about the future (evident in advance belief contrastives) as manifesting an informative distinction between mental contents and the world. In the case of advance belief contrastives, reality is unknown but children talk about

Table 3.6. Total False Belief Contrastives

Child	Age at First Occurrence	2 Years	3 Years	4 Years	5 Years
Adam	3;3	0	10	13	0
Abe	2;9	1	21	12	—
Sarah	4;0	0	0	2	1
Ross	3;3	0	3	7	10
Others	3;8	0	6	0	—
Total		1	0	4	11

beliefs about that reality. In particular, they often admit that the contents of their beliefs may prove to differ from the contents of the world (in such additional comments as, "Let's see," or "I don't know"), thus acknowledging explicitly the critical distinction between beliefs and facts. Adam, Abe, Sarah, and Ross produced 5, 23, 17, and 5 advance belief contrastives respectively. Their first instances were at 3;9, 3;1, 3;3, and 3;3 respectively. (The other children together produced 6 instances from age 2;9 on.)

Altogether it seems to us that these young children recognize a realm of representational mental contents, and talk about that realm in the case of false beliefs, but talk about it in other fashions as well. They do so beginning at just about the time they begin to make genuine reference to thoughts and beliefs. In this regard our data provide no evidence that a representational understanding of beliefs is a significantly later achievement, following only on the heels of an earlier "connections" misconstrual of beliefs. Instead, the data suggest that very soon after children begin to talk about thoughts at all, they discuss a variety of distinctions among mental contents and states of the world, including some that seem to presuppose a representational understanding of mental contents as separate from but about the world.

Think and *Know*, Thoughts and Knowledge

Beyond using a variety of mental terms to refer generally to thoughts and beliefs, children used the terms more specifically and appropriately to refer to specific mental states such as wondering, knowing, and making believe. The examples in Table 3.1 give some sense of these distinctions, but it is useful to consider children's reference to specific mental states via specific terms more directly. We undertake this only for the terms *think* and *know* and the states of thinking and knowing. Ninety-six percent of children's uses of the words we examined involved the terms *think* and *know*, providing sufficient data in these cases to further consider children's understandings and usages.

For adults, *think* and *know* refer, in the main, to different sorts of mental states, or different aspects of one's mental states. Mental states, and their relation to the world, are complicated, and our descriptions of them in language mirror this complexity. Among the complexities are two separable aspects that we regularly consider and talk about: the contents of a person's thoughts—just what, under some description, he or she thinks—and second, beyond their content, whether they correctly describe reality or not. (A third aspect is whether the thinker of the thoughts takes them to describe or represent reality.)

When talking of someone's knowledge using the term *know*, for example, that person's mental states are often being considered from the point of view of their correctness vis à vis the world. To talk about knowledge, we offer a description of the world, presumed to be true, and then claim that the person in question knows 'that'. Similarly, in attributing ignorance, we offer (or at least assume the existence of) a true description of the world and then claim the person does not know that. Talk about knowledge, knowing and not knowing, emphasizes the possession, or lack, of a correct appraisal of the world. For this reason it is easy to imagine that children might conceive of knowledge as something like a connection to a real-world state, as we discussed previously: here is what is so, we posit, and then we ask, is the person connected to (knowledgeable of) that or not?

On the other hand, when we talk of someone's thoughts using the term *think*, we often emphasize the first aspect of mental states, their contents, regardless of how those contents map onto the world. Decidedly fictional imaginings, mental speculations, and firm convictions are all thoughts, and in each case it is worth describing just what the person thinks, what his or her mental contents are. Adult treatment of ignorance versus false belief illustrates this difference. In describing someone's ignorance, we describe something that is true that the person does not *know*. We emphasize what is true. In describing someone's false belief, we describe what he does think even if it is not true. We emphasize the mental contents.

Our language samples reveal that children use *think* and *know* in these distinctive ways, and they do so from the point at which we have credited them with genuine reference to thoughts and beliefs. In using the term *know* to make genuine psychological references, children concern themselves with what is so, and with whether someone does or does not grasp that event, fact, or state of affairs. There is, appropriately, considerable discussion about ignorance in children's use of the term *know*, about true things that people do not know. Table 3.7 presents some typical examples. In using the term *think* to make genuine psychological references, children concern themselves with the contents of person's thoughts, with *what* the person thinks. (Table 3.7).

Children's contrastives provide some of the best evidence as to their distinctive reference to thoughts and knowledge in the uses of the terms *think* versus *know*. As an examination of Tables 3.2 and 3.4 shows, the children's uses of the term *know* in making contrastives involve primarily the ignorance–fact distinction. In talking about knowledge, children appropriately focus on the distinction between the fact that something is true and that the person does not know 'that'. In using the term *think*, however, children often focus essentially on mental contents, encompassing variety of contrastives. Children use the term *think*, at times, to talk about how two people can have two different mental contents, in individual contrastives. They use the term to talk about mental contents that are fictions and fantasies, in fiction–reality contrastives. They also talk about mental contents that the holder takes to be true, beliefs, in advance belief and false belief contrastives. In each of these examples, the emphasis is appropriately on what the thinker thinks, the contents of his or her thoughts.

Know. As just noted, our data for contrastives give a more detailed picture of children's understanding of thoughts and thinking (encompassing such varieties as fictional thoughts, epistemic thoughts, wondering, and believing falsely) than they do for knowledge and knowing. But it is possible also to further explore children's conception of knowledge.

Perner (1991), following earlier analyses (e.g., Richards, 1982), provides an overview of various aspects of an everyday conception of knowledge as referred to by words like *know* and *knew*. In part, knowledge is associated with success;

Table 3.7. Genuine References to Thoughts and Beliefs Using *Think* and *Know*

Think	Know
ADAM (2:11): I thinking 'bout a leaf	ADAM (2;10): What dat?
ROSS (3;3): I think Marky wants to get out. He wants to get out 'cause he splashes.	ADULT: What is this? ADAM: What dat is. Don't know what dat is. Don't know.
(Mother inserts another piece in an incomplete puzzle.)	ROSS (3;2): It disappeared. ADULT: OK. ROSS: And I didn't know where they are.
SARAH (3;5): Oh . . . I think it's a ball. ADULT: You think this is going to be a ball, huh?	(Mother is looking for father's shoes.)
ABE (3;1): I'm thinking. I'm thinking of something I like to eat.	ADULT: Do you know where Daddy's shoes are? NAOMI (2;11): No. Maybe they're in the bathroom.
(Looking at small toys of horse, wagon, donkey, egg.)	ADULT: In the what? NAOMI: I don't know where they are. ADULT: I'll find them. NAOMI: I know where your shoes are.
PETER (2;7): Think this is the horse.	ADULT: Where honey? NAOMI: In the bedroom.
	SARAH (3;6): I know you get a princess phone. You hang it on your wall if you want to. It's on your wall.
	ADULT: What animals do you see here? ABE (2;11): A giraffe and a elephant, a zebra. I don't know those are. ADULT: Those are deer.

when someone knows something she can answer correctly or perform successfully. *Know* is used, therefore, to describe success and successful actions, when, for example, we say we know how to do something, or know an answer meaning we can correctly state it. Knowledge is furthermore claimed to be true. We use *know*, therefore, also to talk about truth, or about factual states of affairs. Our earlier discussion of 'knowing' versus 'thinking' highlights this use of *know*, as do the examples in Table 3.7 for *know* which refer to what is so, or true, or factual. Finally, and this is Perner's emphasis, knowledge is formed by exposure to relevant information or appropriate experiences. It is not enough that a person be correct to be said to *know*; correctness must stem from the proper sources. This aspect of knowledge is clear, for example, in contrasting *know* and *guess*. A lucky guess may turn out true (or a person may accidentally perform successfully), but knowledge more precisely refers to stored facts and skills derived from exposure to relevant information and experience.

Perner argues that children might have little psychological understanding of knowledge, yet be able to use *know* to appropriately refer to successful actions (he ties his shoes correctly, so he knows) and to correspondence with the facts (it really

is in the kitchen, so if he says it's in the kitchen then he knows). A deeper understanding would be that knowledge depends on exposure to proper sources of information. According to Perner, children first use *know* to refer to success and
factuality but fail to make reference to sources of knowledge before about 4 years
of age.

Perner's specific hypotheses are but one example of an increasing interest in
children's understanding of the sources of knowledge. Some investigators (e.g.,
Gopnik & Graf, 1988; O'Neil, Astington, & Flavell, 1992; Wimmer, Hogrefe, &
Perner, 1988) emphasize younger children's failure to appreciate that knowledge
is intimately linked to relevant sources until about 4 years or so; others contend
that even 3-year-olds demonstrate appreciation for this link, for example, in acknowledging that perceptual experience (looking inside an opaque box or not) is
linked to knowledge (knowing or not knowing what is in the box) (Pillow, 1989;
Pratt & Bryant, 1990).

Children's uses of *know* in our data speak to these issues. When children first
use *know* to refer to people's knowledge in our data, in their utterances coded as
genuine psychological references, they primarily refer either to situations involving
successful actions or to correct statements.

> PETER (2;5): I wanted my Daddy . . . is.
> ADULT: What did you say?
> PETER: I said don't know where daddy is.

> ADULT: Who watched you today when you woke up from your nap?
> ABE (2;11): I don't know. Who did it?

> ADAM (2;11): Where dat go? I know where dat go.

> ROSS (2;10): Mommy can't sing it she doesn't know it.

> ROSS (3;0): His daddy said, "Do you know how to read?" And the boy said,
> "No, because I'm not big enough." Then his mommy showed him how to read.

> SARAH (3;6): (naming letters with her mom)
> ADULT: What's that?
> SARAH: "K."
> ADULT: What is it. . . . I'm disappointed in you.
> SARAH: I think I don't know that.

Consistent with Perner's speculations, these are the two most frequent early uses
of the term *know*. Such uses of *know* are appropriate for children, just as for adults,
but they leave open the question of when children refer to knowledge sources.
When do these children appreciate that knowledge rests on exposure to relevant
sources of information and relevant prior experiences?

To address this question, we returned to those utterances coded as genuine
psychological references to sources of knowledge. Clear references to sources of
knowledge came in two primary forms: In one sort of utterance, children explicitly
mentioned not only that someone knew something but also how he or she came to
know it or might come to know it. For example, Ross (3;5) asked, "Do you know

why the Hulk is going? I will tell you if you will listen." Abe (at 3;9) said, "Snakes haveta hear." And when his dad asked why he responded, "Cause they wouldn't know who was gonna kill 'em, if they couldn't hear." In such examples children not only talk about someone's knowledge but refer to relevant sources of information that would influence that knowledge. A second sort of reference to sources of knowledge emerged when children explicitly questioned people about the sources of their knowledge. For example, when an adult told Adam (2;10) that a piece of cloth was a diaper, he asked, "What? How do you know?"

Table 3.8 shows several examples of children's references to sources of knowledge, both assertions about sources and questions about sources. Table 3.9 breaks down the occurrences by age and shows that the children made early consistent reference to sources of knowledge, again beginning at just about the third birthday.

To summarize, it is apparent that children use a variety of mental terms to refer to thoughts and beliefs, and they do so in order to talk about different aspects of

Table 3.8. Sources of Knowledge

Questions about Sources	Assertions about Sources
ADAM (3;0): Dat a duck?	ADAM (3;8): A little boy and a little girl.
ADULT: That's a duck.	ADULT: What're they doing?
ADAM: How do you know dat a duck?	ADAM: I don't know. I don't see it.
ADULT: What about the tails.	ROSS (3;3): I don't know. I don't know the name of the movie I watched.
ADULT: Yes.	ADULT: The movie you watched. You don't know the name of the movie you watched.
PETER (3;1): Yes. yes. It looks like . . . I got this. How did you know I got this?	ROSS: No. Will you tell me?
ABE (3;8): How did you know the caterpillar didn't die?	ADULT: How could I tell a nice hawk from a mean hawk?
ADULT: Cause I saw the pupa. Would he have made a pupa if he would have died?	ABE (3;3): Some hawks eat seashells. If you see a hawk eating a seashell, you know he's mean.
ABE: No. He would have smelled really bad if he had died.	NAOMI (3;5): These are new books. I don't know what they are about so you will have to help me.
SARAH (4;0): Is the swimming pool open?	NAOMI (3;5): Because this not really your game. My game. You don't know what it is. You can't know what it is.
ADULT: Yea.	ADAM (3;8): I don't know, will you tell me?
SARAH: How do you know?	ABE (3;9): Do you know this is wheat bread because it's made from wheat?
	ADULT: Yup, I know that.
	ABE: I didn't know that.
	ADULT: Oh you didn't know until you tasted it?
	ABE: No. I thought it wasn't wheat bread.

Table 3.9. Total References to Knowledge Sources

Child	Age at First Occurrence	2 Years	3 Years	4 Years	5 Years
Adam	2;10	1	14	14	0
Abe	2;11	1	27	19	—
Sarah	3;5	0	3	12	0
Ross	2;8	2	12	11	6
Others	2;11	2	3	0	—
Total		6	59	56	6

mental states and contents. The vast majority of such talk recruits two general terms, *know* and *think*. Children do not use these terms indistinguishably but rather differentially to refer to thoughts versus knowledge.

Mental States of Self versus Others

As mentioned in Chapter 1, an intriguing set of questions concerns children's understanding of and talk about their own mental states in comparison to those of others. References to the self's thoughts occur in first-person statements like "I bet nobody found it because I think it's burned." References to others' thoughts occur in second- and third-person statements like "You don't know what it is, right?" and "They think they are mean animals." (See Tables 3.1, 3.2, and 3.4 for other examples.) In our analyses, uses of "we," such as "We think he's mean," were conservatively considered as references to self.

Three of the children (Eve, Allison, and Nathaniel) had seven or fewer total references to belief. Table 3.10, therefore, includes data only for the children who provided at least minimal samples of genuine talk about beliefs. In Table 3.10, we show the children's age in months at their first (and third) references to their own and others' thoughts or beliefs. These data reveal a tendency for children's first references to thoughts and beliefs to be statements about their own thought or belief. But reference to the beliefs of others follows very quickly thereafter.

Throughout the transcripts, references to one's own mental states predominate; 79% of all genuine references to thoughts or beliefs refer to the child's own states. This proportion remains relatively stable even while decreasing somewhat with age: before the third birthday, 85% of all belief references refer to the self; for 3-year-olds the percentage is 74%, and for 4-year-olds 69%. Long after children clearly refer to the beliefs of both self and other, they predominantly refer to their own beliefs. This overall tendency to simply talk about themselves must be considered in assessing the significance of children's first expressions. We would expect children's first belief references to be to themselves if they *either* (a) simply prefer to talk about themselves, *or* (b) at first conceive of only their own beliefs. If chidren at first do not understand that others even have beliefs, however, the delay between talking about one's own and others' beliefs might be expected to be substantial. Alternatively, if children understand something of others' beliefs and simply prefer to talk about themselves, the delay between self-references and references to others

Table 3.10. Total Utterances Referring to the Beliefs and Thoughts of Self versus Other by Age at First (and Third) Reference

Child		No. of References	Age at First (and Third) Reference
Adam	Self	282	2;11 (2;11)
	Other	102	3;0 (3;0)
Abe	Self	482	2;8 (2;8)
	Other	173	2;10 (2;11)
Sarah	Self	156	2;9 (3;0)
	Other	67	2;10 (3;7)
Ross	Self	194	2;7 (2;11)
	Other	109	3;0 (3;3)
Peter	Self	29	2;4 (2;5)
	Other	3	2;9 (3;1)
Naomi	Self	19	2;11 (2;11)
	Other	6	2;8 (3;3)
Mark	Self	21	3;6 (3;8)
	Other	10	3;5 (3;8)
Subtotal			
	Self	1,183	
	Other	470	
Total utterances		1,653	

could be very short (although reference to the beliefs of others would remain relatively less frequent). It is telling, therefore, that reference to others' beliefs follows so quickly behind the first references to belief at all, as shown in Table 3.10. The average delay between referring to one's own beliefs and thoughts and referring to someone else's is one month.

An alternative way of addressing this question would involve examining each child's very first references to belief. Again, three of the children produced very few genuine references to belief because they were sampled mostly at very young ages. For the other seven children we examined their first 10 references to belief. On average, 2 of these 10 references were to others, ranging from 1 of 10 (for Peter) to 5 of 10 (for Adam). The occurrence of individual contrastives (see Figure 3.3) also demonstrates an early ability to talk about the beliefs of self and of others and moreover to distinguish quite precisely between the content of one's own beliefs and the contrasting content of others'.

Conclusions

Children's use of words such as *think, know,* and *wonder* reveals their emerging concepts of thoughts, beliefs, and knowledge. In our data children begin to use such terms infrequently in the months after their second birthday. These earliest uses are conversational turns of phrase, repetitions, and idiomatic phrases rather than genuine references to mental states. Right before the third birthday, however, genuine references to the mental states of thinking, believing, and knowing appear. These early references to thoughts and beliefs could conceivably be largely mistaken or restricted to only one certain type of mental state or mental content; however, we find no evidence of an early stage in which children erroneously think of thoughts as connections instead of representational mental states, or in which they talk about only one sort of mental state, say, fictional imaginings. Instead, in these transcripts children's early talk about thoughts includes several varieties of mental contents as well as of contrasts between mental contents and the world. Children's flexibility with cognitive constructs is clear in their differing uses of *think* versus *know*. It is clearer still, perhaps, in their expression of several different types of thought–reality contrastives: fiction–reality, ignorance–fact, advance belief, and false belief. In fiction–reality contrastives, the child distinguishes imagined mental contents from the occurrences and contents of the real world. In ignorance-fact contrastives, the child describes some aspect of the real world and claims that a person is ignorant of that aspect. In advance belief contrastives, an opposite sort of distinction is made. The child perceives that believer has mental contents of a particular sort but reality is unknown because it has not yet transpired. Finally, in false belief contrastives, reality, the fact of the matter, is known to the child speaker, but the believer has a mistaken belief about that fact. The fact that the children in our data utter all of these categories of thought–reality contrastives well before 4 years, indeed beginning at just about the third birthday, shows an understanding at an early age of both mind and the realm of mental contents; that is, a person's thoughts may be fictional or about the world, and, if about the world, may incorrectly or correctly represent corresponding reality. These young children also realize that such mental contents exist in others' minds as well as their own.

Notes

1. Note in Figure 3.1 how small the numbers are (0–3%) when expressed as percent of children's total utterances, although the pattern of change is largely similar across the two panels. As noted in Chapter 2, to avoid the problems of dealing with such small numbers we almost always present our findings as percentages of total utterances containing a target belief-desire verb rather than percentage of total utterances. Because we are interested in development within talk about the mind, including making comparisons between talk about thoughts, beliefs, and desires, it is usually more useful to present our results as in Figure 3.1A, that is, as a percentage of total uses of belief-desire terms.

2. Eight utterances identified as genuine references to thoughts and beliefs occurred in the very earliest time periods, 18 to 28 months. Seven of these came from a single precocious child, Eve (whose first genuine psychological reference to belief occurred at 21 months); the remaining early reference to thoughts and beliefs was uttered by Peter at 28 months (2; 4) precisely. With the exception of Eve, therefore, genuine references to belief began to appear only well into the third year, and even Eve had an early period of 3 months where transcripts were available and utterances frequent, but where she produced no genuine references to thoughts and beliefs. (For the other children's data, see Fig. 3.2.)

4

Talk about Desires

Sarah at 2;10

> SARAH: I turn it off.
> MOTHER: You did not.
> SARAH: Yes off.
> MOTHER: Yes you did. Don't!
> SARAH: I want . . . don't want . . . I don't want it on.
> MOTHER: Well, you gotta have it on. Leave it on.

We examined children's use of the terms *want, wish, hope, care,* and *afraid* in order to chart their early understanding of mental states of desire.[1] Together, desires and beliefs constitute the core constructs in our everyday mentalism. Desires, broadly conceived, include a person's goals and motives; they point to what the person wants, or is attracted to. Beliefs cognitively frame these desires. Desires provide the dispositional bedrock of our everyday psychology; we construe human actions as essentially desire-driven, intentional actions motivated by the actor's desires.

Our everyday notion of desire encompasses certain complexities that must be considered in any attempt to unravel children's understanding of this mental state. As depicted in Figure 4.1, when we attribute to someone a desire, we generally also attribute to the person an internal experience, in this case a longing, an urge, a craving for some object, action, or state of affairs.

More specifically, desires are intentional, in the philosopher's sense, that is, they are about, for, or toward some object. In Figure 4.1, John wants an apple; his desire is about that apple, it is for that apple. However, characterizing the object of a desire is not always so simple. The object of a desire may be physical, but it could also be an action or complex states of affairs. John wants an apple, or he wants to raise his arm, or he wants to go home. John might even want an object that does not exist. He might want a unicorn or to be able to hold his breath for three hours. The object of such a desire must therefore be represented as a state of affairs in John's mind rather than in the world. It can be argued that all desires describe mental-content objects, internal states of affairs ''as desired,'' rather than as they really are or really could be.

Despite their variety, in each of these cases it is possible to identify the object of the desire. Desires exist for certain things and not others and therefore are object-

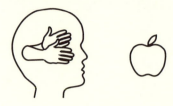

Figure 4.1. Depiction of a person's simple desire.

specific. In this respect, desires can be contrasted with less specific motivational states such as arousal or depression. General arousal causes organisms to move or to act, but arousal is not specifically directed toward some singular object. An apple or a banana will satisfy hunger; water or milk will satisfy thirst. Indeed, one can experience arousal and not know whether it is hunger, thirst, or even some other urge, such as to get warm. Only a specified intentional object, however, satisfies desire. If John wants an apple, an apple and nothing else satisfies his desire.

As the preceding discussion implies, desires not only specify objects; they constitute an experience of the subject or agent. In being experiences, desires differ from overt behavioral descriptions of actions, agents, and objects. Consider the action or behavior of reaching, for example. ''John is reaching for an apple'' is an object-specific description. But such a description refers to an action directed to a target. An attribution of desire specifies a mental attitude toward an object, as opposed to an action toward an object. Thus, a desire is in principle separable from the overt act of reaching for, or getting, the object. Desires consist of wanting an object; they are not the object or the getting of it per se.

A desire is not only object-specific and experiential, it is subject-specific. Recall that in Figure 1.2. John wants an apple, but Bill does not. A desire is a subjective experience that is specific to some person or persons and not others. Desirability, then, is something that inheres ultimately in people's experiential selves, in subjects rather than in objects.

In sum, desires are a special sort of internal-state description. To attribute a desire to a person is to attribute a subjective experience about or for certain objects. In this general way, desires are similar to beliefs; they are mental states about objects, that is, intentional states. Desires are quite different from beliefs, however, in the sort of internal experiential state they encompass, in this case a motivational experience of wanting to obtain an object or wanting a state of affairs to come about.

Both the object-specificity and subjective, motivational nature of desire can be considered in assessing children's understanding of desire and desire's role in action. The terms *want, wish, hope, care* (about), and *afraid* (that) are commonly used by young children for talking about this state. *Want*, in particular, is one of the very first internal-state terms produced by children, who employ it frequently.

Genuine Reference to Desires

It is difficult to simultaneously address all aspects of an understanding of desire in children's utterances about wanting, hoping, wishing, and so forth. For this reason, our coding proceeded in several phases, just as it did for thoughts and beliefs. First, we strove to identify utterances that sensibly referred to something like desire, or an actor's goal—his or her longing to obtain an object, engage in an action, or experience a state of affairs. In additional analyses, focusing often on contrastives, we sought to corroborate the first more general coding and to verify when children clearly understood certain of the aspects of desire just discussed, for example, its experiential core removed from any actions or obtainments.

Our first coding identified children's utterances that sensibly referred to desire in an intentional and psychological sense—or at least those references that would ordinarily qualify as such if produced by an adult. Not all uses of desire terms, even for adults, refer to psychological or intentional states, and we discarded those that potentially did not. For example, we excluded use of desire terms in idiomatic or frozen expressions ("wish upon a star"), for purely social convention ("I don't care" to make a polite denial), or in mere repetition of someone else's utterances (child repeats adult's statement, "I want one)".

In addition, children could conceivably just use desire terms to describe motivational states with no specified object (something like arousal). Utterances like "wanna" or "I don't wanna" may just describe a generalized state of agreeableness or compliance versus disagreeableness or resistance. Objectless statements of desire like "I wanna" were rare, even as sentence fragments, and were simply excluded as genuine reference to desire.

More problematically, children could conceivably use desire terms just to describe behavior. An utterances like "I want to run" might just be behavioral descriptions on the order of "I'm running;" or "I want a cookie" might mean no more than "give me a cookie." The possibility that children might interpret and produce desire terms to mean behavior poses a difficult problem that warrants further discussion. We will proceed by describing (a) a type of behavioral reference that we simply excluded, (b) the sort of utterances we accepted as genuine reference to desires, and (c) a more in-depth view of the connection between behaviors and desires.

A type of utterance classed as mere behavioral reference, and thus simply excluded from further consideration, was the simple, unadorned request for a concrete object, such as saying "I want the ball" when a ball was in plain view. Such a statement could too easily, in the absence of additional context or evidence, be a mere request for an object as in "Give me the ball," or even a polite form of "Hand me the ball." Although we could not of be completely sure that the children's meaning in such unelaborated utterances was simply behavioral, there were numerous other utterances that provided more convincing reference to desire-like states. Simple requests thus were noted as such and not considered further.

What did convincing instances of reference to desire look like? Here are two examples:

> ROSS (2;6): You want it [a button] off?
> FATHER: No, thank you.
> ROSS: You want it on?

> ABE (2;9): Daddy! Fill my squirt gun.
> FATHER: Why?

ABE: Because.
FATHER: Why?
ABE: Because I want to play with it.

In the first example, Ross's initial question might just have been a behavioral request, "Take it off." However, Ross's follow-up question, "You want it on?" suggests a focus on desire rather than on a specific action. That is, the conversation seems to be more than just a behavioral request because Ross did not simply take the button off, or insist that his father do so. Instead, he seems to continue to try to characterize his father's goal, his 'desire,' in the absence of, or in advance of, instrumental actions. Similarly, in the second example Abe seems to be appropriately citing a desire behind a request for action and not, for example, just describing a behavior or outcome. In other words, he describes what was wanted initially (to play with it), in contrast to what action he is specifically requesting (fill the squirt gun). In coding for genuine reference to desires we attempted to identify such sensible uses.

These codings, as reasonable as they seem, do not completely rule out some sorts of potentially behavioral reference. The difficulty becomes evident by supposing that an adult makes a statement like "I want to go to the store" as he is walking out the door. It could be argued conservatively that he is saying nothing more than "I'm going to the store," describing the action (going) and the outcome (to the store) rather than a desire more specifically. Most ordinary uses of desire terms in everyday conversation do not indisputably rule out such possibilities and paraphrases. Talk about desires often necessarily includes talk about actions and outcomes, because of desire's world-to-mind direction of fit, in Searle's (1983) terms.

Desires are internal mental states separable from the world, but by definition they describe an attitude with a world-to-mind direction of fit. This direction of fit involves a pressure for change, for action in the world to satisfy one's desires. If a belief (that an object is an apple) is shown to be false (it's really a funny pear), the pressure is for the belief to change to fit the world (a mind-to-world direction of fit). But if a desire (I want an apple) is unfulfilled (I haven't got one), the pressure is to change the world (buy one, steal one) to fit the desire (world-to-mind direction of fit). The attitudinal force of a desire is to change things—to get, obtain, have, experience the intended object. It is because desires have this direction of fit that they configure motivation, designating the sorts of mental states directed toward (desired) objects that cause people to act. Part of the notion of 'desire,' therefore, encompasses information about acting to obtain something, in real-world terms. To be sure, desires are not the obtainment, but they are desires-for-obtainment.

Talk about desire, then, is often talk about actions and obtainment as well. That is why the statement "I want an apple" functions so well as a request; announcing the desire institutes a press for its fulfillment. Similarly, announcing a desire to act, "I want to go," is often announcing an intention to act: "I plan to go," "I'm going to go," "I'm going." Thus, conversation about desire is intimately intertwined with goal-directed behavioral descriptions and behavioral expectations.

Several aspects of adult talk helps us more confidently conclude that such uses as "I want to go to the store" are talk about desires, beyond being talk about actions and objects. As an example, adults also tend to produce more explicit utterances that contrast desires with actions: "I want to hit him, but I won't," or, "I wanted to win the award but I didn't; I still want it, but it's just not going to happen." In such statements, adults reveal a conception of desires as contrasting with associated actions, outcomes, and world changes.

As with belief terms, our method relied on analyzing children's desire talk in multiple fashions. After coding for genuine reference to desire, we undertook additional corroborative analyses, especially including more precise codings of contrastives in children's talk. Such contrastives do appear for children, at least at certain ages and in certain contexts.

Having an initial broad and perhaps lenient coding, coupled with additional more precise analyses, had several advantages. One was that the initial coding provided a larger, comprehensive picture. Adults or children rarely need to be as explicit as they are in utterances like contrastives. Much legitimate talk about desire would have undoubtedly been excluded if only contrastives were examined. Moreover, an initial somewhat lenient coding was important for an investigation of development because it was unlikely that a genuine understanding of desire would emerge full-blown, all at once. Young children's initial understanding may be sensible but partial, or holistic rather than precise. For example, a child might see a person as wanting an object in an internal motivational sense, without firmly separating the internal state from the behavioral act; the wanting and the acting to obtain might be inextricable. In our first coding, we looked for sensible understanding without requiring full evidence of complete and precise understanding. We wished to exclude obvious cases of mere behavioral reference, but we did not wish to err by excluding genuine references to desires just because they were intimately bound up with descriptions of actions and action-goals. However, this sort of initial comprehensive consideration of children's utterances required follow-up analyses in order to determine more precisely the nature and limits of children's understanding of talk about desires.

Coding for Genuine Reference to Desire

Each utterance using any of the various focal verbs of desire was coded in the general fashion described in the preceding section for sensible reference to desire. To be included as a genuine reference to psychological state, an utterance had to present definite contextual evidence of reference to desire states.

Just as different belief terms mark different states and shades of conviction, different desire terms, for example, *want* versus *wish*, mark a variety of kinds of desire. The differences, at least in our adult understanding of the terms, provided both special difficulties and opportunities for coding. What follows is a description of the basic considerations we adopted for coding utterances using the different verbs. As noted in Chapter 2, the vast majority of utterances in fact used some form of the verb *want* (e.g., "want," "wanna," "wanted"), so we begin there.

Want. The core psychological sense that we sought was defined as an expression of desire for a specified object, an expression often intimately linked to intention or goal-directed action.

> ADAM (2;6): Sit on the front of the truck, Adam, and ride now.
> ADAM: No wanta sit there.
> ADULT: You don't want to sit there? Are you tired, Adam?
> ADAM: No, I don't want to sit seat.
>
> ADAM (2;7): Eat mommy.
> ADULT: Eat?
> ADAM: Yeah.
> ADULT: I'm not hungry.
> ADAM: Want spoon?
> ADULT: No thank you.
> ADAM: OK. You don't want a spoon. You don't want a spoon.
>
> SARAH (2;8): My new book.
> ADULT: A new book.
> SARAH: New book. Wan' go read it? Go . . . see new book?
>
> SARAH (3;10): I don't like my own house.
> ADULT: I don't like this house either, but . . . we have to stay here for another year
> or two.
> SARAH: I want to . . . buy another house. Don't like this house. Do you?
>
> ROSS (2;6): He scratched me.
> ADULT: Didn't it hurt?
> ROSS: Yeah. I want a Band-Aid. The boy hurt me.
> ADULT: The boy hurt you? How did the boy hurt you?
> ROSS: The boy wanted to.
>
> MOTHER: Did you like those cranberry muffins, Stan?
> FATHER: Yeah. They were alright.
> ABE (2;5): I wanna cranberry muffin. I like them.
>
> ADULT: Ice cream tastes good. It's cold.
> ABE (2;8): I don't want it cold. I want it warm.
> ADULT: You want warm ice cream.
> ABE: I want you put hot chocolate on it.

As these examples show, the intentional object involved could be an action ("don't want to sit") or a state of affairs ("want to . . . buy another house"), not just a physical object. Expressions of a desire connected to the child's own action, for example, "I want to move this block" said while the child is pushing a block across the room, were included as references to desire when the child seemed to be commenting on an attitude toward the act in addition to describing his own action (i.e. not just announcing "I'm moving this block," but in addition expressing his experience of wanting).

Some uses of *want* referred more to a wish, that is, to a desire for something recognized as unobtainable (e.g., "I want to be 7 years old"), without any commitment to action. These uses were noted for further consideration, on the assumption that they might, like *wish* and *hope*, be especially revealing of an understanding of mental states independent of action or reality. Similarly, uses of the past tense ''wanted'' were considered as likely places to find explicit distinctions between desire and outcome (e.g., ''but I wanted the red one'').

Uses of *want* to request an available object (e.g., ''I want an apple'') were coded as ''want-as-request'' instead of as genuine psychological references, because they could be simply paraphrased as ''give me'' statements.

Wish. Uses of *wish* in situations similar to those just described for *want* referred to psychological states of desire. *Wish* additionally referred to desires less connected to definite, purposeful action. At one extreme, *wish* could even refer to seemingly unobtainable desires in the face of the child's knowledge that he or she would not act or that the desire was impossible to actualize (e.g., ''I wish I was a boy''). These types of utterances had a special potential for revealing instances of children's understanding of the distinction between desires and actions or outcomes.

> ADAM (3;5): I wish I could play with this.
> ADULT: Ask your mother.
> ADAM: Can I open it?
> MOTHER: Yes.

> ROSS (3;7): Daddy, I wish we could go back to that store where Marky and me ride that white horse.

> ABE (4;2): I wish we had gotted some mail today.

> ROSS (4;3): I wish there was blue Jell-o.
> ADULT: That's nice. Is that your favorite color?
> ROSS: Yeah. And then I might turn into Captain America.

Hope. The important senses of *hope* were either an expression of desire as in wanting (e.g., ''I hope I can climb to the top'') or wishing (e.g., ''I hope Santa comes at Easter''):

> ADAM (4;4): That's a water fountain.
> ADULT: A water fountain.
> ADAM: I'm getting me some more. I'm gonna see. I hope this water.

> SARAH (4;2): Now I'm gonna cut it out. I hope I don't hurt it. Once I hurt myself.

> ABE (3;5): Daddy, I hope my toast will pop up.
> FATHER: It will.
> ABE: I hope it will because I'm so hungry.

Use of *hope* to refer to wish-like desires had the same potential as *wish* for marking contrasts between desires and outcomes. Conversational uses (e.g., ''I hope you aren't going to bother me'') to soften a command or make an indirect request were excluded.

Care. Uses noting a preference (e.g. "Do you care if you have red or green candy?") or lack of preference (e.g., "No, I don't care") were coded as referring to relevant states of desire.

> ROSS (5;6): I don't care if we go to Denny's or Arby's or McDonald's. I just want to go to a place that has food.
>
> ADAM (4;6): I don't care if Renny [the dog] makes . . . I don't care if she bites me.
> ADULT: I don't think you'd like for Renny to bite you.
> ADAM: I don't care. She won't make me . . .

"Taking care" of someone or "caring for" them were excluded as behavioral references, because these uses described acts of nurturance or help rather than an internal state of desire or preference. For example, Ross (5;11) said, "I really do care about my brother." Lack of preference ("don't care") was especially frequent and seemed potentially informative about instances of lack of desire, which could also reveal children's understanding of the distinction between action and desires (e.g., "I'll take that one, but I don't care").

Afraid was regarded as a psychological desire term only when it was used propositionally (e.g., "I'm afraid that we'll be rained on"). Adam (4;9) presents an example: "Do they have worms at the pond? I'm afraid they don't." References to simple fears (e.g., "I'm afraid of dogs") or being scared (e.g., "I'm afraid") were considered to be primarily emotional in substance and therefore were not counted as genuine reference to desires. Use of *afraid* to genuinely refer to desires also had potential for revealing contrasts between desires and outcome, because *afraid* often expresses a desire to avoid something that in fact happens; that is, it refers to not wanting something that actually occurred (e.g., "I was afraid that it would fall").

Since 97% of all uses of these desire terms in fact were uses of the term *want*, our principal aim (by design and necessity) was to identify sensible reference to a generic desire-like state (that is, positive and negative attitudes toward objects) rather than to differentiate precisely among children's understanding of wants, hopes, and wishes.

Children's Reference to Desires

Based on the coding considerations above, each use of the verbs *want, wish, care, hope,* and *afraid* fell into one of four exhaustive and mutually exclusive categories: genuine psychological reference; other substantive uses, including behavioral requests such as "I want that" or "I'm taking care of him," along with objectless uses such as "I wanna"; conversational uses, including direct repetitions and idiomatic expressions like "wish on a star"; and a residual set of uncodable utterances. There was a total of 7,507 uses of these verbs, of which 1,646 (22%) were other substantive uses (largely simple requests), 49 (1%) were conversational uses, and 254 (3%) were uncodable. That left 5,558 (74%) instances referring to genuine psychological states of desire as we have defined it. There were approximately 200,000 child utterances in the entire data set, so on average sensible reference to desire occurred about once in every 35 to 40 utterances. Of course, this rate of production changed with age.

Figure 4.2 shows the children's genuine psychological reference to desire at the various ages. Figure 4.2A, which presents the data as a percentage of total utterances using any belief-desire term, gives the impression that reference to desire may begin to decrease at about 3 years. In fact, this apparent decrease reflects the

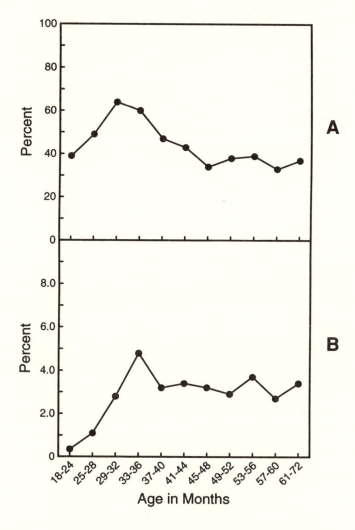

Figure 4.2. Genuine psychological reference to desires, shown as a percent of all utterances using terms of desire, thought, and belief (A), or as a percent of total utterances (B).

rapid increase in children's use of belief terms at this age (see Table 2.5). As Figure 4.2B shows, children's genuine reference to desire as a percentage of all their utterances increases from 2 to 3 years and is relatively constant thereafter. As both graphs in the figure show, genuine reference to desire occurs very early and is well established by 2 years of age; the data portray the relatively frequent and consistent use of desire terms to make sensible reference to desire-like states across all the years represented.

Of course, this figure portrays the group data. Figure 4.3 shows the data for psychological reference to desire for each of the 10 subjects. Our data for belief revealed an early age at which there was no genuine reference to thoughts and beliefs, followed by the onset of such references. All 10 children, however, refer

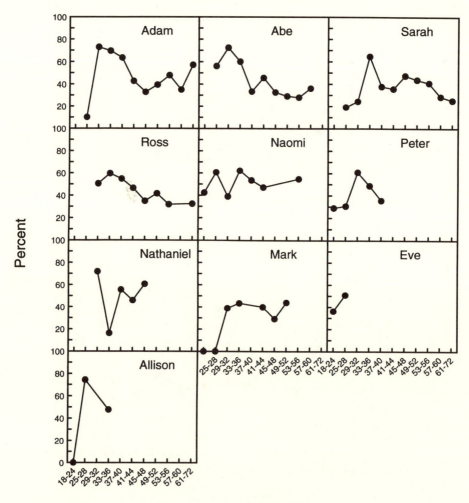

Age in months

Figure 4.3. Genuine psychological references to desires for the ten individual children, shown as a percent of all mental-term uses.

Table 4.1. Age at Children's First (and Third) Use of Desire Terms and Genuine Reference to Desire

Child	Age at First Available Transcript	First Use of Desire Term	First Genuine Reference to Desire
Adam	2;3	2;3 (2;3)	2;4 (2;6)
Abe	2;4	2;4 (2;4)	2;4 (2;4)
Sarah	2;3	2;3 (2;3)	2;3 (2;4)
Ross	2;6	2;6 (2;6)	2;6 (2;6)
Naomi	1;8	1;8 (1;10)	1;10 (1;10)
Allison	1;4	2;4 (2;4)	2;4 (2;4)
Eve	1;6	1;6 (1;6)	1;6 (1;7)
Nathaniel	2;6	2;6 (2;6)	2;6 (2;6)
Peter	1;9	1;10 (2;0)	1;10 (2;1)
Mark	0;10	1;6 (2;5)	2;5 (2;7)

quite early to states of desire. Table 4.1 makes this clearer by showing the month in which each child's first sensible reference to desire was found in comparison to his or her use of desire terms at all, regardless of meaning. Also shown is the first month of transcription. For 7 of 10 children, desire references and other uses occur together, in the first transcripts available. Of course, as Table 2.2 showed, our earliest transcripts for many of the children reflect periods at or just beyond their second birthday. Nevertheless, 3 children have a considerable amount of early data: Eve, Peter, and Naomi, with transcripts beginning at 1;6, 1;9, and 1;8 respectively. As Table 4.1 shows, the talk of these youngest children suggests that genuine reference to desire via such terms as *want* begins very early, perhaps as soon as children use such desire terms at all.

Additional Concerns and Analyses

These data demonstrate that a concept of desire is available to children quite early, at least from the second birthday on. Additional analyses reinforce and amplify this characterization. Consider, for example, whether these early uses of desire terms could be simply descriptions of overt behavior. In addressing this question, it is useful to distinguish two different sorts of descriptions: physical behaviors versus goal-directed actions (see Huttenlocher et al., 1983). Some things that people do are described in terms of overt behavioral movements alone: jumping, running, sneezing. Other acts are described in terms of goals and outcomes rather than specific behaviors themselves: taking off a coat, buying groceries, going to the beach. An action described as going to the beach may involve any of several sorts of movements (e.g., running, walking, or driving). What is described is the change in affairs that occurs or the goal obtained, rather than physical movement. We will call the first sort of descriptions behaviors, and the second goal-directed actions.

Desire term uses that we accepted as sensible reference to psychological state certainly encompassed more than simple physical descriptions of behavior. Genuine psychological references to desire, as we coded them, often referred not to behaviors but to goals and intentions. Examples were "I want it back" (2;5), "I wanna cookie'' (1;11), ''I want take that'' (2;1), and ''Wanna put them away'' (1;10). In these examples, children refer to object goals of the actor (a cookie) and or to a goal-directed action (put them away). At the very least, these statements specify an agent and an object that is a goal, or an agent and a goal-directed action, not physical descriptions of movements alone.

To ascertain whether even children's earliest desire statements indeed fit this characterization, we examined each child's first 10 utterances coded as genuine reference to desire, sorting out those which mentioned specific goals from those that talked only about behavior. Reliability was calculated on 100% of the data, and agreement was 91% (Cohen's kappa = .82). Out of their first 10 genuine desire references, children averaged 5 goal-mentioning utterances, ranging from 2 to 9. It seemed unlikely from these data that early utterances coded as genuine reference to desires were ingenious behavioral descriptions instead.

However, there remains an important difference between a goal-directed action (''I put them away'') and a desire (''I want to put them away''). Thus, there is still the question of whether children refer to desires as well as to goal-directed actions. Not only is there a conceptual difference between these two notions, there is a difference in adult talk about these two things. Talk about goal-directed intentional acts (''put them away'') typically uses an intentional action verb (put, take, open, etc.). Talk about desires (''I want to put them away''), for adults, also uses a verb of desire (*want, wish, desire,* etc.). The desire statement can include a description of a goal-directed act but additionally includes specific mention of a mental attitude toward that act, via a verb of desire. What about children's early references to desire?

Our coding for genuine reference to desire focused on desire verbs. All these utterances, therefore, necessarily included such verbs. However, in some cases the desire term was the only verb in the sentence (e.g., ''I want a doll''). In such cases, it was conceivable that the child was doing nothing more than using a desire verb (*want*) as a substitute for some intentional action verb (e.g., *get*), and thus was describing actions (''Get me a doll'') instead of desires (''I want a doll''). However, children often used a desire verb along with an intentional action verb, for example, ''I want put them away.'' If the child simply was describing the goal-directed action—''put them away''—there was no need to add the desire word as well—''want to put them away.'' When children, like adults, sensibly and appropriately mention a verb of desire as well as a verb of action, then this provides support for the notion that they are engaging in reference to desires, not just actions. So we coded children's genuine references to desire into two types of utterances: those with a single verb of desire (''I want cookie''); and those with two verbs, one of desire and one of action (''I want ride the pony''). Using this simple distinction, we examined the first 10 genuine desire utterances made by each child. Reliability was assessed on 100% of the data, and there was 100% agreement between two independent coders.

We found that even in our earliest samples, children often used desire terms appropriately in conjunction with descriptions of goal-directed actions that could have stood on their own. That is, many of children's genuine references to desire used the two-verb form. Out of their first 10 genuine desire utterances, children averaged 6 two-verb usages, ranging from 3 to 9. To reinforce this finding, we expanded our examination to the children's first 50 genuine desire utterances (again, agreement between two coders on all the data was perfect). Eve is the subject for whom we have the largest sample of utterances at the youngest age. Her first 50 uses of desire terms, beginning at age 18 months, were comprised of 30% two-verb uses. While other children varied in their earliest age available, their two-verb uses averaged 68% of their first 50 genuine psychological references for desire (ranging from 38% to 86%).

From our earliest transcripts, children used desire terms for more than reference to either physical movements or goal-directed actions; they also used desire terms to express an actor's attitude about or for that action or goal. Further corroboration of these children's understanding of desire is available from their contrastive utterances and conversations.

Contrastives

Paralleling our analyses of belief, we identified more extended instances of speech about desires where the child contrasted reference to a desire with reference to another related aspect of the situation. For example, when an adult said, "Oh, you mean a candy dot. . . . Sandra wouldn't give ya the purple one," Sarah at 3;8 shook her head "no" and replied, "But I wanted it." Here, Sarah describes her desire while acknowledging that it has not been satisfied, thus revealing that she distinguishes between the desire and the outcome or the relevant action (getting the candy).

Desire contrastives come in several overlapping varieties: those contrasting desires and outcomes, those contrasting desires with actions, those contrasting desires at one time with a later changed state, those contrasting the desires of two different people, and so forth. As an initial categorization within this variety, and again paralleling our procedures for belief utterances, we identified two general kinds of contrasts: the child contrasts the desire with its concomitant fulfillment or with related goal-directed actions, as in the above example (desire–outcome contrastives); or the child contrasts one person's desires with another's (individual contrastives). An example individual contrastive is

> SARAH (3;11): You wanta take that one off?
> ADULT: No, I don't wanta take that one off.
> SARAH: I did . . . wanta take this one off.

Table 4.2 presents several further examples of desire–outcome and individual contrastives. Because of our interest in early uses, the table presents examples from children considerably younger than 4 years of age.

Figure 4.4 presents data on the appearance of both types of contrastives in children's speech. These contrastive uses are once again portrayed as a proportion of all mental term uses, but because contrastives are less frequent than ordinary uses of the terms, the scale is altered, so that the top of the scale is 10% of the

Table 4.2. Contrastives for Desire

Individual Contrastives	**Desire–Outcome Contrastives**
ADULT: I want you to tell her about this book.	ABE (2;6): Get a circle one for me [a telephone].
ADAM (2;8): Don't want book.	ADULT: No, I won't get you a [telephone] . . .
ADULT: You don't want to tell her about the book.	ABE: I want one. When I grow big I get one.
ADAM: No.	
ADULT: I'd like to see you draw on one.	(A toy is gone)
NAOMI (2;7): No, I don't want to.	ADAM (2;7): I don't want it to leave it. Momma, why it leave?
ADULT: No? I'd like to see you draw so much.	
NAOMI: No.	
SARAH (2;11): Eat water?	ADULT: Don't push that button.
ADULT: Huh?	NAOMI (2;11): I want push on this one.
SARAH: Eat; you eat water?	ADULT: No. That's the one you're not supposed to.
ADULT: No, I don't want any water.	
SARAH: I want some.	
SARAH (3;6): Now which color you want? I want blue. What color you want?	ROSS (3;0): He [toy cookie monster] gonna eat my other raisins and I'm gonna eat these raisins. I want some cookies.
	ADULT: We don't have any.
	ROSS: My cookie monster wants my mommy to make some cookies for him.
ABE (3;7): I don't want to. I don't want to play baseball. Don't you want to? I don't want to.	SARAH (3;10): Turtle. Turtle. I want a turtle, but I can't have one.
ADULT: I want to.	
ABE: I don't want to. I want to stay home.	

total data. Contrastives account for 13% of all genuine psychological references to desire and 10% of all uses of desire terms.

Desire contrastives were produced by each child from very early ages. To consider individual patterns, however, it is once again useful to refer to Abe, Ross, Adam, and Sarah (Fig. 4.5). These four children provided 79% of all the belief-desire uses in the data; they similarly provided 76% of all desire contrastives. For each child, the data for contrastives mimic the overall data for genuine reference to desire.

Just as for belief, our coding for contrastives included both explicit and implicit contrastives. In explicit contrastives, the child explicitly mentioned both a desire and its outcome, or the desires of two different persons. Thus in Table 4.2 Adam at 2;7 says, "I don't want it to leave . . . why it leave?" mentioning both the desire and contrasting reality. And Sarah at 3;6 says, "Which color you want? I want blue," specifically referring to both her known and her mother's unknown desires. In implicit contrastives, the child also acknowledged both alternatives, but explicitly mentioned only one, contrasting it to an alternative expressed by someone else.

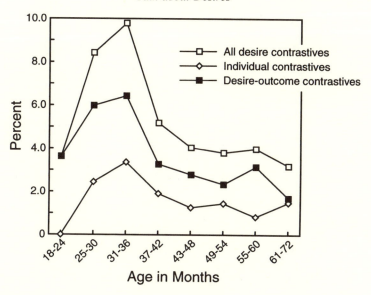

Figure 4.4. Contrastives for desire.

In Table 4.2, for example, Naomi at 2;7 says, "No, I don't want to," in response to her mother's stated desire, definitely but implicitly contrasting her desire with her mother's.

Paralleling our analyses for beliefs, we examined each child's first 10 desire–outcome contrastives and their first 10 individual contrastives (or all contrastives for children who had fewer than 10 contrastives of each type). We coded each contrastive as explicit or implicit as just described. Two independent coders examined a sample of 40% of the desire contrastives. Percent agreement was 91% (Cohen's kappa = .74). Disagreements were resolved in discussion. Overall, 18% of children's first desire–outcome contrastives were explicit. Excluding Allison (who produced only 2 desire contrastives total), individuals' data ranged from 1 of 10 explicit contrastives (for Eve, Nathaniel, Mark, and Peter) to 3 of 10 (for Ross and Naomi). Overall, 20% of the children's first individual contrastives for desire were explicit. Excluding Allison and Eve (who had no individual contrastives), individuals' data ranged from 1 of 10 explicit contrastives (for Peter) to 5 of 10 (for Sarah) and 2 of 3 (for Mark).

The production of contrastives further corroborates the richness and appropriateness of children's early references to desires. When children distinguish one person's desires from another's, as in individual contrastives, they reveal a person-specific understanding of desires. When they distinguish desires from the outcomes or actions that fulfill them, as in desire–outcome contrastives, they demonstrate an understanding of desires as something like a personal disposition or experiential state.

The data also suggest that for these children contrastives first appear at just about the same age as does psychological reference to desire, or only slightly

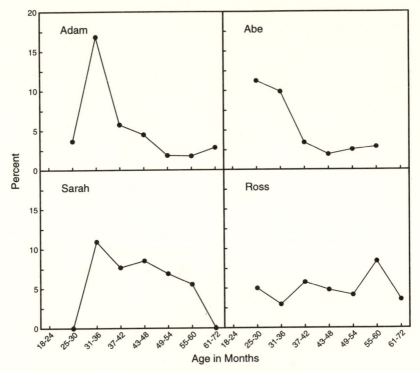

Figure 4.5. Contrastives for desire for the four primary children.

thereafter (Table 4.3). The most informative data for comparing the appearance of contrastives and genuine reference to desire comes from the three children for whom we have large samples of very early language: Eve, Peter, and Naomi. Table 4.3 shows that these children, too, produced desire contrastives almost as soon as any references to desire. In short, even if we confine ourselves to the evidence from contrastives (or even to explicit contrastives), genuine reference to desire

Table 4.3. Age at First (and Third) Desire Contrastives as Compared to Genuine References to Desire

Child	First Genuine Reference to Desire		First Desire Contrastive	
Adam	2;4	(2;6)	2;6	(2;6)
Abe	2;4	(2;4)	2;5	(2;5)
Sarah	2;3	(2;4)	2;9	(2;9)
Ross	2;6	(2;6)	2;6	(2;6)
Naomi	1;10	(1;10)	1;11	(2;1)
Allison	2;4	(2;4)	2;4	(2;10)
Eve	1;6	(1;7)	1;7	(1;8)
Nathaniel	2;6	(2;6)	2;6	(2;6)
Peter	1;10	(2;1)	1;10	(2;1)
Mark	2;5	(2;7)	2;10	(3;6)

seems well documented in these children's speech very early in life, often before the second birthday.

Further Analyses of Contrastives

It is important to scrutinize children's desire contrastives further, to better understand their variety and to better understand what they tell us about children's conception of desire.

Conflicts

Contrastives typically appear over two or three conversational turns (see Table 4.2) as the child tries to make clearer his meaning or interest to a conversational partner. Not surprisingly, perhaps, extended talk and clarification about desires is often the result of a conflict in desires or an unclearness about the desires of the speech partner; many of the contrastives revolve around conflicts, or potential conflicts, between the goals, intentions, and desired outcomes of two different persons. A deeper analysis of these conflicts begins a deeper analysis of desire contrastives.[2]

In our analysis of desire conflicts, we coded each party's conflicting desires according to a standardized template. The template captures something like the full potential information about a person's expressed desire. In abstract form the template is *desirer* wants *someone* to do *something sometime*. For example, "I want you to turn on the TV now." The four italicized terms represent open slots in the template that can be filled in various fashions. The *desirer* is the person spoken of, perhaps the speaker ("I") or somebody else. *Someone* is the subject of the content of the desire, perhaps the speaker (I want "me" to turn on the TV) or someone else. *Something* is what the desirer wants *someone* to do, have, or experience, perhaps a physical object (a bicycle) or action (to turn on the TV) or a state of affairs (to have a fun birthday). Of course, the *desirer* can want *someone* to do *something* or not to do *something*. *Sometime* concerns the timing of the desired act or event—now, later, never, quickly, tomorrow, and so on. Children's (and adults') desire statements can be easily coded in this fashion, as shown in Table 4.4.

This scheme for analyzing desire expressions makes it easy to portray talk about conflict between persons' desires. Several such conversations are depicted in Table 4.5. In the schematized column the point(s) of conflict are italicized. These conversations each capture a difference between the desire of one desirer and another. Beyond that, the desires in question can conflict with regard to the actor or experiencer—the *someone* slot. Ross (2;10), for instance, wants the father to read; the father wants the mother to read. The conflict can also be about the action or experience or item involved—the *something*. For instance, Sarah (2;10) wants a Band-Aid on; the mother wants a Band-Aid off. And the conflict can be about the time of the event in question—*sometime*—which in these examples essentially has to do with now versus later. The conflict also can involve several of these factors, as the last two examples in the table demonstrate.

Table 4.4. Application of the Schema for Desire–Actual Utterances

Age	Child's Actual Utterances	Phrased Schematically
2;10	Want go	Child wants child to go. (Desirer wants someone to do something.)
2;10	I want you to read my new books.	Child wants adult to read books. (Desirer wants someone to do something.)
3;0	I want sweater.	Child wants child to have a sweater.
3;0	I don't wanna look both ways.	Child wants child to not look both ways.
2;9	I wanna watch TV . . . I wanna watch something now.	Child wants child to watch TV, immediately.
2;11	I want the tempra ones oh mix up. You mix em.	Child wants mother to mix paints.
2;11	I didn't want my hand hold.	Child wanted father not to help.

Because the conversations in Table 4.5 concerning conflicting desires are all contrastives, the child shows some awareness of or some questioning of both parts of the conflict: what one party wants and what the other party wants (or might want). The child need not explicitly mention both desires in the conflict, although that often happens. Nonetheless the child recognizes the conflicting positions in some obvious fashion. For example, in the first conversation in Table 4.5, Sarah (2;10) insists and argues for her desire, against her mother's.

Table 4.6 presents a tabulation of the children's conflicts for each of the different slots in this template. Analyzing their conversations in this fashion gives a useful summary of the nature of children's articulated conflicts (with adult partners at least). More important, however, this analysis fleshes out the nature of children's underlying conception of desire. In particular, conflicts around each of the slots in the hypothetical template for describing desires (*desirer, someone, something,* and *sometime*) appear in children's talk. That is, in their various disputes children acknowledge that desires are possessed by specific desirers (they are person-specific) and that they involve complex objects, encompassing the desire that someone (not necessarily the self) have or experience something at some time. These separable aspects of a sensible reference to desire are the same in adults and very young children.

Subjective Contrastives

The analysis of conflicts constitutes one step in a further analysis of individual contrastives. Children acknowledge (and argue about) quite a few differences between the desires of different persons: I want (me) to do X, but you want me not to; he wants to do X now, but she wants him to do it later. These conflicts explicitly acknowledge desire differences among people. At the least, therefore, these conflicts show that children understand such individuation; desires are experienced by persons, and persons have differing desires. In our data young children certainly do not presume that desires are universally shared by all and sundry, nor do they

Table 4.5. Verbatim and Schematic Portrayals of Desire Conflicts

Verbatim	Schematized
SARAH (2;10): I wan' see *Romper Room.*	Mother wants child to see TV *later.*
ADULT: *Romper Room*'s all over. Get up in the chair.	Child wants child to see TV *now.*[c]
SARAH: Wan' see measles.	
ADULT: You can see the measles later.	
SARAH: I wan' do it.	
ADULT: Don't.	Mother wants child *to have* a Band-Aid on.
SARAH (2;10): I want . . . don't want . . . I don't want it on [a Band-Aid].	Child wants child *not to have* a Band-Aid on.[b]
ADULT: Well you gotta have it on. Leave it on.	
SARAH: No.	
ABE (2;9): I wanna, I wanna watch TV.	Adult wants child to watch TV *later.*
ADULT: You can in a little while.	Child wants child to watch TV *now.*[c]
ABE: I wanna watch something now.	
FATHER: Mommy'll read it to you.	Father wants *mother* to read books.
ROSS (2;10): I want you read my new books.	Child wants *father* to read.[a]
ADULT: We'll turn it on later.	Adult wants adult to turn TV on *later*
ABE (2;10): You turn it on later?	Child wants adult to turn TV on *now.*[c]
ADULT: Yep.	
ABE: No. I don't want it on later . . . I want it on now. You said you will turn the cowboys on?	
ADULT: I said I'll turn them on later.	
ADAM (2;10): More milk.	Adult wants child *not to have* milk.
ADULT: You don't need milk.	Child wants child *to have* milk.[b]
ADAM: Why not? Want some milk in it.	
ADULT: Oh, you're going to put it on?	Child wants *child to have* some.
ADAM (2;7): Want some? [to adult]	Adult wants *adult not to have* some.[a,b,d]
ADULT: No, I don't want some.	
ADAM: OK, I want some. You don't want some.	
ADAM (2;10): [to first adult] Do want more coffee please?	Adult₁ wants *adult₁ not to have* coffee.
ADULT: No, I don't think so.	Adult₂ wants *adult₂ to have* coffee?[a,b,d]
ADAM: [turns to different adult] Want more . . . want more coffee?	

[a]The desires in question can conflict with regard to the actor or experiencer (the *someone* slot).

[b]The conflict can be about the action, experience, or item involved (the *something* slot).

[c]The conflict can be about the time of the event in question (the *sometime* slot).

[d]The conflict can involve a combination of factors.

Table 4.6. Number of Conflicts that Evidence Desire Discrepancies of Various Sorts

Child	Before 2½ Years			2½ to 3 Years			3 to 4 Years			After 4 Years		
	Someone	Something	Sometime	Someone	Something	Sometime	Someone	Something	Sometime	Someone	Something	Sometime
Adam	2	2	0	11	52	0	19	22	0	3	7	1
Abe	1	7	1	4	28	20	6	9	7	3	4	0
Sarah	0	0	0	6	10	3	6	16	4	5	9	3
Ross	0	1	0	0	4	0	1	16	3	4	10	3
Others	1	37	6	8	34	0	4	14	0	0	8	5
Total	4	47	7	29	128	23	36	77	14	15	38	12

Note: All conflicts represented in this table also involve a discrepancy between the desires of two persons, that is, the desirers.

egocentrically think only of their own desires without recognition of the conflicting desires of others. To the contrary, discussing recognized conflicts over desires is common in the speech of quite young children.

A deeper question, however, concerns children's understanding of the subjectivity of desire. As discussed in the introduction, an important distinction exists between an understanding of mental states, such as desire, as subjective and a misunderstanding of such states as objective. Referring back to Figure 1.2, when do these children understand that one person may find an object (physical object, action, or situation) desirable while another finds the exact same object undesirable? An objective misconstrual would view desirability as inherent in objects, not subjects; the intentional objects of mental states are simply desirable (or not) in themselves, and hence experienced similarly by all who encounter them.

Note that children's understanding of conflicting desires, as analyzed above, does not necessarily indicate an understanding of subjectivity. Take the example of a child saying "I want to watch TV now," then acknowledging that the adult says, "I want to watch TV later." On the one hand, such a conflict shows understanding that desires differ in some manners across persons, but, on the other hand, both persons actually want to watch TV. The conflict is about when—now or later. In another example, Adam at 3;0 says he wants to smoke a cigarette. His mother says no, she doesn't want him to, while smoking herself. Both persons seem to see smoking a cigarette as desirable, although there is still a conflict about the child's actually smoking one. In short, as Astington and Gopnik (1991) put it, "understanding that desires may be different for different people isn't the same as understanding that what is desirable may be different for different people" (p. 43).

In contrast to the previous examples, imagine that a child said something like, "Here, look at this object. Well, you like it, but I don't. You think it's nice and want to have it; I think it's rotten and want nothing to do with it." If children said something like that, then this would indicate a subjective understanding of desires. In such a statement, a single object has been spotlighted for both of us and we differ as to its inherent desirability. In fact, children do at times make such statements, which we term subjective contrastives:

ADAM (3;9): Can you eat snails?
ADULT: Some people eat snails, yes.
ADAM: Why?
ADULT: Because they like them.
ADAM: Mommy, do you want to eat snails?
ADULT: No, I don't think I'd like to eat snails.
ADAM: I don't like to eat snails. . . . People eat snails.

ADAM (2;7): Want some? [to adult]
ADULT: No. I don't want some.
ADAM: OK. Want some.

ROSS (2;9): That's kind of scary.
ADULT: Well, but it's neat. I like it.
ROSS: But I don't like it.

ADULT: Because we like it hot. Don't you?
ABE (2;10): No. I like it warm. This is hot. I want it to be cold.

ABE (2;10): No.
ADULT: You don't like it?
ABE: You like it?
ADULT: Yes, I do.
ABE: But I don't like it.

ADULT: No, I don't want any [water poured on her].
SARAH (2;11): Why?
ADULT: Because I don't like to get wet.
SARAH: Huh. Don't like to get wet? Swim? You want you swim?
ADULT: No, I don't wanna swim.
SARAH: OK. I like swim.

ADAM (3;0): I don't like shaving cream.
ADULT: You don't like shaving cream?
ADAM: No. Daddy like shaving cream.

ROSS (3;3): Do you like mushrooms?
ADULT: Yes. Do you like mushrooms?
ROSS: No. I hate them.

ROSS (3;3): Why do you have coffee?
ADULT: Because I like it.
ROSS: I don't like coffee.

ABE (3;7): This, what I got on my bread, was sour on my tongue. . . . I don't like
it [hands bread to his father].
ADULT: Why do I have to eat it?
ABE: Because I don't like the sour part.
ADULT: What makes you think that daddy's going to like it?
ABE: You are . . . because you like sour stuff. So eat it.

In the first example, Adam asks if his mother wants to eat snails, and seems to be
genuinely struggling with whether she or someone else could ever find them desirable. Subjective contrastives defined in this fashion form a subset of individual
contrastives, a subset that focuses on differences in desirability of the same objects.

Note in the examples above that children's distinctions between desires per se
and desirability more generally—between what someone may want right now versus their more enduring, generalized preferences—are often expressed or clarified
via the term "like." We did not include the term "like" in our initial examination
of children's understanding of desires (see note 1), however, the term "like" is
especially helpful in examining children's understanding of the desirability of certain objects removed from a here-and-now desire to have (or not to have) one. In
coding for subjective contrastives regarding desirability, therefore, we examined all
children's individual contrastives coded for the terms *want, wish, hope, care,* and
afraid, and we coded all children's utterances with the word "like" for subjective
contrastives as well.[3]

This scrutiny of desire utterances, as well as utterances with the term *like,*

Table 4.7. Total Subjective Contrastives for Desire Terms and for Like

Child	Age at First Occurrence	2 Years	3 Years	4 Years	5 Years
Adam	2;6	13	25	4	1
Abe	2;5	14	18	8	—
Sarah	2;10	6	7	15	0
Ross	2;9	3	9	6	2
Others	2;4	16	8	5	—
Total		52	67	38	3

searching for clear instances of subjective contrastives yielded the data in Table 4.7. As can be seen there, subjective contrastives appear in these children's talk at about 2½ years of age. These analyses confirm that the children's understanding of desires is at least at times appropriately subjective, even at very early ages.

Desire–Outcome Contrastives

Two analyses of subsets of the desire–outcome contrastives allowed us to examine children's understanding of the distinction between desires and outcomes or desires and actions.

To begin with, consider a sample of the sorts of conversations coded as desire–outcome contrastives (in addition to the five such examples in Table 4.2).

ABE (2;9): I wanna watch TV, I wanna watch TV.
ADULT: You can in a little while.
ABE: I wanna watch something now.
ADULT: Nothing good is on until 11 o'clock. Why don't we practice tumbling for a while.
ABE: I don't wanna tumble.

ABE (2;10): I want put this on.
ADULT: Wait. Dad hasn't finished yet.
ABE: Wanta put this on.
ADULT: OK. Just a second. Let me get . . . pour one more glass.
ABE: I wanna put this on. Let me put this on.

ADULT: What comes from the yellow one or the red one?
ADAM (2;9): Dis one [a pen that isn't working]. Want to write. Huh?
ADULT: I don't think that one writes.

ADAM (2;10): More milk.
ADULT: You don't need milk.
ADAM: Why not? Want some milk in it.
ADULT: You take that in [you put the glass away].

SARAH (2;10): I wan' see *Romper Room*.
ADULT: *Romper Room*'s all over. Get up in the chair.
SARAH: Wan' see measles.
ADULT: You can see the measles later.
SARAH: I wan' do it.

ROSS (2;7): I want my glasses, sun.
ADULT: They're inside.
ROSS: I want it back.

In each of these instances, the child commented on someone's desire while at the same time acknowledging in some fashion the independence of that desire from its concomitant action or outcome. Very often this contrast between desire and outcome or action occurred because the child expressed his or her desire for something that he or she also acknowledged as not currently obtainable. Sometimes this contrast occurred explicitly, as in the last example in Table 4.2. At other times, the contrast was more implicit but still apparent. Consider the second example in Table 4.2. First, the child states a desire for cookies and finally, by changing it to a desire to make some cookies, acknowledges that his desire is at present unmet. The desire (wanting cookies) is in that sense distinct from its concomitant outcome (having cookies). Or consider the first example above. Here the child understands that the TV is off but expresses a desire to have it on. Indeed, the whole conversation is senseless unless the child is acknowledging both these contrasting aspects: his desire (for TV to be on) and the current contrasting situation (the TV is off).

In one regard these desire–outcome contrastives seem unsurprising; the child is announcing a desire so that it will be fulfilled. This sort of talk simply refers to desire's direction of fit (world-to-mind); desires are states of not having an object encompassing a pressure to change the world to obtain the object. For adults, of course, such statements as in Table 4.2 and above are unremarkable. They simply, correctly, use a desire term to describe a goal, an intention, a state of desire that guides actions or requests to obtain; they refer to a desire to make the world come to fit a (desired) goal state. Albeit unremarkable for adults, this ordinary understanding of desire-states (as separable from but propelling efforts toward obtainment) is exactly what we wish to document in young children. That is, as we have acknowledged before, young children might misunderstand talk via desire terms to simply be about the actions themselves (making a cookie) or about the obtainment itself (getting a cookie). Ordinary desire–outcome contrastives, of the sort illustrated in the examples given, document instead that children recognize an important distinction between desires and related actions or obtainments.

Some of our examples of desire–outcome contrastives seem more clear and explicit than others, and across the examples it seems that children might be referring to several different sorts of contrasts between desires and their related actions or outcomes. In our further analyses of desire–outcome contrastives, therefore, we identified some clear and separable cases. We term these more precise and distinctive contrastives unfulfilled desire and advance desire contrastives.

Unfulfilled Desire Contrastives. One important distinction between desires and the actions or objects desired concerns the issue of satisfaction or fulfillment. A person can have a desire for something but not get it, and indeed realize that he or she is unlikely to obtain the desired object, that the desire will continue to go unfulfilled. In this case, a positive desire contrasts with a negative outcome, and awareness of this difference constitutes a clear distinction between goals and acts or outcomes.

Indeed, this is a very important distinction—wanting something does not necessarily mean getting it; wanting to do something does not necessarily mean doing it, or being able to do it—and these mismatches separate desires and outcomes.

Many of the utterances coded as desire–outcome contrastives are references to desire that are not now fulfilled, but that may well soon be fulfilled. This sort of comment about one's desire often is designed to encourage or insure its fulfillment. In the subcategory called unfulfilled desires we identified instances in which the child commented explicitly that a desire was in fact unfulfilled. An example is Abe's (3;6) statement, "I said I wanted some and you didn't get me any," explicitly noting the desire and its unfulfillment. In this example, Abe does more than simply announce a desire that is as yet recognizably unfulfilled; he comments on both the desire and its discrepant outcome, thereby more explicitly acknowledging this crucial distinction between desires and the acts or objects that satisfy them. Additional examples are presented in Table 4.8.

Advance Desire. A different forum for noting the independence of desire from actions is the case of planning future acts or agendas, in which current desires remain unenacted now but carry the expectation that they will be enacted after a considerable delay.

Bratman (1984) speaks of the two faces of intention. One is intention's face in ongoing intentional actions, or intention-in-action; my acts are intentional because I'm doing them on purpose, for a current goal. Such acts embody or enact a desire. The other face of intention, however, is its future-directed face; not intentional action, but intention to act later. "I'm planning [now] to go to Paris for Christmas" shows this separation of the intention from intentional action. So too for desire: "I want [now] to buy [next month] a gift for your birthday" conceptually separates desire and action.

Bratman argues that it is necessary to separate future intentions from intentional actions in order to undertake effective planning in the case of several or conflicting intentions. If I intend to go to the store and intend to go to the bank and intend to go to the ball game, planning allows me to make one trip to the bank first and then go to the ball game, saving the store for tomorrow. Intentions, separated from embodied actions, are necessary for and reflected in advance planning. So too for desires: planning to enact one's desires later clearly separates a notion of desire from actions to obtain the desire. Expressions of desire (now) for objects or actions to be enacted later, reflect a conceptual separation of desire from action. Such expressions are what we mean by advance desire contrastives.

The need for planning, for talk about desires related to future intentions, is often occasioned not just by one's conflicting solitary desires, but by social necessities. One must often separate desires (now) from plans of action (perhaps later) in order to coordinate plans with partners. Young children do talk about their desires socially with others, as we have seen in their desire conflicts. Often in these discussions they insist on immediate fulfillment of their desires, but at other times they argue for and negotiate for delayed fulfillment of their desires. They do so, for example, in order to plan with their parents future courses of action. Table 4.8 presents several examples of such advance desire contrastives.

Table 4.8. Desire–Outcome Contrastives

Unfulfilled Desire	**Advance Desire**

Unfulfilled Desire

ROSS (3;2):   Daddy, I want to go to MacDonald's and you didn't say so [= you didn't let me go].

ABE (2;10):   I want pull up.
ADULT: No, you do it with this.
ABE: I can't do it. Want some.

ROSS (3;4):   Well, 'cause I wanted to be a sun day but it didn't.
ADULT: What? Sunday. You wanted it to be a Sunday, but it wasn't?
ROSS: No, No. I wanted it to be a sun day, 'cause the sun didn't come out.
ADULT: Oh you wanted it to be a sunny day, yeah.
ROSS: I wanted to be sun.

ADAM (2;10):   I simply don't want it.
ADULT: Don't want what?
ADAM: Simply don't want it.
ADULT;   You simply don't want what?
ADAM: Don't . . . want beans inneere.
ADULT: Want beans in there?
ADAM: Yes.
ADULT: How do you know beans are in there. . . .
ADAM: They don't come out.

ADULT: We'll turn it on later.
ABE (2;10):   I don't want it on later. . . . I want it on. I want it on now. [said while TV is clearly off and remains off]

NAOMI (2;5):   I wanna take your stockings off. I wanna take your . . . I can't take your stockings off. Let's take off your stockings off.
ADULT: They're too tight, Naomi.

PETER (2;8):   I wanna come out. I can't come out.

ABE (3;6):   How come we're not doing what I wanted?

ADULT: Do you remember [what you got as a present]?
ABE (3;3):   A net. [a basketball hoop]
ADULT: Uh huh.
ABE: 'Cept I didn't want it. I wanted a bat and baseball.

Advance Desire

ABE (2;6):   Get a circle one for me [a kind of telephone].
ADULT: No, I won't get you a [telephone] . . .
ABE: I want one. When I grow big, I get one.

ABE (2;9):   I wanna get something . . . I want to get something we go at the football game.
ADULT: You might.
ABE: I want some candy.
ADULT: I don't know if they have candy at football games.
ABE: When we go at the football game, I get some candy, OK?

(In a conversation with an unrelated adult)
ADULT: Where are you going?
PETER (2;9): Gimme another picture Mommy. Wanna do it. I'm gonna be right back. I'm gonna to tell Mommy I want paper.

(In a talk about birthdays)
SARAH (2;9): Dere.
ADULT: Yes. Would you like one of those?
SARAH: I want have one of dose.
ADULT: Tell Daddy. [said by mother]
SARAH: I want have dose.
ADULT: For your birthday?
SARAH: Yeah, for my birthday.

ABE (3;0):   When mommy gets home. . . . When mommy's at school, don't put me to bed. When mommy gets home. Don't put me in bed. When mommy gets home, her's going to put me in bed and read to me.
ADULT: I'll read to you tonight.
ABE: How come. I want mommy to.

ROSS (3;6):   Are you going to die?
ADULT: Not until you get to be an old man.
ROSS: If you die, I want mommy to get another you.
ADULT: Another me?
ROSS: Yea, another Brian.

90

Table 4.8. (continued)

Unfulfilled Desire	Advance Desire
ADULT: You mean a candy dot. . . . Sandra wouldn't give you the purple one? SARAH (3;8): [shakes her head no] But I wanted it.	
ADULT: What about your ax? ADAM (3;2): Yeah, I still want a ax	

Findings. Table 4.9 shows the combined data for unfulfilled desire and advance desire contrastives. We reiterate that these subcategories reflect two different sorts of evidence of children's recognition of the general distinction between desires as experienced, versus actions or outcomes. The table indicates the presence of such contrastives in these children's speech from about the middle of the third year. Together with the subjective contrastives discussed earlier, these unfulfilled and advance desire contrastives suggest a rather firm understanding of desire.

Beyond corroborating our earlier codings, these additional analyses help detail an understanding of three separable aspects of desire; they indicate a rich and precise understanding of desires as not only something like goals embodied in concomitant intentional (goal-directed) acts, but as individuated experiences, subjective in character, and separable from the acts they propel. Young children understand that (a) actions can fail to fulfill desires that linger beyond their acts, (b) desires exist in advance of and removed from acts that may only be executed in the distant future, and (c) identical outcomes or acts may or may not be desired by different persons.

Desires of Self versus Other

When do children begin to talk about the desires of others as well as their own? In our sample, children talked about their own desires in first-person statements, such as (2;2) "I wanna sit back here." References to others' desires occurred in second-person statements, like (2;3) "You want me get it?" and third-person utterances, like (2;3) "Marky wants to pee in the tub." For our comparison of references to self versus other, we considered first-person plural statements, for example (4;3) "We hope so," as referring to the self.

Table 4.9. Total Unfulfilled Desire and Advance Desire Contrastives

Child	Age at First Occurrence	2 Years	3 Years	4 Years	5 Years
Adam	2;10	5	10	3	1
Abe	2;6	13	18	6	—
Sarah	2;9	4	3	9	0
Ross	2;10	3	7	4	3
Others	2;1	12	3	1	—
Total		37	41	23	4

Table 4.10 summarizes the data for children's references to their own and others' desires. In the table, we show the children's ages in months at their first (and third) references to their own and others' desires, as well as total references to each. One child (Nathaniel) refers to others' desires well in advance of talking about his own, three children begin self and other reference in the same month, and six children's references to self precede references to others. For all three children for whom we have large amounts of data at very early ages (Naomi, Eve, and Peter) self references precede other references. The data, therefore, reveal a tendency for children's first references to desires to be to their own desires. Just as for references to beliefs, however, reference to others' desires follows relatively quickly thereafter. The average delay between self and other references is just less than two months, and even excluding Nathaniel, it is just less than three months. An alternative measure involves examining each child's first genuine desire utterances. Seven of the 10 children referred to others' desires at least once in their first 10 references to desire; across the 10 subjects, the average was 2 of 10, ranging from 0 of 10 (for Naomi, Allison, and Peter) to 6 of 10 (for Ross).

As Table 4.10 also shows, and as was the case for belief, in all of the transcripts references to one's own desires predominate; 71% of all genuine references to

Table 4.10. Total Utterances Referring to the Desires of Self versus Other by Age at First (and Third) Reference

Child		No. of References	Age at First (and Third) Reference
Adam	Self	509	2;4 (2;6)
	Other	752	2;6 (2;6)
Abe	Self	1,340	2;4 (2;4)
	Other	198	2;4 (2;6)
Sarah	Self	482	2;3 (2;4)
	Other	232	2;9 (2;9)
Ross	Self	543	2;6 (2;6)
	Other	197	2;6 (2;6)
Naomi	Self	282	1;10 (1;10)
	Other	73	2;4 (2;4)
Allison	Self	40	2;4 (2;4)
	Other	11	2;4 (2;4)
Eve	Self	97	1;6 (1;7)
	Other	26	1;9 (1;10)
Nathaniel	Self	186	2;6 (2;6)
	Other	7	1;11 (1;11)
Peter	Self	358	2;0 (2;1)
	Other	104	2;3 (2;5)
Mark	Self	58	2;5 (2;7)
	Other	18	2;11 (3;8)
Subtotal			
	Self	3,895	
	Other	1,618	
Total utterances		5,513	

desire refer to the child's own desire. This predominance of self-reference over other-reference continues across all ages. Before the third birthday, 70% of all desire references refer to the self; after the third birthday, 66% do so. Children have a decided preference for talking about themselves, but they also refer to the desires of others, and they begin to do so shortly after their first reference to desire at all.

Conclusions

Children's use of words such as *want, wish,* and *care* reveal their conceptions of desires. The children studied here began to use these words very early in life, by 1½ to 2 years, which is consistent with other reports (e.g., Bretherton & Beeghly, 1982). Conceivably, children's early uses of these terms could be largely nonpsychological, perhaps references to overt behaviors or goal-directed actions. However, in our data the children's early uses of desire terms in fact encompass substantial genuine reference to psychological states of desire in themselves and others. Moreover, at around the second birthday, as the children became able to engage in increasingly extended conversations, they talked more extensively and revealingly about desires. In their disputes with parents about desired activities, they revealed an understanding that *desirers* want *someone* to do, have, or experience *something sometime*. In their contrastive utterances, these young children revealed an understanding that different people have different desires; identical objects may differ in desirability among different people; and desires are essentially experiential states that motivate action but that are also separable from the external world of overt acts and outcomes. We believe that this early conception of desire establishes an initial foundation for the child's continuing efforts to understand the mind.

Notes

1. We did not systematically examine all possible terms for desire. For example, we did not examine the term *desire* itself. *Desire* was almost never used by children, and only after age 5. Two other terms were used by young children and have been included as expressions of desire by other investigators: *need* (Bretherton & Beeghly, 1982) and *like* (Brown & Dunn, 1991). For adults, *need* refers prototypically to objects required or necessary for some function, or compulsory because of some rule or convention, not merely desired. Gerhardt (1991) argues that by age 3 children distinguish needs, regulations, and desires via the verbs *needta, hafta,* and *wanta.* We focused on *want* as more directly referencing desires.

Like refers to a general preference or trait rather than a specific and present desire. If an adult says, "I like strawberries," she might be indicating indirectly or politely a desire for a strawberry. But more precisely or directly, such a use of *like* refers to a generalized preference for strawberries, a preference she would have even though she does not desire a strawberry right now. This distinction between desires and likes can be made quite explicit, for example, "You like strawberries, and I do not, but neither of us wants a strawberry now." Thus, while 'likes' are often linked to desiring something at some time, such a general preference is not itself the desire; initially we did not examine use of *like* on these grounds.

However, we later undertook a partial examination of children's uses of the term *like*, as we report in this chapter, in order to complement our initial analyses.

We do not claim to have exhaustively captured all of the children's references to desires, but we are confident we have analyzed large samples of children's very early references to desires. We have done so by focusing primarily on the term *want*, complemented by analysis of *like* and related terms such as *wish* and *hope*. The term *want* is used very frequently by young children to straightforwardly refer to desires, as we will show, and is used more frequently than *need* or *like* and earlier than *need*. For example, in Bretherton and Beeghly's (1982) sample of 30 28-month-olds, 93% used *want* to refer to desires. In comparison, only 67% used the term *need*. Of course, more could be learned about children's very early conceptions of internal states by precisely contrasting their understanding of desires, needs, and likes. This remains as a project for future research.

2. We searched both individual and desire–outcome contrastives for instances of desire conflict as well as several other subcategories of contrastives: subjective, unfulfilled desire, and advance desire (detailed in the remainder of the chapter). These categories were not exhaustive or mutually exclusive, although in fact only a few contrastives fell into more than one category. Of the total 720 desire contrastives, 149 were coded further by two independent coders. The 149 were selected randomly but with the constraints of representing roughly equally productions from both before and after 37 months and both desire–outcome and individual contrastives. For desire conflicts, agreement was 97% (Cohen's kappa = .93). Reliabilities for the other subcategories were: subjective contrastives, 99% (kappa = .96), unfulfilled–desire contrastives, (100%), and advance desire 100%.

3. Children begin to use the term "like" at about the same time that they use *want*, that is, sometime before the second birthday. Abe, Adam, Sarah, and Ross, for example, were already using *like* at the time of their first transcripts. The vast majority of children's uses of the term *like* at all ages are for comparatives, such as "This one is red like that one." At times, however, children use "like" to refer to general preferences. As explained in note 1, we did not initially include children's use of "like" in our analyses; but we added it in the current analysis of subjective contrastives, because it was especially relevant here and to help corroborate our analyses of *want*.

5

Desires and Beliefs

Adam (3;10) is trying to pull a scooter behind a trike but it keeps untying and coming off.

ADAM: Can I tie it again? I want to tie it. I don't want it to keep coming off. Mommy, I don't know how to tie everything.
MOTHER: Why are you tying it?
ADAM: Because I want it to ride in de back. Why do that? Do you think it's going to stay on dere?
MOTHER: No, I don't really think so.
ADAM: It is so.

In the two previous chapters, we have considered children's talk about desires and beliefs separately. Here we consider them together. Substantively, our everyday mentalism involves appeals to both beliefs and desires, the core constructs of a theory of mind. Furthermore, children talk about both these states; the children talking about thoughts and beliefs in Chapter 3 are the same children talking about desires in Chapter 4. At times, children talk about beliefs and desires in the same breath, as in the example above. So an important question is how children's developing understanding and talk about these two constructs relate. When and how does reference to thought and belief emerge in relation to reference to desire? There are theoretical and methodological reasons to address this question.

To understand the theoretical motivation, consider again Figure 1.3. It certainly seems possible to conceive of a simplified understanding of desire, as depicted in Figure 1.3A, one which requires no conception of representational mental states. In this simplified conception, John has an internal longing for an external apple. In such a connectionist conception, as discussed before, there exists only one realm of "contents": real apples, in this figure, or real behaviors, or real states of affairs. A person is simply either connected to those contents or not. Perhaps the person is connected to these things behaviorally by reaching for them, touching them, or manipulating them, perceptually by seeing them or hearing them, affectively by fearing them or liking them, motivationally by wanting them. In contrast, our ordinary conception of belief construes the believer as representing the apple, as dealing with a realm of mental contents in addition to real-world contents. This sort of distinction between potentially different conceptions of mental states fuels a serious hypothesis, namely, that understanding people's desires precedes under-

95

standing their beliefs (e.g., Astington & Gopnik, 1991; Woolley & Wellman, 1990). If such a hypothesis is correct, then there may well be an early age at which children talk sensibly about desires but fail to talk sensibly about beliefs, or fail to talk about beliefs at all. More generally, if we find that reasoning about desires precedes reasoning about beliefs, or vice versa, this would contribute important information to our efforts to chart and understand children's developing conceptions of mind.

It is, moreover, methodologically important to consider children's talk about beliefs and desires together. Children's talk about one mental state provides needed controls for interpreting developments in their talk about the other, as we will show.

Talk about Desires Precedes Talk about Beliefs

In Chapter 3 we reported that reference to mental states of thought and belief emerges at around the third birthday. In Chapter 4 we demonstrated that reference to persons' desires is apparent very early in the children's speech, in the earliest transcripts we possess. Figure 5.1 shows this relation between reference to desires versus beliefs directly. The figure clearly depicts an early period when children talk about desires but make no reference to thoughts generally or beliefs specifically. This developmental pattern is confirmed in the individual data of the 10 children, shown in Figure 5.2. The data for Adam, Abe, Ross, and Sarah, those children with the most complete longitudinal records, replicate the overall pattern in each case. Naomi, Nathan, Peter, and Mark demonstrate the same pattern in somewhat attenuated forms; for each child, reference to desire is apparent throughout but reference to belief is at first absent and only begins to emerge later. Eve and Allison offer the earliest data, and each has an early period when they refer to desires but not to beliefs. Table 5.1 shows the data for first (and third) occurrence of genuine reference to desires versus beliefs for all 10 children. On average the delay is 7 months, which is an underestimation because half of the children were already making consistent reference to desires in their very first transcripts (Abe, Sarah, Ross, Eve, and Nathaniel).

Do these data demonstrate a real and important phenomenon in children's talk about the mind, or might they instead be an artifact of our codings? It is unlikely, for the reasons outlined in Chapters 3 and 4, that our coding procedures simply misattributed reference to desire or to belief to children where there was none. Nonetheless, it is possible that our codings for these two different conceptions vary in sensitivity relative to one another. For example, perhaps our codings for belief are overly conservative, failing to credit children with some early but genuine references to belief. Conversely, perhaps our codings for desire are overly lenient, tending to credit young children with genuine reference to desire too readily. Either case could produce the observed developmental trend.

Consider first whether our codings for belief are too strict, relative to our codings for desire. Perhaps early uses that we coded as conversational or behavioral actually reflect genuine, however unconvincing, instances of reference to belief.

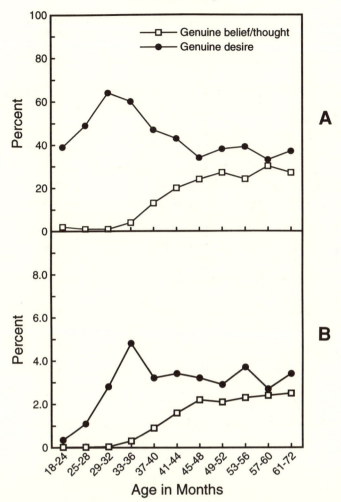

Figure 5.1. Genuine psychological references to desires and to thoughts and beliefs, shown as a percent of all utterances using terms of desire, thought, and belief (A), or as a percent of total utterances (B).

This concern can be addressed by considering more lenient criteria. In this regard, the most lenient possible criteria would be to simply accept any production of mental terms, such as *think* and *know*, as representing genuine reference to mental state. But Table 2.5 in Chapter 2 shows that simply looking at mere occurrence of the relevant terms yields the same developmental trend: frequent mention of desire terms precedes any mention of belief terms whatever.

The opposite possibility is that our coding for genuine reference to desire was too lenient. Perhaps early use of desire terms, even those we coded as genuine reference to desire, really only referred to overt aspects of behavior and action. As explained in Chapter 4, we purposely made broad codings for genuine reference to desire. Perhaps as a consequence, 74% of children's utterances using desire terms

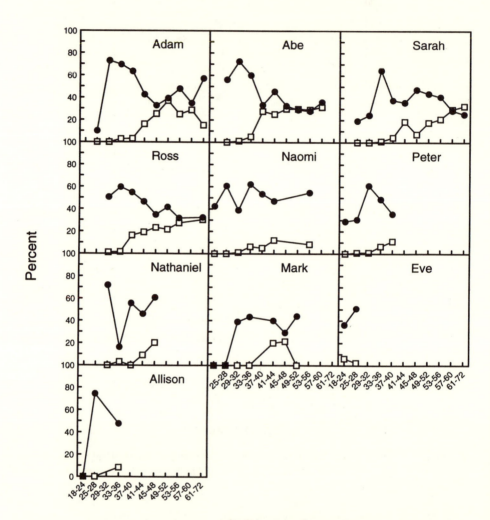

Figure 5.2. Genuine psychological references for the ten individual children, shown as a percent of all mental-term uses.

were accepted as genuine references to desire (see Chapter 4), whereas in comparison 39% of children's utterances using terms for thoughts and beliefs were accepted as genuine references (see Chapter 3).

The possible influence of differential leniency in our desire and belief codings can be addressed by considering stricter, more conservative classification schemes. Contrastive utterances provide a more conservative assessment. It is extremely unlikely that utterances classed as contrastives for desire represent mere behavioral

Table 5.1. Age at First (and Third) Genuine Reference to Thoughts and Beliefs versus Desires

Child	Thoughts and Beliefs	Desires
Adam	2;11 (2;11)	2;4 (2;4)
Abe	2;8 (2;8)	2;4 (2;4)
Sarah	2;9 (2;10)	2;3 (2;3)
Ross	2;7 (2;11)	2;6 (2;6)
Naomi	2;8 (2;11)	1;10 (1;10)
Allison	2;10 (2;10)	2;4 (2;4)
Eve	1;9 (1;11)	1;6 (1;7)
Nathaniel	3;5 (3;9)	2;6 (2;6)
Peter	2;4 (2;5)	1;10 (2;1)
Mark	3;5 (3;7)	2;5 (2;7)

reference instead. Moreover, codings for contrastives seem more comparable across belief and desire; for both belief and desire terms we similarly identified individual contrastives, and desire–outcome contrastives are roughly comparable to thought–reality contrastives in that each require children to acknowledge a key difference between mental states and realities.

Figure 5.3 compares children's references to desires versus beliefs, now using only contrastive utterances as a stricter, more comparable, criterion. That figure shows the same developmental pattern of reference to desire preceding reference to belief. Figure 5.4 shows the same data for the four major children individually, confirming the overall pattern in each case. These data suggest that it is unlikely that the developmental sequence, from first talking about desires to later talking about beliefs, results from adopting too lenient a criterion for the attribution of reference to desire relative to the criterion for belief.

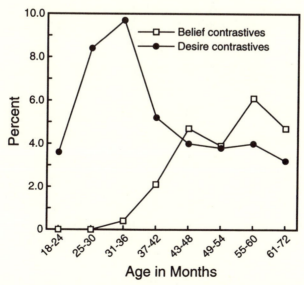

Figure 5.3. Contrastives for desire and for thoughts and beliefs.

It might be objected, however, that even this overall comparison between contrastives for desire and belief is not precise or strict enough. Chapters 3 and 4
discuss several sorts of differences that leave ample room for the speculation that
our methods for belief were stricter than our methods for desire. For example, in
Chapter 3 we noted that individual contrastives for belief were all examples of
subjective contrastives as well, a conceptually more precise category. In Chapter
4, we reported that individual contrastives for desire involve a variety of contrasts,
only a subset of which were, strictly speaking, subjective contrastives as well. An
overall comparison between individual contrastives, therefore, may give a false
picture of talk about desire preceding talk about belief, inasmuch as these may be
noncomparable codings.

Fortunately, further analyses comparing contrastive talk about desires with
strictly comparable talk about beliefs are possible. One concerns the comparison
just alluded to, of subjective contrastives for desire versus subjective contrastives
for belief. Table 5.2 compares these data, primarily for the four focal children, and
indicates that subjective contrastives for desire precede subjective contrastives for
belief.

Other similarly precise comparisons are possible. For example, for both desires
and beliefs, children at times explicitly contrast a person's current mental state with
a reality that will only be encountered later. They do so for desire in advance desire
contrastives (see Table 3.3) and for belief in advance belief contrastives (see

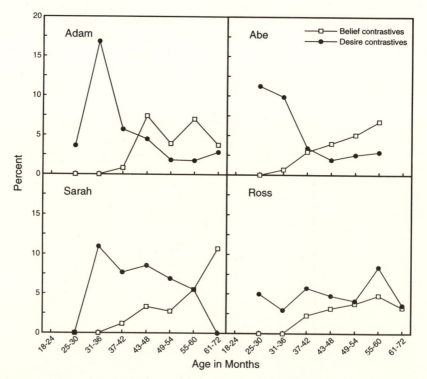

Figure 5.4. Contrastives for desires and for thoughts and beliefs (percent of all mental-term
uses) for the four primary children.

Table 4.8). A comparison of these contrastives also indicates earlier talk about desires than beliefs, in this case earlier production of advance desire contrastives than advance belief contrastives. Although contrastives of this sort are infrequent, each of the four children for whom we have the most data (Adam, Abe, Sarah, and Ross) talks about advance desires prior to advance beliefs. Adam's first advance desire contrastives appear at 2;10, and his first advance belief contrastive appears at 3;9. For Abe the delay is from 2;8 to 3;1, for Sarah from 2;9 to 3;3, and for Ross from 3;0 to 3;3.

These comparisons within subjective and advance contrastives confirm that, even in the case of strictly comparable talk about desires and beliefs, reasoning about and reference to desire precedes reasoning about and reference to belief. These data illuminate the nature of children's understandings. Mental states of desire and belief differ considerably. However, both mental states are similarly subjective; they refer to an individual's internal experience of an object, not its external objective reality. Children appreciate this subjective quality of mental experience for desires—people's preferences for and attraction to various objects—before they do so for beliefs, that is, people's representations of various states of affairs. Furthermore, beliefs and desires as mental states can both be about or refer to future as yet unknown possibilities. However, children seem to understand that a person can want something that can be obtained only later, before they understand that a person can think something that can be confirmed only later. More generally, the realm of desires may constitute a proving ground or launching pad for children's understanding of mental states, that is, an arena for reasoning out and talking about features of mental experiences that will later come to be seen and discussed as features of beliefs, thoughts, and knowledge as well.

This theoretical possibility raises another methodological concern about our claims as to early understanding of thoughts and beliefs. Thoughts and beliefs come in several varieties, some of which were discussed in Chapter 3. One additional distinction is what Flavell, Flavell, Green, and Moses (1990) have termed value beliefs versus fact beliefs. Fact beliefs encompass beliefs such as that "my shoes are in the closet" or "the earth is the third planet from the sun." Value beliefs encompass beliefs such as that "earrings are beautiful" or "beer is delicious." Value beliefs share obvious properties with desires and preferences; thinking that beer is delicious is arguably comparable to liking or preferring beer. In their research, Flavell et al. demonstrated that an understanding of value beliefs appeared

Table 5.2. Total Subjective Contrastives

	Age at First Occurrence		2 Years		3 Years		4 Years	
Child	Desire	Belief	Desire	Belief	Desire	Belief	Desire	Belief
Adam	2;6	3;3	13	0	25	7	4	11
Abe	2;5	2;8	14	4	18	19	8	10
Sarah	2;11	3;7	6	0	7	2	15	17
Ross	2;9	3;2	3	0	9	10	6	4
Others	2;0	2;9	16	2	8	5	5	0
Total			52	6	67	43	38	42

earlier than an understanding of fact beliefs in young children, and they speculated that this may be because children can simply interpret statements of value belief as being statements of desires and preferences.

In our data the related concern is that we may have credited children with early reference to thoughts and beliefs when they were really only referring to desires and preferences, in the guise of value beliefs. For example, consider Ross's (3;7) statement, "We think God is mean" or Abe at 3;3, "I think they are good animals."

To assess this possibility, we examined the first 10 genuine references to belief for the terms *think* and *know* for each of the four primary individuals (Adam, Abe, Sarah, and Ross). We coded these utterances as fact beliefs or as value beliefs. Fact beliefs referred to ascertainable matters of possible fact such as something's name, identity, or location. Value beliefs included potential references to desires or preferences, via such phrases as "I think it's *good*," or *bad, yucky, delicious,* and also included potential references to intended or desired actions, via such phrases as "I think I'll do that." In coding for value beliefs, we attempted to be as lenient as possible. For example, when Adam at 3;3 said, "Can I keep de train? I want to keep de train. I think I will keep my train," we coded his statement as a value belief in the sense of potential reference to a preferred or desired outcome or action.

Two independent coders examined the entire set of 80 utterances. Agreement was 95% (Cohen's kappa = .81). The four disagreements were resolved in discussion.

None of these children's first uses of *know* were value beliefs. Instead, children uniformly referred to knowledge about where things were, what things were called, and so on (see, e.g., Table 3.1 or 3.4). Two of Adam's first 10 genuine psychological uses of *think* were coded as value beliefs, including the example above. The frequencies for Abe, Sarah, and Ross were 4 of 10, 1 of 10, and 5 of 10 respectively. For Adam, Sarah, and Ross, their first genuine psychological use of *think* referred to clear fact beliefs; Abe's first reference (at 2;8) was a value belief "think it's pretty," but his second (also at 2;8) was a clear fact belief, "Mommy, I think everyone gots some presents for you."

Our earlier analysis of contrastives (see Chapter 3) also argues against the idea that these children's early references to thoughts and beliefs were solely references to value beliefs or to desires, preferences, and intentions phrased via cognitive terms such as *think* and *know*. In the majority of the examples in Tables 3.2 and 3.4 it is clear that children are referring primarily to matters of fact in their references to thinking and knowing. In general, therefore, our data document an early genuine reference to thoughts and beliefs distinguished from a still earlier reference to desires, preferences, and intentions.

Alternative Explanations

This primary pattern of results, indicating reference to desire preceding reference to belief, depends essentially on the finding that talk about beliefs is at first absent and only emerges around the third birthday. How should this finding be interpreted? One possibility that we favor is that this trend represents an important conceptual development. Emerging talk about thoughts and beliefs reflects children's emerging conception of such representational mental states. According to this account, young children do not talk about people's thoughts generally and beliefs specifically because they do not conceive of persons as having such mental states. They do not yet construe people in terms of internal mental contents separate from the real world but depicting either the world or fictional, not-real situations.

There are, of course, alternatives to this conceptual account. For example, perhaps children conceive of persons as having thoughts and beliefs but just do not talk about such states. After all, if the data on children's understanding of desires are to be believed, then young children do construe persons as having some mental states, specifically desires. Perhaps they are also aware of persons' thoughts and beliefs but for some reason do not or cannot talk about them appropriately.

In principle, it is impossible to prove definitively that young children lack a particular conception; no matter how sensitive our methods, it remains possible that we have simply failed to discover a conception that children, nonetheless, genuinely possess. However, it is possible to make the hypothesis that children lack a conception increasingly compelling. We can do so by addressing competing alternative hypotheses and ruling them out, and by considering additional implications of the conceptual account and confirming those implications empirically.

One obvious alternative hypothesis to consider is that young children have not yet learned the words they need to express concepts they understand. Without the words to talk about beliefs, children could not, in the present research, have demonstrated their conceptions. Data for testing this possibility in a straightforward manner are available. Table 2.5 shows that, as a group, the children used terms for belief, essentially *think* and *know*, as young 2-year-olds. However, they only began to refer to the mental states of thinking and believing later in the third year. At first the children used belief terms for conversational uses alone, such as capturing someone else's attention in phrases like "Know what?" Shatz, et al. (1983) first documented this phenomenon for a single child, Abe. Our data show more generally that the appropriate mental-state terms are available to and used by many children in advance of their making reference to thoughts and beliefs. As shown in Table 5.3, for each of the 10 children, conversational and other uses of *think* and *know* preceded psychological uses of those terms, and they did so by an average of five months. Lack of appropriate terms does not seem to have been the limiting factor; instead there was a substantial period when children used the requisite belief terms, but not with reference to mental states. More generally, it seems unlikely that word learning per se strongly limited the children's expression at this age. Even at earlier ages, children are learning hundreds of new words a month (e.g., McCarthy, 1954; Nelson, 1973) to talk about objects, people, and states. It is unlikely that simply lacking the necessary vocabulary accounts for the trend we report.

A stronger possibility is that other aspects of language competence limit children's expression. Everyday talk about beliefs is relatively complex in several fashions. Consider the statement, "He thinks that Ronald Reagan is the President."

Table 5.3. First (and Third) Genuine Psychological Reference to Thoughts and Beliefs versus Other Belief Term Uses

Child	Nonmental uses		Mental references	
Adam	2;4	(2;4)	2;11	(2;11)
Abe	2;4	(2;6)	2;8	(2;8)
Sarah	2;5	(2;7)	2;9	(3;0)
Ross	2;6	(2;6)	2;7	(2;11)
Naomi	2;3	(2;5)	2;8	(2;11)
Allison	2;10	(2;10)	2;10	(2;10)
Eve	1;8	(1;9)	1;9	(1;11)
Nathaniel	2;7	(2;7)	3;5	(3;9)
Peter	1;11	(2;2)	2;4	(2;5)
Mark	2;6	(3;5)	3;5	(3;7)

Talk about mental states, as in this example, often involves use of two verbs (thinks, is) with one verb phrase (Ronald Reagan is the President) providing the sentential complement of the mental verb (thinks). Moreover, the sentential complement is typically marked by use of a complement term of some sort, such as "that" (or "to" or "when, where, how, what"). Thus at 3;11 Mark said, "I thought they were . . . that . . . there was a real man." Because talk about mental states refers to a mental attitude about an object describable in sentential terms, this sort of complex syntax is often recruited to refer to mental states (see also Bloom et al., 1989). Perhaps talking about representational states depends on this sort of advanced language competence and thus, although young children understand the notion of a person's beliefs, talk about that notion awaits later linguistic developments.

In considering the merits of this argument, we first note that talk about beliefs does not in fact require this sort of complement language. We can refer to thoughts and beliefs in statements like "I think so," "He knows," and "I wonder." Note, however, that in our coding system, as described in Chapter 3, these sorts of shorter objectless statements were regarded with suspicion. In our endeavor not to mistakenly attribute reference to belief when it was not really present, such sentences often offered too little evidence of children's underlying meaning for confident interpretation. More complex sentences, such as "I thought that there was a real man," in appropriate contexts, were more likely to reveal a sufficiently appropriate conception. In short, even if complex sentential constructions are not necessary to talk about the mind, they may have been necessary to utter the kinds of statements we took to be indicative of psychological references to belief.

In general, however, we are doubtful that syntactic competence is the limiting factor. More important, in the period when children were failing to make genuine reference to belief they were systematically making reference to desires. Yet talk about desires also often uses complex syntax of a similar sort. The utterance "He wants to go home" also includes two verbs (wants, go) connected by a complement term (to). This complexity is often useful because desires are also mental states about objects describable in sentential constructions of their own (to go home). If young children can make cogent reference to desires, they probably possess the linguistic wherewithal to refer to beliefs as well; yet they do not.

In addition to raising these various hypotheses, we can test them empirically. For example, since utterances such as "I thought that there was a real man" require children to coordinate two verbs (thought, was) in one sentence, perhaps an early inability to express complex ideas connecting two sentential thoughts in a single utterance limits children's ability to refer to beliefs. As a simple but direct test of this possibility, we considered children's talk about desires before the onset of their talk about beliefs.

We began by finding the earliest age at which each child produced genuine references to belief (Table 5.4). We then examined for each child an earlier set of utterances that had been coded as genuine psychological references to desire. We examined the first psychological desire references up to either the first psychological belief reference or up through the first 50 psychological desire references, whichever came first. The size of each of these samples is indicated in Table 5.4. Then we simply tabulated whether these desire sentences used one verb (e.g., "Want that") or two (e.g., "Want ride" or "Want me get out?"). Table 5.4 thus also shows for each child the proportion of two-verb versus one-verb utterances for desire in these earliest samples. The children's early psychological references to desire often revealed use of two-verb constructions; with the exception of Eve, such constructions comprised from 36% to 86% of children's earliest references to desires (ranging from 6 to 43 utterances). Hence, talk about belief does not await an ability to connect two sentential ideas in a two-verb utterance; that ability is in place at substantially earlier ages, as is evident in children's early talk about desires.

Sentences such as "I thought that there was a real man" contain not only two verbs, but more specifically one verb phrase (there was a real man) that is indicated to be the predicate complement of the other (I thought) by an explicit complement term (that). In a further analysis, therefore, we examined the early desire utterances described in Table 5.4 more closely for the presence of clear predicate comple-

Table 5.4. Total Two-Verb versus One-Verb Utterances Prior to First Genuine Reference to Thoughts and Beliefs

	Age at First Genuine Reference to Belief	No. of Genuine References to Desire Prior to First Reference to Belief (or max. of 50)	No. (and Proportion) of 2-Verb Utterances Referring to Desire Prior to First Genuine Reference to Belief	No. of 1-Verb Utterances Within First 20 References to Belief
Adam	2;11	50 (of 195)	33 (.66)	6/20
Abe	2;8	50 (of 219)	43 (.86)	8/20
Sarah	2;9	11	9 (.82)	9/20
Ross	2;7	18	7 (.39)	1/20
Naomi	2;8	50 (of 162)	18 (.36)	0/20
Allison	2;10	36	24 (.67)	0/1
Eve	1;9	3	0	0/9
Nathaniel	3;5	50 (of 183)	41 (.82)	0/3
Peter	2;4	28	18 (.64)	2/20
Mark	3;5	8	6 (.75)	6/20
Total		304	199 (.65)	32/153

mentation (e.g., "Want to take top off"). Adam, Abe, Sarah, and Ross produced 92 predicate complement utterances in their references to desire, again all in advance of their first genuine reference to belief (ranging from 7 for Ross to 43 for Abe). The other children produced 107 predicate complement utterances for desire before their first reference to belief. In short, predicate complementation is apparent well before children begin to refer to beliefs.

As the example above indicates, however, predicate complementation in talk about desires often relies on the specific complement term "to." In fact, all the instances of predicate complementation found in early references to desire, and tabulated in Table 5.4, involve to- complementation (see also Bloom et al., 1984). As the "I thought that there was a real man" example indicates, predicate complementation for thoughts, beliefs, and knowledge more typically involves that-complementation or wh- complementation (as in, "I wonder where it is?"). Maybe children's delay in talking about beliefs, relative to desires, stems from a lack of ability to use these very specific predicate complement constructions.

As a test of this possibility, we examined the speech of the four children who provide the majority of the data (Abe, Adam, Ross, and Sarah). We again chose the age at which each child produced his or her first genuine reference to belief, as shown in Table 5.4, and then examined the child's language prior to that time. In this case, we conducted entirely new computerized word searches for the terms "that, why, what, where, who," and "how." Most of children's talk with "that" used the term as a demonstrative (e.g., "that's the one," "What's that?"). Most of children's use of the wh- terms were for questions (e.g., "Where's Paul?" or "Who did?"). But these various terms were also used as complement connectors in predicate complement constructions:

> (2;4) Look what Jean gotted for me.
> (2;5) I see that's something on the door.
> (2;5) The boy is glad that the grass is good.
> (2;6) Dad, see that it's round in circles.
> (2;7) My mommy said that we make popcorn.

For three of the four children, we found that predicate complementation using explicit that- and wh- complements was well established before the advent of reference to belief. The examples above are all instances of those early predicate complements. These early uses of that- and wh- complements occurred almost exclusively in utterances about perception and utterances about speaking. Table 5.5 shows the early occurrence of these sorts of predicate utterances. These instances, of course, reveal only explicit complementation, the production of utterances that explicitly mention the that- and wh- complements. Implicit complementation is also apparent during these early times (e.g., (2;5) "See [what] Adam did") but our data do not include that. Considering only explicit complements shows that use of that- and wh- complements precedes genuine reference to belief for Abe, Adam, and Ross.

Table 5.5 also shows that Sarah manifests a different, but equally revealing, pattern. For Sarah, explicit complementation with that- and wh- complements ap-

Table 5.5. Comparison of Children's Ages with Reference to Beliefs and Explicit That- and Wh- Predicate Complementation

Child	First Transcript	First Genuine Reference to Belief	First Predicate Complement Construction	No. of Predicate Complement Constructions Before First Genuine Reference to Belief
Adam	2;3	2;11	2;4	10
Abe	2;4	2;8	2;4	10
Sarah	2;3	2;9	3;2	0
Ross	2;6	2;7	2;6	3

pears only well after the emergence of genuine reference to belief. That is, Sarah's early uses of the belief verbs studied here, *think, know, wonder,* and so on, are all lacking that- and wh- complementation. This means that Sarah makes early genuine reference to belief, as we coded it, without any use of explicit predicate complementation. More generally, children could, and did, make reference to persons' thoughts and beliefs without any use of complex sentential constructions.[1]

To further demonstrate this fact, we looked at the children's first 20 psychological belief references (or as many as they produced if less than 20) and counted the number that were simple one-verb utterances. These utterances revealed 32 psychological belief references that involved only one verb, out of 153 utterances, and coming from 6 of the 10 children. An example of such a psychological belief reference is the following exchange involving Adam, aged 3;0:

> ADULT: What happened to Tom?
> ADAM: I don't know.
> ADULT: What happened to him?
> ADAM: I don't know. He ran down the street?

Another example involves Sarah, aged 3;3:

> SARAH: Where is it? It's not in the closet, Mommy.
> (Sarah wanders out of her bedroom into the hall in search of the book.)
> MOTHER: No, it's in your toy box.
> SARAH: Oh, I think so.

These examples show how utterances could qualify as psychological belief references without involving the construction of two-verb statements, and while being quite simple, as in ''I don't know'' or ''I think so.''

In summary, these analyses make it exceedingly unlikely that reference to belief awaits the development of a later, advanced language competence, one not available to children before their third birthday or one required to refer to beliefs but not desires. On the one hand, many early references to beliefs are simple, straightforward single-verb utterances well within the capacities of much younger children. On the other hand, children produce complex predicate complement constructions, of the sort often used by adults to refer to beliefs, well before they make reference to people's thoughts and beliefs. To the extent that children have both the words and the necessary syntax, either simple or complex, and still do not talk about thoughts and beliefs, it becomes increasingly likely that our data are charting a conceptual and not a linguistic transition.

A third alternative explanation, however, is that young children understand that people possess beliefs, but for some reason do not see thoughts and beliefs as a proper topic of conversation. This might happen, for example, if adults talked to children about desires but not beliefs. If parents did not talk to young children about beliefs, then children might fail to consider beliefs as an appropriate conversational topic. This possibility is one of a larger class of possibilities that would suggest that very young children's talk about beliefs is extremely limited, or absent, because parental input about beliefs or belief terms is extremely limited or absent. For example, consider again the word learning hypothesis. If certain words were missing or extremely rare in the input to young children, they could not learn them, no matter how competent at word learning they might be.

The data discussed earlier, showing that children learn and produce such words as *think* and *know* five to six months before making reference to thoughts and beliefs (see Table 5.3), demonstrate that children must be exposed to such terms, in their input, well before they talk about the mental states of thoughts, beliefs, and knowledge. It remains possible, however, that in adults' early talk to children genuine reference to belief is absent. Perhaps adults use such terms as *think* and *know* in talk to young children merely for conversational functions, reserving genuine reference to belief until a later age. If so, children's progression from conversational use to genuine reference would make sense, and children might fail to consider beliefs a proper discourse topic.

We tested this hypothesis by looking to see whether parents do or do not talk to their 2-year-olds about thoughts and beliefs. Because our transcripts included parental talk (in the presence of the child) as well as children's talk, we were able to simply examine the extent to which parents used belief terms in the relevant psychological senses. Again, we conducted this analysis for the four children who contributed the most data, Adam, Sarah, Ross, and Abe. For these children, we examined all utterances using *think* and *know* from all adults who appeared in the transcripts. We focused on *think* and *know* because these were the terms most used by children and adults. We coded each adult utterance, according to the scheme described in Chapter 3, as evidencing genuine reference to thoughts and beliefs or not. Reliabilities between two independent coders were assessed on 100% of the data from the largest contributor and yielded agreements ranging between 84% and 92% (Cohen's kappas between .62 and .72).

For each of the four children, the child's versus the adults' genuine references to belief are compared in Figure 5.5. In each case, it is evident that adults are using the terms *think* and *know* to refer to psychological states and acts, even in the earliest available transcripts (in the 25–28 month age bracket for each child). Not only do parents make some genuine references to thoughts and beliefs, such references are the predominant usage for parents, as shown in Table 5.6. Genuine reference to belief by parents greatly overshadows conversational, uncodable, and

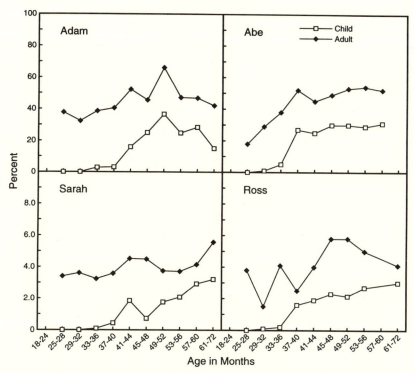

Figure 5.5. Comparison of adults' and children's genuine references to thoughts and beliefs.

other substantive uses of *think* and *know* at even the earliest ages. Parents use belief terms such as *think* and *know* in their speech to very young children and they use these terms predominantly to refer to persons' psychological states, their thoughts, beliefs, and knowledge.

Even though adults genuinely refer to thoughts and beliefs in their talk to young children, a related possibility is that such references may be rare. Specifically, it is possible that references to thoughts and beliefs may be comparatively rare relative to adult references to desire. If so, then reference to beliefs, however genuine, may be swamped by references to desire in the young child's input. To consider this

Table 5.6. Adult Genuine Psychological References to Thoughts and Beliefs as a Proportion of Total Thought and Belief Term Uses by Child's Age in Months

Child	25–28	29–32	33–36	37–40	41–44	45–48	Mean[a]
Adam	.82	.71	.74	.76	.83	.71	.76
Abe	.70	.76	.82	.83	.82	.79	.81
Sarah	.70	.75	.68	.61	.63	.64	.64
Ross	—	.62	.65	.63	.75	.87	.87
Mean	.75	.73	.73	.73	.76	.72	.74

[a]Proportions were calculated by dividing adults' genuine psychological references to belief by their total *think* and *know* uses, within each age period. Total belief references from adults for any given age period ranged from 10 to 336, averaging 151. Means were calculated from the raw data, not by averaging the proportions for each age period.

possibility we again examined adult talk to Adam, Sarah, Ross, and Abe, this time focusing on adult reference to desire in the earliest months available to us (the 25–28 and 29–32 month periods). We examined all utterances using the term *want*, and using the scheme in Chapter 4 coded those utterances as evidencing genuine reference to desire or not.

Table 5.7 presents these data and explicitly compares adult references to desire (via *want*) with that to thoughts and beliefs (via *think* and *know*). These data show considerable variability in input to the four children. For Abe and Ross, parental references to desire significantly exceed parental reference to belief, although genuine reference to thoughts and beliefs still represent about 20% of the speech to the child using any of these terms. For Adam and Sarah, early adult reference to thoughts and beliefs nearly equals or even exceeds reference to desire. Recall the hypothesis we are considering here: infrequency of reference to thoughts and beliefs (relative to desires) in adult speech to children accounts for children's delay in referring to thoughts and beliefs (relative to desires). Given that hypothesis and the patterns evident in Table 5.7, we should predict that Adam and Sarah would be advanced in their reference to thoughts and beliefs in comparison to Abe and Ross. The data, however, consistently go in the opposite direction: Abe and Ross make genuine reference to thoughts and beliefs in advance of Adam and Sarah (see, e.g., Table 5.1) and consistently produce more explicit talk about beliefs, such as contrastives, at earlier ages (e.g., Table 5.2).

In Chapter 7 we more systematically describe certain individual differences in children's talk about the mind and relate some of those differences to features of parents' speech to their children. The current data alone are sufficient, however, to make it unlikely that the consistent developmental progression evident in our study—of children referring to thoughts and beliefs only well after making earlier references to desires—is simply the result of lack of sufficient reference to thoughts and beliefs in their parent's speech.

Indeed, in examining the parental data it now seems obvious to us that parents would find it extremely hard not to refer to beliefs and thoughts. In our adult folk psychology, psychological explanation requires appeal to several sorts of mental states, prototypically beliefs and desires. We suspect that even if instructed to do so, parents would find it extremely difficult to talk about persons mentalistically and yet not refer to thoughts, beliefs, and knowledge. When their children are still very young, parents begin to talk to them about psychological states. At this point,

Table 5.7. Adult Genuine Psychological Reference to Desires versus Beliefs (via the terms *want, think, know*) as a Proportion of All Uses of the Terms

Child	25–28 mos		29–32 mos	
	Desire	Belief	Desire	Belief
Adam	.30	.37	.24	.44
Abe	.71	.18	.53	.29
Sarah	.46	.35	.41	.39
Ross	—	—	.66	.15

Note: The remaining uses of these terms are coded as repetitions and conversational uses, with some uninterpretable utterances—all uses judged not to represent genuine psychological reference.

parents do not limit themselves to talking about desires without beliefs; they probably could not do so if they tried. Because parents talk to young children about desires and beliefs from a very young age, children hear references to both these states; thus both states ought to seem equally appropriate topics of conversation to children. Nonetheless, young children talk about desires but not about thoughts and beliefs.

Conclusions

Although adult folk psychology seems to be indelibly a belief-desire psychology, young children's folk psychology may not be. The young child's construal of people may be bereft of a conception of thoughts and beliefs. At least in their everyday conversations, the 10 children in our study first discussed people in terms of desires without reference to thoughts and beliefs, and only later incorporated reference to cognitive mental states as well. These young children's talk about desires without beliefs cannot be explained by their deficient word learning, by inadequate expressive language, or by absences in parental input. It could be explained by conceptual development. If children did not conceive of persons as having thoughts, beliefs, and knowledge, then in spite of hearing and even using words like *think* and *know*, in spite of possessing the language competence to talk about beliefs, in spite of talking about desires, in spite of hearing adults talk of beliefs often and systematically, they could not genuinely refer to thoughts and beliefs.

Note

1. Bloom et al. (1989) present some related information. They studied the development of implicit and explicit complementation in four children for the verbs *think, know, see, look* from ages 2 to 3. They show that even early in that time period (Time 1 in their analyses, roughly from 2 to 2½) young children often express complex sentential ideas, although typically without use of explicit complementation (see their Table 9.3). They report that uses of *think* and *know* were associated with two somewhat different complement types (termed sentential complements for *think* and wh- complements for *know*), but found both subtypes also apparent in children's use of *look* and especially *see*. They do not report precisely whether they found complement structures apparent for *see* and *look* before *think* and *know* (nor do they identify genuine mental references for these latter verbs), but their analyses make it clear that predicate complement structures were developed well before 3 years of age in their data, which also is well before the children in our data began to make genuine references to thoughts and beliefs.

6

Explanations and Arguments

In their early conversations, young children first reveal a mentalistic understanding of desires and, somewhat later, of thoughts and beliefs as well. We believe that children's early understanding of desires and beliefs is part of a larger conceptual enterprise, an understanding of persons' actions, minds, and lives. To explore this larger understanding, we must characterize children's references to beliefs and desires in reasoning about and with people. There are two obvious sorts of extended reasoning to consider: children's explanations of action, and their disputes with others. Children's explanations of action bear on the larger topic of their understanding of causality and early talk about causation (e.g., Hood & Bloom, 1979). Children's disputes are part of the larger topic of how their understanding of mind affects their real-life social relations (e.g., Dunn, 1994).

Explaining Action

Adam (3;7) tastes some glue.

> ADAM: I don't like it.
> ADULT: Why would you put that in your mouth?
> ADAM: I thought that was good.

In this example, Adam explains his action to an adult: he licked the glue because he *thought* that it would taste good. Mental explanations of this sort, in which actions are explained by appeal to the actor's mental states, beliefs, and desires, provide some especially revealing samples of talk about the mind.

When we characterize naive psychology as a theory of mind, we are saying that it encompasses certain categories or concepts—specifically, mental constructs such as beliefs and desires—but also that these concepts and understandings cohere into an explanatory system of understanding. Theories explain phenomena; theoretical thinking is explanation-driven. Theories provide a system of concepts and propositions designed to explain and interpret phenomena in their domains. In this way, causal-explanatory reasoning is at the heart of theories, even naive theories. To this point, however, we have had little to say about explanation.

In some accounts, the explanatory structure of our naive psychology is simple and clear-cut. Overt human actions are the phenomena to be explained; mental attitudes—beliefs and desires—are the explanatory constructs.

> So what is a theory of mind? The events to be explained and predicted are talk and action (some would say behavior). The theoretical concepts are those of belief, desire, intention, and feeling. And, third, these concepts may be used to explain and predict the events in the referential domain, namely talk and action. (Olson, Astington, & Harris, 1988, p. 3)

We examine exactly this sort of explanatory reasoning: specifically, children's explanation of action via such constructs and terms as beliefs and desires. But we begin with the acknowledgment that explanation of action by appeal to belief and desire is only part of a larger picture.

Figure 1.1 depicts something of the explanatory scope of our naive theory of mind. This sort of depiction has several implications for the current discussion. First, it is important to note that the phenomena or events to be explained by a theory of mind include much more than action and talk. Beliefs and desires explain actions but also much more. We appeal to beliefs and desires to explain emotional reactions: "Why is he so sad? He *wanted* a pet but didn't get one." We appeal to beliefs and desires to explain beliefs and desires themselves: "Why did he think pears are red? He *knew* that apples are red and *thought* pears would be similar." Or, "Why did he want to go to to the store? He *wanted* an ice cream, and *thought* he could get one at the store." Belief-desire reasoning provides explanations for emotions, perceptions, and states of mind, as well as talk and action.

Moreover, the explanations provided by our theory of mind—the explanatory constructs to be employed—also include more than beliefs and desires. At a minimum, everyday psychological explanation attempts to account both for how world influences mind and how mind influences world: how extra-mental phenomena cause beliefs and desires, and how beliefs and desires cause actions (reactions and so on). More specifically, as shown in Figure 1.1, in our everyday understanding perceptions cause beliefs; perceptions also trigger desires. Physiological states such as deprivation cause desires. Basic emotional reactions, such as fear or disgust, spur more specific desires, such as the desire to avoid some situation. Indeed, even actions themselves cause beliefs and desires. For example, actions lead to outcomes in the world (e.g., Sam reached for but missed the apple) that result in emotional reactions (surprise and disappointment), which in turn shape further beliefs and desires (a renewed, perhaps increased, desire for the apple and the belief that the apple is farther away than Sam first thought).

In short, a theory, such as our naive theory of mind, provides a network of constructs embedded in an intricate web of causal-explanatory connections. Naive theories explain any number of things via the exploitation of any number of theoretic connections.

We find a variety of mental explanations in children's talk about the mind, including all the possibilities outlined thus far. Children talk about how emotions arise and influence actions:

> ADAM (3;9): I finished playing with it.
> ADULT: You didn't play with it much.

> ADAM: I frightened of it.
> ADULT: Look how nice and soft it is.
> ADAM: I don't like it.

They talk about how perceptions of the world cause beliefs and desires about the world:

> (Dog is barking in the back hall)
> ADAM (4;2): She hears you, doesn't she?
> ADULT: I think she heard me coming in the door.
> ADAM: She thought that was a tiger. Mommy, didn't Rinnie, huh?

> ABE (3;9): This is wheat bread. . . Do you know this is wheat bread because it's made from wheat?
> ADULT: Yep, I know that.
> ABE: I didn't know that.
> ADULT: Then how come you told me?
> ABE: Because I tasted it.
> ADULT: You didn't know until you tasted it?
> ABE: No, I thought it wasn't wheat bread.

Children talk about how mental states relate to other mental states:

> ADULT: Would you like to have a cookie?
> EVE (2;3): I want some cookie. Cookies, that make me happy.

> ABE (4;1): I holded my eyes because I scared myself. I thought the castle was a giant's castle.

> SARAH (3;7): I wan' get my pencil. Where is it?
> ADULT: Why? What do you want your pencil for?
> SARAH: I wan wite [write].

And they talk about how mind causes talk and action:

> ROSS (3;10): I said I'm not ready to go. When I think I'm ready to go to preschool, then I will go. But not right now. I'm not ready to go.

In fact, in the prior chapters we have already presented many examples of psychological explanation of one sort or another. In our assessments of children's references to mental states, we have used their explanations as an important, at times even determining, marker. For example, to assess whether young children employed desire terms to make genuine reference to desire (rather than hollow or conversational use of a term), we considered in depth how the child used the term at issue (see Chapter 4). Often it was how the child used the term for some sort of explanation that enabled us to confidently separate mental reference from other uses. Consider the following use of the term *want* by a young child.

ADAM (3;4): I talking very quiet.
ADULT: You're talking very quiet, why?
ADAM: Because I don't want somebody to woke me up.

That use of the term *want* was coded as a genuine reference to desire. Such an interpretation seemed compelling (in part) because the child used the term for the purpose of reasoning about relevant phenomena. In this case, the sort of reasoning expressed is explanatory; the child talked about desire in order to explain an action.

Or consider the following use of the term *think*:

ABE (4;8): Did you see the clouds?
ADULT: That was smoke left over from the fireworks.
ABE: You thought that, but I thought they was clouds.

This use of *thought* was coded as a genuine reference to belief and also as an individual contrastive. Such an interpretation becomes compelling, again, because of the child's larger appropriate reference and reasoning. In this case, the child not only notes the presence of these two states in the two persons, he seems to acknowledge how those states arise from the same perceptual experience. Such causal-explanatory understandings of mind, therefore, have been thoroughly embedded in our analyses of children's conceptual understanding of beliefs and desires all along.

Now we wish to turn the spotlight on these explanations themselves. Our primary focus will be on the very obvious case of children's use of beliefs and desires to explain actions. This is the paradigm case of children's causal-explanatory reasoning about the mind, but, as we have just argued, such explanations are only one sort of a variety of mental explanations.

Talk about Desires

Children's (and adults') genuine references to desire often provide an explanation of action. A child moves to the door and says, "I want to go outside." Such comments describe movement (moving thus and so toward the door) in intentional terms (going outside). Moreover, such utterances appropriately use the language of desire to describe the actor's goal (to go outside). Such talk refers to desires, but it also explains an act by describing that action in intentional terms, by specifying the target or goal of the action.

As noted in Chapter 4, from the earliest transcripts, children's genuine references to desire includes a substantial proportion of such intentional descriptions of action, especially in two-verb utterances such as

ALLISON (2;6): Want to ride truck.
ROSS (2;6): Bear wanna sleep with me.
PETER (2;1): I wanna put the toys away.

In these utterances, the children use a verb of desire (*want*) but also verbalize the sort of goal-directed action that is desired (e.g., put the toys away). Such talk about desires, coded as genuine reference to desire, involves a minimal but non-trivial explanation of action. Actions are described in terms of the actors' intentions, specifically their desires, thereby explaining the goal behind an action or a request.

Those contrastives that we analyzed in Chapter 4 as conflicts often make es-pecially clear the way in which mere reference to desires can constitute an expla-nation of an action as well. In these conflicts, the parties have two different action proposals, and they argue about and defend their respective action proposals by citing the desires that motivate the actions.

> ADAM (2;10): More milk
> ADULT: You don't need milk.
> ADAM: Why not? Want some milk in it.
>
> ADULT: I'd like to see you draw more.
> NAOMI (2;9): No, I don't want to.
> ADULT: No? I'd like to see you draw so much.
> NAOMI: No, you.

From its earliest appearance, talk about desires seems to rationalize, to explain, and at times to argue for certain actions by appeal to the actor's wants. Still, in these sorts of utterances, it is not necessarily clear that the speaker deliberately intends to explain actions in some explicit sense. When interpreted by an adult listener, this sort of talk does provide action explanations. But the child may simply be stating desires, via an ordinary linguistic expression of desire, and not really attempting to provide explanations of action per se. In this chapter, therefore, we report analyses of conversations in which the child explicitly explains a target action by saying the actor did that because he wanted to. We look at these desire explanations together with a similar set of belief explanations—statements in which the child explains a target action by saying that the actor acted because he thought something.

Analysis of Action Explanations

We were interested in explicit action explanations for several reasons. First, iden-tifying such explicit explanations of action is in keeping with the general analysis strategy we have used throughout this book. In general, we have undertaken several broad and inclusive analyses, such as coding for genuine reference to thoughts and beliefs, and then taken care to corroborate those initial impressions with more explicit and precise coding of children's meanings, such as contrastives for thought and belief. With regard to desire explanations, examination of action explanations provided a more precise test of our general impression, that from an early age children explain actors' actions in their everyday talk about actors' desires.

A further reason for identifying explicit explanations of action was to allow for a more thorough comparison between talk about thoughts and beliefs and talk about desires. While many of the children's genuine references to desire may have implicitly explained actions, the same was not true for genuine references to belief. Children's, and adults', references to genuine states of thought and belief tended to occur in statements like this one:

> ADULT: Where is that thing?
> SARAH (3;7): I think it disappeared. You think it does?
> ADULT: Yeah. I think it disappeared.

Such statements emphasize states of affairs (it disappeared) more than actors' actions ("Bear wanna sleep with me"; "I want to ride truck"). That is, ordinary utterances about thought and belief (I think it disappeared) versus desire ("Bear wanna sleep with me") may differentially encompass action descriptions to begin with. Yet both beliefs and desires can explain actions explicitly. The excerpt at the start of this chapter provides an example. When explicitly asked why he did something, Adam (3;7) cites his belief (a belief about a relevant state of affairs). One of our aims was to compare explanation of actions by appeal to desires versus by appeal to thoughts and beliefs. To make this comparison meaningful, we wished to consider comparable explanations; and so we specifically examined children's talk in conversational situations in which a direct explanation seemed required.

Our analysis of action explanations began with a reexamination of all children's utterances coded as genuine references to desire or to thoughts and beliefs. We identified cases in which the child explicitly explained action (or inaction) by invoking the actor's beliefs or desires. Such explicit explanations often occurred in the context of implicit or explicit "why" questions, on the lines of "Why did he do that?" Explicit explanations often included the use of such implicit or explicit connectives as "because", "so" and "for." Hood and Bloom (1979) report an extensive analysis of 2-year-olds' causal explanations in their natural language exchanges; our procedures for identifying causal utterances generally followed their formal and semantic criteria (see their p. 4). Table 6.1 provides several examples of the sorts of explicit explanations of action that we identified.

Two coders, one blind to the nature of the study hypotheses, independently examined approximately 25% of the *think, know,* and *want* psychological references. For utterances with the belief terms *think* and *know,* agreement on explanations was 94% (Cohen's kappa = .88). For the desire term *want,* agreement was 89% (Cohen's kappa = .74). Disagreements were settled in discussion by the two authors.

Figure 6.1 summarizes the explanation data; and Table 6.2 individually details those data for the four major children. These data confirm the pattern now familiar from Chapter 5: children make early reference to desires, from about age 2 years on, followed by later reference to thoughts and beliefs. In this case, we see early explanation of action by appeal to desires, followed by later explanation of action by appeal to beliefs.[1] As noted in Chapter 5, a pattern of findings of this sort carries with it some of its own controls. For example, when children explain action by referring to a person's desires, we know that they are able to explain behavior by citing mental states. Their failure to explain action by citing thoughts or beliefs, therefore, cannot be due to some general inability to conceive of or to express

Table 6.1. Explanations of Action

Desire	Belief
ROSS (2;6): The boy hurt me.	ABE (3;6): I'm gonna take this out too.
ADULT: The boy hurt you? How did the boy hurt you?	ADULT: How come you're taking your boat?
ROSS: The boy wanted to.	ABE: Because I think it's nice to take my boat out.
ADULT: The boy wanted to?	
ROSS: Yeah.	ADULT: You try to hurt people?
	ROSS (4;4): No.
ADULT: Why do you keep saying "why"?	ADULT: Well then, you're not really bad.
ROSS (2;7): I want to say "why."	ROSS: I only hurt them is because I don't know the way.
ADULT: You want to say "why"? Why do you want to say "why"?	ADULT: You don't know the right way to work?
ROSS: I just want to.	ROSS: Yeah.
ROSS (2;10): Look, there's a car up in the air. [on a hoist]	ROSS (4;5): Dad, why do they call Han Solo handsome?
ADULT: Oh. Why is it up there?	ADULT: I don't know.
ROSS: Man put it up there.	ROSS: Because they think he is?
ADULT: Why did he put it up there?	ADULT: Yeah.
ROSS: He want to fix it.	ABE (3;11): Rufus [the dog] is barking so loud.
ADULT: Did he have breakfast?	ADULT: Why do you think she's barking?
SARAH (3;1): No.	
ADULT: No? Why not?	ABE: Sometimes Rufus knows if somebody's outside.
SARAH: He don't wanna.	ADULT: Is that why she barks?
ADULT: Why'd you come in?	ABE: Yeah.
ABE (3;4): Because I didn't want to be out.	SARAH (4;10): I thought I saw his ugly-looking face, so I looked back.
ADULT: Why did she tie it to your wrist? [A teacher had tied the child's balloon to his wrist.]	ADULT: Why did he suck it then?
ABE (3;4): Just a second. I can't talk now. My mouth is full, mom. Because the teacher tied it on. They . . . because they don't want it to blow away.	ROSS (4;3): Because he's just a baby. And he thinks he's a baby, but he's not.

mentalistic explanations. Similarly, we know that young children can respond sensibly to "why" questions and can reason sensibly using implicit or explicit "because" and "so" connectives for the purpose of explaining action; they do so in their explanations via desire. Yet young children still fail to explain action in the same way by appeal to the actor's beliefs. In short, the analysis of explanations reveals a general pattern similar to that for genuine psychological references and for contrastives: sensible reference to desire appears considerably in advance of sensible reference to thought and belief.

The data in Figure 6.1 indicate where belief explanations fit within the larger picture of mentalistic explanation of action. A different but equally important question concerns where belief explanations of action fit within the pattern of children's early emerging talk about thoughts and beliefs. Here another informative pattern emerges: children talk about belief cogently and sensibly before they use thoughts

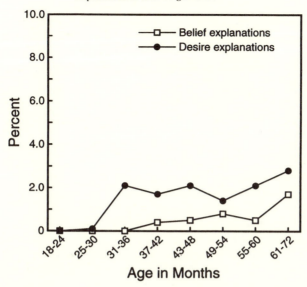

Figure 6.1. Explanations of action by appeal to desires or to thoughts and beliefs.

and beliefs to explain action. Table 6.3 shows (primarily for Adam, Abe, Sarah, and Ross) the pattern of belief explanations in comparison to genuine psychological reference to thought and belief. In each case, the child talks sensibly about beliefs considerably in advance of explaining actions by appeal to beliefs. Thus Adam's first genuine reference to belief appeared at age 2;11, whereas his first belief explanation was at 3;6, seven months later. For Abe, genuine reference to belief appeared at 2;8; belief explanation appeared three months later. Three children never gave belief explanations in our samples. For the remaining children, the median delay between explaining actions by citing a person's beliefs versus genuinely referring to beliefs was six and a half months.

Of course, belief explanations and utterances coded as genuine reference to thought and belief are noncomparable in several fashions. Belief explanation is a much more precise, explicit, and infrequent category in our scheme of codings than is genuine reference to belief. A better comparison, therefore, is between children's belief explanations and their thought–reality contrastives. Thought–reality contras-

Table 6.2. Total Explanations of Action

Child	Age at First Occurrence		2 Years		3 Years		4 Years	
	Desire	Belief	Desire	Belief	Desire	Belief	Desire	Belief
Adam	2;6	3;6	5	0	18	2	6	3
Abe	2;5	2;11	23	1	29	11	14	3
Sarah	2;10	4;10	6	0	10	0	10	1
Ross	2;6	3;7	24	0	16	3	9	9
Others	2;1	3;1	16	0	12	2	6	1
Total			74	1	85	18	45	17

tives are a circumscribed subset of thought and belief references, and expression of such contrastives requires the child to explicitly talk about the mind beyond simply referring to belief. Moreover, thought–reality contrastives parallel belief explanations in form, in the sense that each requires the child to acknowledge and connect together two different descriptions or statements. In thought–reality contrastives the child must acknowledge and/or describe both a real state of affairs and a thought corresponding to that situation ("It's a bus; I thought it was a taxi"). In belief explanations the child must acknowledge and/or describe an action and a belief causal to that action ("Why do they call Han Solo handsome? . . . Because they think he is?").

Table 6.3 also summarizes this more conservative comparison, revealing a lag in belief explanations relative to thought–reality contrastives. In spite of the similarities between the two categories, in coding specificity, explicitness, and form, children uttered thought–reality contrastives well before they explained actions in terms of the actor's thought or belief. Thus, Adam's first thought–reality contrastive appeared at 3;3 whereas his first belief explanation appeared at 3;6. Across all the children in Table 6.3, belief explanations first appeared, on average, five months after the children were explicitly distinguishing beliefs from reality in thought–reality contrastives.[2]

These data raise the question of what function children's earliest references to thoughts and beliefs typically serve, if they do not serve to explain action. That is, if children are talking cogently about thoughts and beliefs at an early age, but not for the purpose of explaining actions, what is the nature of those references to belief?

The answer to this question, in retrospect, seems straightforward. The vast majority of children's first references to thoughts and beliefs seem designed to simply state the existence and the nature of an experienced representational state. That is, children talk about thoughts and beliefs to comment on the nature of someone's mental state or experience and especially to express and make public their own. The implicit question most often being addressed, therefore, is not "Why did someone do that?" but rather "What is someone thinking [*knowing, believing*]?" Following are some examples, and also note the examples of talk about thoughts and beliefs presented thus far (e.g., Tables 3.1, 3.2, and 3.4).

Table 6.3. Age at First (and Third) Appearance of Various Types of Reference

Child	Genuine Reference to Belief	Thought-Reality Contrastives	Belief Explanations
Adam	2;11 (2;11)	3;3 (3;5)	3;6 (4;1)
Abe	2;8 (2;8)	2;9 (2;11)	2;11 (3;2)
Sarah	2;9 (3;0)	3;3 (3;5)	4;10
Ross	2;7 (2;11)	3;3 (3;5)	3;7 (3;10)
Others:			
Naomi	2;8 (2;11)	2;8 (2;11)	3;5
Peter	2;4 (2;5)	2;9 (3;1)	3;1
Mark	3;5 (3;7)	3;8 (3;8)	3;11

Note: To be included in this table, a child needed to have data for all three columns; only seven children had sufficient data. Allison, Nathaniel, and Peter were not sampled late enough to provide sufficient talk about belief (e.g., Allison's last transcript was at 34 mos).

ADULT: Do you know where daddy's shoes are?
NAOMI (2;11): No. Maybe they're in the bathroom
ADULT: In the what?
NAOMI: I don't know where they is.

ABE (3;0): I thoughted you eated mine. I thought daddy eat my bacon.

ADULT: Why don't you go hide and I'll get you a small surprise, OK?
ABE (3;1): OK. I'm gonna go hide.
ADULT: OK, go ahead.
ABE: I think it's gumdrops . . . nope.

ADAM (3;2): I hear it, mommy.
ADULT: You do? Where is it? Meeow.
ADAM: Is it a cat?
ADULT: Meeow.
ADAM: I don't see it mommy. I wonder where the cat is.

ADAM (3;5): It doesn't talk. Does he think it talks?

(Mark sees a piece of red paper on the top of the Raisin Bran.)
MARK (3;8): Oooo blood!
[Adult takes it off.]
ADULT: It's paper.
ROSS: We thought it was yucky stuff.
ADULT: You did?
MARK: Yea, me and Rossy [his brother] did.

As these examples show, often the conversational goal of reference to thoughts and beliefs seems to be simply to describe and communicate mental experience, ideas, and states of mind. Children's early talk about thoughts and beliefs seems to reflect their assumption that knowledge, beliefs, and thoughts are nonobvious mental states, that must be verbalized in order to be shared or understood by another person. The earliest talk about thoughts and beliefs does not seem motivated by a need to explain actions; rather, it seems motivated by a need to translate private states into a public medium, namely, speech. Children's earliest talk about thoughts and beliefs seems to simply express states of mind. Somewhat later, states of belief are invoked as explanations of action as well.

Explaining actions by appeals to belief appears later than references to belief in these data. Why might that be so? One possibility is that when children first acquire an understanding of thoughts and beliefs they already have an adequate means of explaining actions mentalistically, namely, by appeal to the actor's desires. Simply recognizing that an actor has beliefs does not entail invoking those beliefs to explain his or her acts; appeal to desires may do that adequately (if not fully) on its own. Even for adults, desires often provide sufficient explanations or at least the first line of explanation. For young children, such explanations may be at first their only recourse, but even later they may still be sufficient. From this perspective, what the appearance of belief explanations reveals is the emerging importance of a conception of belief for children's understanding of mental life in general. A conception of beliefs becomes so central that it becomes necessary to mention the actor's beliefs, as well as desires, in order to optimally explain some acts. Belief explanations, therefore, do not mark children's first understanding of thoughts and beliefs. (Genuine reference to thoughts and beliefs is a more sensitive measure of that.) Instead, belief explanations index an increasingly important role for a conception of thoughts and beliefs in children's larger understanding of persons, actions, and minds.

Conflicts or Disputes

Ross at 3;10

> ROSS: Leslie make me angry.
> ADULT: Why?
> ROSS: If she thinks something is silly. I don't think it's silly at all.
> ADULT: Oh, you had a disagreement.
> ROSS: Uh huh. She thought her necklace was silly.
> ADULT: She thought it was silly?
> ROSS: Yeah. But I didn't think it was.

Children can use mental constructs not only in reasoning about people, such as in explaining their actions, but also in reasoning with them, that is, in disputing different positions, attempting to persuade one another to different points of view, or taking sides in or trying to resolve various conflicts. Some disputes revolve around people's physical aspects (e.g., who is bigger or stronger), some around aspects of social interchange (e.g., whose turn it is or who possesses certain objects), but others involve specifically psychological aspects (e.g., whose desires will prevail or whose beliefs are correct). The conversation at the beginning of this section provides one example of a dispute about beliefs. Young children who are acquiring basic psychological construals of persons are also acquiring an understanding of the grounds for psychological disputes. In this sense, children's psychological disputes should reflect their developing psychological notions. Specifically, if children move from a conception of persons in terms of desires to a conception that includes beliefs, that transition should influence the nature of their disputes and conflicts.

In Chapter 4 we considered the existence and nature of children's disputes with others over conflicting desires. Awareness of differences in desires, and conflicts over whose desires are to be satisfied, were found to be common in the very early talk of children in our data. Here we present some parallel data for thoughts and beliefs, disputes about whose representations of reality are correct. As a preface to presenting these analyses, we note that when we examined children's disputes by focusing on their use of terms such as *think* and *know*, the data reflected the now common trend: disputes about desire preceded disputes about beliefs by many months. Tested in this fashion, however, the results simply manifest the results already reported. That is, we know (from Chapter 5) that genuine reference to desire precedes genuine reference to belief. We know also (from Chapter 4) that desire conflicts are apparent, indeed frequent, in the children's earliest genuine references to desire. Hence, desire conflicts must precede thought or belief conflicts in the children's talk as we have examined it thus far.

However, it is conceivable that children may engage in conflicts over beliefs without using such belief terms as *think, know,* and *wonder.* They might say simply, for example, "you're wrong and I'm right," or "that's not true," or "it is so." Children use such terms as "right" and "so" well before their third birthday, and perhaps through them they argue about beliefs. In what follows, therefore, we have undertaken an analysis of children's disputes involving such terms, in addition to terms such as *think* and *know.* This expanded analysis serves as yet another test of whether these young children may have a conception of a person's thoughts and beliefs at a very early age and simply not express that conception via such terms as *think* and *know.*

In this analysis, we once again focused on Adam, Abe, Sarah, and Ross, the four children who contributed the majority of the data. We searched for use of the words *true, false, right, wrong, so* (not so), and *mistake.* Our goal was to find conversations in which children used these terms to argue about beliefs, opinions, or facts in the sense of what is right or true or so. For example:

> ADAM (3;3): Yeah
> MOTHER: That's not right. I'm sorry to say but that's wrong.
> ADAM: It's . . . it's right.

> ADAM (3;5): Mr. Peanut Butter.
> ADULT: Mr. Peanut. He's not peanut butter yet.
> ADAM: He is so.
> ADULT: Mr. Peanut.
> ADAM: No.

> ADULT: Your blanket is wet.
> ROSS (3;5): It's not true, daddy. It's not true what you said. My blanket is not wet.
> ADULT: Yeah. But it's dirty.

> ADAM (3;7): That is so fingerpaint.
> ADULT: No. It's not fingerpaint.
> ADAM: It is fingerpaint!
> ADULT: You're silly.

> (Abe and his father are watching a TV program about snakes with a female narrator.)
> ABE (3;8): Is that a poisonous snake, dad?
> ADULT: No.
> ABE: I think if she tells about it. . . . I think if she says it's a poisonous snake . . . you're gonna be wrong.
> ADULT: You're right, I would be wrong. But it's not a poisonous snake, she just said it wasn't.
> ABE: It looks like a poisonous snake.
> ADULT: Yeah. But it's not.

SARAH (4;6): This one?
ADULT: No. [but then they try it]
SARAH: I was right.
ADULT: You were right.

Children used these terms frequently, especially *right* and *so*. Each child has multiple instances of using the terms *right* and *so* in the very first months of their transcripts; the vast majority of these uses, however, do not refer to beliefs or opinions. For *right*, the majority of uses are indications of temporal or spatial position, as in (2;3) "Tractor go right there," or (2;3) "Adam shoe right here." The majority of uses for *so* were for emphasis or comparison, as in (2;9) "You so big," or for making causal connections, as in (2;11) "We going to turn light on, so you can't see me." In spite of these early uses of such terms, their use to dispute opinions and beliefs began to appear only later, at about 3 years of age.

We also identified examples of disputes about thoughts and beliefs as expressed by children in their use of the belief terms analyzed in Chapter 3: *think, know, wonder, believe, expect,* and *dream.* In this analysis, we simply examined belief term utterances and identified those that were parts of disputes about beliefs, such as

ADAM (3;3): Does you think have sugar. . . some sugar in here?
ADULT: I don't have any sugar.
ADAM: I think you have sugar.

Two independent coders examined a sample of more than 200 conversational excerpts in which children used the terms *right, so, true, wrong,* and *mistake.* Agreement as to which excerpts represented disputes about thoughts and beliefs was 95% (Cohen's kappa = .89). Disagreements were resolved by discussion.

Figure 6.2 presents the data for children's disputes about desires and about thoughts and beliefs. Those data show that once again talk about desires precedes comparable talk about thoughts and beliefs. In this case, young children are regularly involved in arguments with others about desires, that is, one party claiming the priority of his or her desires over those of someone else. Only substantially later do children become involved in similar disputes about beliefs, namely, one party claiming the correctness of his or her beliefs over those of someone else. Table 6.4 shows that this lag between arguments about desire and arguments about belief is apparent in the talk of each of the four primary children. On average, disputes about desires precede disputes about thoughts and beliefs by six months.

Children's frequent engagement in psychological disputes—conflicts with others about beliefs and desires—suggests a larger hypothesis. Perhaps such disputes provide formative experiences for children, heightening their awareness that psychological states differ across persons and that psychological contents can certainly differ from the real-world state of affairs that they are about. Piaget (1932) advanced such an hypothesis, but he emphasized children's conflicts with peers in the school years. The current data underwrite the ubiquity of conflicts at much

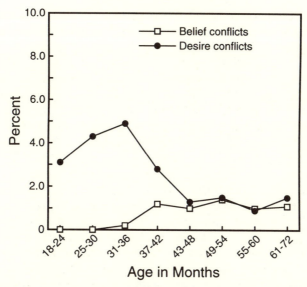

Figure 6.2. Psychological disputes about desires or about thoughts and beliefs.

younger ages and also with parents, suggesting the possibility of a still larger role for such experiences in shaping children's social cognition.

Conclusions

Children's reference to thoughts, beliefs, and desires in their reasoning about and with other people, that is, their explanations of action and their disputes about psychological states, follows the same pattern charted in Chapter 5: talk about desires precedes talk about thoughts and beliefs. The data here provide a further test of that developmental description. More generally, the data speak to the larger importance of an understanding of mental states in children's social lives.

Interest in and research into the development of children's concepts of mental states has expanded rapidly in the past 10 years. The interest and the research is based, in part, on the assumption that such conceptions affect children's larger

Table 6.4. Total Psychological Disputes

Child	Age at First Occurrence		2 Years		3 Years		4 Years	
	Desire	Belief	Desire	Belief	Desire	Belief	Desire	Belief
Adam	2;6	3;3	55	0	24	14	7	10
Abe	2;5	2;8	57	5	17	24	5	11
Sarah	2;10	3;3	14	0	21	2	12	6
Ross	2;6	3;2	5	0	20	12	9	5
Total			131	5	82	52	33	32

understanding of human behavior and indeed their social interactions. Relatively little research, however, has actually explored the nature of the presumed links between knowing about beliefs and desires and children's larger explanations (for an exception, see Bartsch & Wellman, 1989b) or between knowing about beliefs and desires and children's social interactions (for exceptions, see Chandler, La-londe, Fritz, & Hala, 1991; Dunn, in press). Of course, a considerable body of current research has been directed at the hypothesis that autistic children are se-verely deficient in their understanding of mind (see Baron-Cohen, 1990, for a re-view). The presumption behind this work is that such a conceptual deficit accounts for peculiarities in autistic children'scausal understanding (Baron-Cohen, Leslie, & Frith, 1986) as well as for their deficiencies in social interaction, pretense, and communication (e.g., Leslie, 1991). But as Chandler et al. (1991) point out, this literature on autism does not serve to answer related questions for normal devel-opment, such as what the other understandings and social interactional competen-cies are that accompany, or change in response to, children's acquisition of an understanding of beliefs and desires. Demonstrations that developing notions of mind actually correlate with everyday explanations of behavior, or with everyday aspects of social discourse and interaction have been notably absent.

The data presented in this chapter begin to fill the gap. We have documented something of the developing nature of children's explanations of human behavior and one very frequent sort of human interaction, verbal arguments. Developmental changes in children's notions of the mind are mirrored in their explanations and arguments. General conception of and reference to mental states at first include desires but only later encompass thoughts and beliefs; this change influences the ways in which children explain human actions and how they argue with others.

Notes

1. For this analysis, if children mentioned both beliefs and desires (which seldom hap-pened), we considered it as appeal to beliefs. In this respect, the codings were designed to be as sensitive as possible to the earliest occurrence of explanation of action by appeal to belief.

2. In contrast, a parallel analysis for desire, comparing desire explanations with desire–outcome contrastives, showed explanations for desire emerging at essentially the same time as desire–outcome contrastives. In this analysis, desire explanations preceded desire–out-come contrastives for two children, succeeded them for four children, and appeared at the same time for 4 children. The average delay between desire contrastives and desire expla-nations was one and a half months.

7

Individual Differences

Abe at 2;11

ABE: I don't like . . . I don't want to babysit Andy.

ADULT: How come?

ABE: Because he cries when everybody hits him.

ADULT: Gosh, I would cry too, if someone hit me.

ABE: I will not cry when someone hit me.

ADULT: Does it hurt when people hit you?

ABE: Uh-uh [no]. I don't hurt when people hit me.

ADULT: I see. You think it hurts when people hit Andy?

ABE: Yeah.

Sarah at 2;11

(Mother pours water on Sarah, in bath.)

SARAH: What that? What you doing?

MOTHER: I put some water on your hair.

SARAH: I pour you some.

MOTHER: No, I don't want any.

SARAH: Why?

MOTHER: Because, I don't like to get wet.

SARAH: Huh? Don't like . . . go wet . . . swim? You want, you swim?

MOTHER: No, I don't wanna swim.

SARAH: No?

MOTHER: No.

SARAH: OK. I swim.

In prior chapters, piecing together a composite picture of early talk about the mind was only possible because of certain important commonalities in young children's talk about these topics; the composite picture mirrored the individual developments of 10 children. However, there are obvious and striking differences among these children as well. Consider the excerpts above, which are among the early subjective contrastives for Abe and Sarah respectively, utterances in which the child acknowledges that two people can have very different attitudes about the same state of affairs. However, Abe's subjective contrastives began at 2;5, Sarah's began at 2;10; Abe produced 55 such contrastives before his fourth birthday, Sarah produced 15. Differences such as these in the onset and frequency of individuals' references to mental states are intriguing in their own right, and they provide insight into several larger issues, especially the correlates and antecedents of an understanding of mind.

In this chapter we address the topic of individual differences in early talk about and understanding of the mind. Because our data are limited to only 10 children (and in many specific analyses fewer than that), we are necessarily limited in our ability to examine differences. Any relationships we detect must be large indeed in order to be significant with so few cases. At the same time, any apparent findings must be regarded as tentative, potentially unreplicable in a different, larger, or more representative sample.

To set the stage for further analyses, consider Figure 7.1. In Chapter 3 we showed graphs depicting the onset of genuine reference to thoughts and beliefs for each of the children. Figure 7.1 depicts these separate trajectories together on one graph. Figure 7.1A plots children's references to thoughts and beliefs as a percent

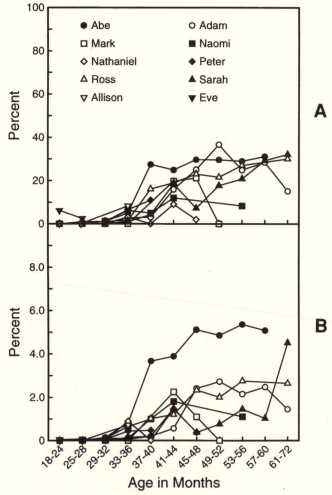

Figure 7.1. Genuine references to thoughts and beliefs, shown as a percent of each child's utterances using terms of desire, thought, and belief (A), or as a percent of each child's total utterances (B).

of all utterances using belief-desire verbs; Figure 7.1B portrays the same data as a percent of all the children's utterances. Immediately obvious in this figure is the uniformity across children; a similar onset and increase in genuine reference to belief essentially occurs within the limited time period of from about 2;6 to 3;6. At the same time, there is obvious variation on two fronts. The first concerns the onset of references to thoughts and beliefs. First genuine reference to belief ranges from Eve's precocious first reference at 21 months to first references by Nathan and Mark at 41 months, a discrepancy of one and a half years. This variation among the children suggests differences in when belief understanding is acquired, as indexed by our coding schemes. Second, there is variation in terms of frequency or fluency. The frequency with which children refer to thoughts and beliefs, relative to other mental state talk, differs both across these ages and at any given age.

The overall similarity across children apparent in Figure 7.1 is a reflection of still deeper uniformities, in particular, the strikingly uniform sequence of acquisition evident in a consideration of both belief and desire references. Much of what is discussed in earlier chapters concerns this sequence. For example, a sequence from understanding desire to understanding belief to invoking an actor's beliefs in order to explain his or her actions is consistent with the data for all 10 individual children, as discussed in Chapter 6.

But what about the variations in timing of the steps in this sequence as well as in the frequency with which children mention these topics? This variation can be brought to life by comparing two children, specifically Sarah and Abe. Our data include numerous transcripts from both these children, ranging in age from 28 to 60 months (see Table 2.2). Yet these children differ in important ways. Abe is the son of a language investigator (a graduate student at the time data were collected), and Sarah comes from a working-class family. At the third birthday, Abe's mean length of utterances (MLU) was 6.0 compared to Sarah's 2.3, the largest difference in our sample.

How do these two children compare in their development of belief and desire reference? Table 7.1 compares the children's age at first observed reference for many of the categories discussed in prior chapters. Both children, like others in

Table 7.1. Age at First (and Third) Reference

	Abe		Sarah	
Desire				
Genuine desire	2;4[a]	(2;4)	2;3[a]	(2;3)
Individual contrastives	2;5	(2;6)	2;11	(2;11)
Desire–outcome contrastives	2;5	(2;5)	2;9	(2;9)
Desire explanation	2;5	(2;7)	2;10	(2;11)
Thoughts and belief				
Genuine belief	2;8	(2;8)	2;9	(3;0)
Individual contrastives	2;8	(2;10)	3;7	(3;10)
Thought–reality contrastives	2;9	(2;11)	3;3	(3;5)
Belief explanation	2;11	(3;2)	4;10	

[a]First age transcripts available

our sample, are credited with references to genuine desire in their earliest transcripts (at 2;3 for Sarah and 2;4 for Abe), so a comparison of acquisition using this measure is not meaningful. All other measures indicate earlier acquisitions for Abe. Moreover, Table 7.1 suggests that the gap between Abe and Sarah widens rather than narrows over time, with the various earlier-appearing desire indicators showing lesser gaps between the two children, and the later-appearing belief measures indicating larger discrepancies. On the various desire measures, Abe is ahead of Sarah by an average of five months (discounting the genuine desire references because of their artificial constraint). On the belief measures, the gap averages eight months.

Not only do Abe and Sarah differ in the onset of various belief and desire references, they also differ in the relative frequency of these sorts of talk, albeit again within an overall similar pattern. The graphs in Figure 7.2 reveal these differences in the relative frequencies of belief and desire references. Abe talks more about desire than does Sarah early on; he then talks more about thoughts and beliefs than does Sarah later on. What accounts for, or at least covaries with, these differences?

Focus and Questions

In simplified form, investigations of developmental differences first focus on some target attribute that varies across individuals, and then consider how other factors, for example, individual or group membership differences, covary with or account for that variation. Our target is talk about thoughts and beliefs. There are practical and theoretical reasons for this focus. Practically, our data are more complete for belief than desire, in the sense that we have more completely captured the developmental trajectories involved. As shown in Figure 7.1, our data for belief include the initial onset of talk about thoughts and beliefs as well as initial and later frequencies in such talk. In contrast, for desire our data typically begin after the child's first talk about desire has started, in mid-trajectory so to speak. More specifically, we will focus on children's genuine references to thoughts and beliefs. Among the many coding categories for thoughts and beliefs described in Chapter 3, the genuine references to belief represent more of the children and systematically include large rather than small samples of utterances.

Theoretically, our focus on children's understanding of thoughts and beliefs parallels the current emphasis in the literature; considerable attention has been paid in cross-sectional, experimental research to children's early developing conceptions of belief and false belief. Understanding differences in and associates of children's understanding of belief is, therefore, an obvious place to begin. "If the growth of this ability is such a central aspect of human development, the question of what influences differences in its developmental course, is surely important" (Dunn et al., 1991b, p. 1353).

Yet consideration of individual differences in children's conceptions of mind generally or belief specifically has barely begun. For example, to what extent are differences in children's responses to laboratory questions about beliefs attributable to differences in verbal ability alone? This question becomes even more pressing in regard to our own conversational measures of an understanding of thought and

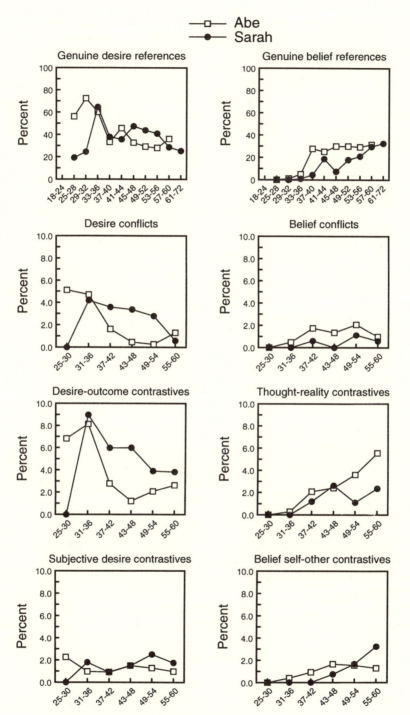

Figure 7.2. Comparison of eight categories of references to desires and to thoughts and beliefs for Abe and Sarah, grouped by age in months.

belief. Could the differences on our measures, and even the basic sequence of findings, be due simply to differences in, and developmental increases in, linguistic fluency? If the differences are due to conceptual changes, other issues arise that deserve exploration: given our findings in Chapter 5, it is reasonable to hypothesize that understanding thoughts and beliefs not only succeeds an understanding of desires, but builds on it, or relates to that earlier understanding in some systematic fashion. Regarding either language or conceptual developments, what role might be played by parental talk? Is it not reasonable to suppose that a parent's talk about the mind influences the child's talk, and that certain family conversations about mental states may foster children's understandings. Obviously, children neither grow up as isolated individuals, nor are their conversations merely reflections of individual understandings; rather, these conversations, embedded in social inter-actions, are two-way channels, with children both evincing their own understanding and probably gaining insights from an exchange with others. In this chapter we offer some analyses concerning differences in timing and frequency of children's talk about beliefs as related to verbal ability, to earlier talk about desires, and to parent-child talk about these topics.

To reiterate, any relationships we discover must be considered tentative at best. Fortunately, the last few years have seen a beginning interest in differences in theory of mind understandings, inspired in large part by Judy Dunn's ongoing research. We can compare our preliminary findings to hers.

Background Variables: Verbal Ability

Several background factors might influence children's developing understanding of mind, for example, the general economic and social status of the child's family, the child's developing verbal abilities, and the culture in which the child is raised. Our limited sample does not permit us to examine cultural variation or socioeco-nomic status properly. All 10 children are English-speaking native-born U.S. citizens. Sarah is the only child from a working-class family (as opposed to middle- or upper-middle-class), as characterized by the original investigators. Adam is the only nonwhite participate. However, we can examine verbal ability because we have measures of the children's MLU. Using MLU as assessed at the third birthday, we looked for relationships between general language competence and both the onset and frequency of children's genuine references to belief. (Only Eve was excluded from this analysis because she had no transcripts at the third birthday.) No relationship was found between MLU and children's age at first genuine reference to belief, $r(7) = -.19$, n.s. What did emerge, however, was evidence for a relationship between children's MLU and the frequency of genuine belief talk at 37 to 40 months, $r(5) = .66$, $p < .06$.[1] That is, children who were more fluent at 3 years of age talked relatively more about belief in the first part of their fourth year.

This is a comforting pair of findings: MLU is unrelated to onset but related to frequency. Initially, a distinct possibility was that our data were just too limited or noisy for any significant findings to emerge. The relation of MLU to frequency of talk about thoughts and beliefs counteracts this suspicion, providing a sensible and even predictable finding. Children who are more fluent, in the sense of using longer utterances, are also more fluent in their talk about belief; that is, they talk about thoughts and beliefs relatively more frequently. But this finding raises the question of whether all of our measures are just proxies for verbal facility. In this vein, for example, one could also hypothesize that as children's language advances they become able to talk about rarer conversational topics, and it is then that talk about thoughts and beliefs emerges. However, in our data MLU is in fact unrelated to onset of talk about belief, that is, unrelated to age at first genuine reference. This zero-order relationship, in conjunction with the significant relation between MLU and frequency, corroborates our arguments in Chapter 5 that long or complex sentences are not necessary to refer to beliefs.

These findings emphasize that in our data genuinely referring to a concept or distinction is not the same as mentioning it frequently. More generally, possessing a concept is not the same as employing it often. Fortunately, our data allow us reasonable measures of both sorts: age at initial acquisition as well as relative frequency of mention. In our data, age at first genuine reference to belief is not significantly correlated with frequency of mention of beliefs thereafter, r (7) = $-.38$, n.s. It is a strength of the sort of densely sampled longitudinal data provided by our investigation that we can examine the onset of certain references rather than just differential frequencies of mention.

Relation of Talk about Desires to Later Talk about Beliefs

If children's later talk about beliefs represents an extension and expansion of their earlier talk about desires, then some telling relations should exist between these earlier and later references. We cannot look at how age of onset of talk about desire relates to later talk about belief; we simply do not have measures of first genuine reference to desire for most children. But we can examine the relative frequency of children's earlier talk about desire to see if it relates to later talk about belief. In this calculation we chose an early time period that maximized the number of children included: at 29 to 32 months we have transcripts for 8 of the 10 children (excluding only Eve and Allison). We then related frequency of genuine references to desire at this age to the child's age of onset for belief references; r (7) = $-.24$, n.s. We also related this measure of early desire frequency to a measure of later frequency of talk about belief—in this case frequency of belief references at 37 to 40 months (which includes all the children except Mark and Eve); r (6) = $.27$, n.s. Thus it is *not* the case in our sample that children who talk more about desire early on then talked more or at earlier ages about belief.

However, we do have evidence that some aspects of early desire talk sensibly relate to later belief talk. In this regard, we reasoned that children's explanations appealing to desires might be of special importance to their larger understanding of persons and minds. It is often argued that children's understanding of mental states provides the constructs used to understand the causes and explanations of action, and that causal-explanatory understandings are particularly central to any theory of mind. A child who early understands and attends to how desires cause people's behavior is attending to and mentioning a special aspect of mind, and therefore this special sort of talk about desires may be related to later understandings about mind and action. Indeed, in our data, age of onset for desire explanations was correlated to age of onset for genuine belief references, $r (8) = .84$, $p < .01$. At the very least, these data provide some evidence for a basic continuity in children's talk about the mind: earlier understanding of an important aspect of desire states relates to earlier understanding of belief states. Once again, however, measures of onset and of frequency differ. Frequency of desire explanations (at 29–32 months) did not significantly relate to onset of belief references, $r (6) = -.36$, or to the frequency of belief references (at 37–40 months), $r (5) = .33$.

Another sort of continuity is also apparent in children's talk about desires and beliefs. This continuity concerns children's tendency to make predominantly self or other references. In Chapters 3 and 4 we described young children's preference for talking about their own beliefs and desires in comparison to others' beliefs and desires. This preference also varied across the individual children. While all the children in our sample tended to talk about themselves, some did so almost exclusively whereas some made relatively more frequent references to others. To compare earlier talk about desires with later talk about beliefs, we looked at each child's first 10 genuine desire utterances and calculated the proportion of self references. We then looked at each child's first 10 genuine belief utterances (or as many such references as there were as long as there were 5 or more) and calculated the proportion of self references. (Nathaniel and Allison were the only children excluded from this analysis; each had fewer than 5 genuine references to belief.) Children who were most likely to refer to their own rather than others' desires early on were also most likely to refer to their own beliefs later; $r (6) = .59$, $p < .10$.

Parental Talk and Parent–Child Interaction

An important potential source of differences in children's reference to and understanding of beliefs is parents' talk to children. In Chapter 5 we reported an analysis of parents' genuine references to beliefs and desires in their early speech to Adam, Abe, Sarah, and Ross. Primarily, these analyses reassured us that from a very early age parents do talk to children about beliefs as well as desires. Parents used both belief and desire terms in their talk with very young children, and indeed the vast majority of their talk to young children using these terms involved genuine references to mental states. Additionally, however, in the data for these four children, it looked like it might be early parental talk to children about desires, rather than beliefs, that was related to the children's later acquisition of talk about belief. Why might early talk about desires be especially related to later understanding of beliefs? One possibility is that young children's early understanding of mental states revolves around desires. Since they have, according to our data, no concomitant understanding of thoughts and beliefs, then it is via talking and thinking about desires that the children develop a deeper understanding of persons and minds. This increasing understanding eventually leads to an understanding of belief. Thus, what may be helpful initially is to foster the children's developing mentalism via conversations about desires, rather than by mentioning thoughts and beliefs. Of course, an opposing hypothesis would be that parental talk about beliefs is the crucial factor. That is, frequently mentioning thoughts and beliefs directly fosters children's understanding of these mental states.

We can test these two hypotheses, at least tentatively, in our data. In this analysis we began by tabulating early parental use of belief and desire terms. Because the analysis in Chapter 5 for the four children showed that most adult uses of these terms were genuine psychological references, and in order to shortcut the large amount of coding needed to assess whether all parental uses were genuine psychological reference, we simply counted the number of uses of the terms *think*, *know*, and *want* in the adult talk in each child's transcripts. We then calculated the proportion of total uses of belief talk versus desire talk. These two numbers were inverse; if 40% of such talk involved thought and belief terms, then 60% involved desire terms. The hypothesis that frequent early parental talk about beliefs leads to earlier onset of a child's talk about belief predicts a significant negative relation between parent and child measure, that is, frequent parental talk about belief leads to a younger age of onset for the child's talk about belief. Conversely, if parental talk about desire was the crucial factor, the significant negative relation would be between parental use of desire terms and child onset of talk about belief, that is, frequent early parental talk about desire leads to earlier onset of the child's talk about belief. Relative frequencies of adult talk at the 29 to 32 month period were used, again to maximize the number of children that could be included. (Only Eve and Allison had no transcripts and hence no adult data at this time.) Adult *desire* talk, rather than belief talk, was significantly negatively related to the age of onset of belief references in the child, r (6) = $-.59$, $p < .10$. That is, children in our sample whose parents (and other adult contacts) talked about desire frequently and early on were the ones who made earliest reference to beliefs.

We also compared these adult belief-desire frequencies with later child frequency (again at 37–40 months) of genuine belief reference. Our hypothesis was that early adult desire talk would predict a significant positive relation between the adult and child measures—that frequent early parental talk about desire should lead to more frequent child talk about belief. Conversely, the hypothesis that parental belief talk was the relevant factor would predict a positive relation to exist for belief talk; that is, frequent early parental talk about belief should lead to more frequent child talk about belief. In this case, the relation was not significant, but it was positive for parental desire talk, r (5) = .43, rather than for belief talk, r (5) = $-.43$. Taken together, these correlations suggest that the relative frequency of adult talk about desires when children are younger is related to the age at which children begin to understand belief, such that more adult desire talk predicts earlier belief talk acquisition.

These analyses of parent and child talk might evoke the picture of a child simply listening to adult talk about desires, digesting it, and being informed by it. This picture is too passive, however; young children are also talking about desires, expressing themselves, and learning from conversational interaction. We have one conversational measure that is considerably more interactive, our measure of children's disputes with adults about desires. An intriguing possibility, alluded to in Chapter 6, is that conflicts about desires may be an especially fertile breeding ground for a deeper understanding of desires, subjectivity, and mind. Children's early interactions centering on what different people want may galvanize the thought progressions that culminate in reasoning about beliefs along with desires. We began to examine this possibility by comparing children's early desire conflicts, encounters in which the child verbalized a conflict about desires between two persons, with their later belief talk. One analysis compared the children's ages at their first desire conflicts in relation to age of onset for first genuine reference to belief; r (8) $= .88$, $p < .01$. We also compared the relative frequency of early desire conflicts (at 29–32 months) to both the onset of belief references, r (7) $= .19$, n.s., and the later relative frequency of belief talk, r (5) $= -.23$, n.s. The significant positive relationship between first desire conflicts and first genuine references to belief is consistent with the notion that early experience with desire conflict facilitates other, later understandings of mind, including a concept of belief. One might also have expected frequency of desire conflicts to matter. However, in general our analyses based on frequencies of certain sorts of child talk yielded little other than relations to MLU.

Summary. Accounting for individual differences in the development of an understanding of mental states was not a primary goal of our study; it could not be a major focus given our very small sample. Nevertheless, our data yield some provocative preliminary findings. First, MLU relates to how much these children talk about thoughts and beliefs, but it is relatively unrelated to the timing of this important milestone. Second, children's earlier talk about desires is systematically related to their later talk about beliefs. For example, earlier talk about desire predicted earlier talk about thought and belief. Moreover, a tendency to talk mostly about one's own desires predicted a later tendency to talk mostly about one's own beliefs. These data suggest that talk about desire and talk about beliefs may be linked in children's developing conceptions, not just in our eyes as adult investigators. Indeed, third, adult talk about desires and child–adult discourse about desire conflicts when the child is younger both relate to the onset of talk about belief.

Even if we had larger samples and could conduct analyses replicating these findings, these sorts of correlational results are subject to a variety of alternative interpretations. In particular, no conclusion about the causal significance of these various predictors of later talk about belief can be drawn from our correlational data. Consider our finding that children's early talk about desires relates to their later talk about belief. Perhaps, as previously hypothesized, early consideration of persons' desires advances the child's thinking about persons and minds, leading to an understanding of belief. Alternatively, perhaps these data simply capture differences in cognitive maturity among children: those who are more mature in their talk about desire, and in their talk about conflicting desires, also mature earlier in their talk about beliefs. That is, they make genuine reference to thoughts and beliefs at an earlier rather than a later age. In this regard, it is noteworthy that children who talk earlier about beliefs are not just more mature on all available measures. For example, they are not more mature in their language acquisition, at least as measured by MLU. Nonetheless, this general possibility cannot be ruled out, and we simply do not have the sorts of data or samples needed to systematically tackle alternative causal hypotheses. Given this caution, it is also the case that these preliminary data are consistent with some more intriguing possibilities worthy of further research. Most notably, it is possible that early talk about desire, and participation with others in talk about persons' desires, contributes to children's understanding of mental life generally and to their eventual understanding of thoughts and beliefs specifically.

Other Research Targeting Individual Differences

While accounting for individual differences in the development of an understanding of mental states was not the primary goal of our study, it has been focal in other research. In particular, in research that provides an excellent complement to our own, Dunn and her colleagues have been directly investigating individual differences in children's conversations and reasoning about persons (e.g., Brown & Dunn, 1991; Dunn, 1988; Dunn, Brown, & Beardsall, 1991a; Dunn et al., 1991b). Dunn's studies encompass a variety of specific sources of individual differences, including children's social characteristics, social environments, and social interactions. Here, we will consider where her studies corroborate our tentative conclusions and where they diverge or provide additional information.

Dunn's research, like our own, depends largely on sampling natural conversation. However, her research differs in several fashions from our study. In general, she observes a larger number of children but collects smaller language samples and at many fewer time periods (typically once every six months or once a year). Such samples cannot provide the sensitive measures of differences in age of onset that we have emphasized; her measures of differences focus on frequencies of expression. At the same time, Dunn has collected several other measures of children's social interactions and has administered laboratory-type tests, in addition to considering children's talk. Finally, Dunn has been most concerned with young children's talk about feeling states, their talk about emotions, preferences, and affective reactions.

To illustrate, in a study of young children's developing understanding of people's feelings and beliefs, Dunn et al. (1991b) observed and tested 50 second-born children. At 33 months of age, the children were observed at home with their mothers and siblings on two occasions, generating a two-hour language sample for each child. From this sample, measures were taken of conversational turns, MLU, talk about feelings and emotions, talk about causality, and interactions between mothers, children, and siblings. At 40 months of age, the children were given false-belief reasoning tasks and affective role-taking tasks. The false-belief tasks (from Bartsch & Wellman, 1989b) involved both predicting action from information about a puppet's false belief and explaining a puppet's action in terms of false belief. The affective role-taking tasks (from Denham, 1986) involved inferring the emotion of a puppet in a variety of everyday situations, such as seeing a parent off on a trip.

This report is one of several (see also Brown & Dunn, 1992; Dunn & Brown, 1993; Dunn, 1994) from an ongoing longitudinal study of these 50 children. In total, the children and families have been examined at 33, 40, and 47 months. At each time period, two one-hour observations are made, recording everyday conversations. At 40 months, as described above, several experimental tasks were also administered. In addition, Brown and Dunn (1991) report data on conversations about feelings, desires, and thoughts from a smaller sample of six young second-born children, observed with their mothers and siblings. Two one-hour audiotapes were recorded for each child at six two-month intervals, yielding data at 24, 26, 28, 30, 33, and 36 months.

How do Dunn's analyses compare with what we have observed? Consider first some of our basic descriptive findings. In the Brown and Dunn (1991) report about six young children, all six were talking about desires and feelings when first observed at 24 months. More precisely, they were using such desire and emotion terms as *want, need, afraid, love,* and *happy*; Brown and Dunn did not undertake detailed codings of the meaning of the children's use of these terms. Nonetheless, very young children used these terms, and with increasing frequency over the course of the third year, from 24 to 36 months. This observation corresponds to our data for references to desire in Chapter 4. As shown in Figure 4.1, we found genuine references to desire well in place by 24 months but also found increases in such references from 24 to 36 months.

In contrast to their use of feeling-state and desire terms, none of the six children in Brown and Dunn's (1991) study made any reference to thoughts and beliefs at 24 months; that is, they did not use terms such as *know, think, pretend,* and *wonder* (which the authors called mental-state terms). The earliest such reference was at 28 months. By 36 months, however, all six children were making at least some infrequent use of these terms. These data correspond to our own in Figure 7.1 charting the onset of genuine reference to thoughts and beliefs. In our data, as in Brown and Dunn's, reference to thoughts and beliefs typically appears in the months just before the third birthday.

Brown and Dunn's (1991) data for parental talk also parallel our own in several fashions. Mothers in Brown and Dunn's study talked not only about desires and feelings to their 24-month-olds, they also talked about thoughts and beliefs. On average, parental talk about desires and feelings outweighed talk about thoughts and beliefs; nonetheless, all mothers consistently referred to thoughts and beliefs in even the earliest time samples. As we reported in Chapter 5, parents in our study also made consistent genuine reference to thoughts and beliefs when their children were very young. In the last three months of the third year (33 and 36 months), Brown and Dunn's mothers' use of mental-state terms increased (from about 2% to 3.8% of all utterances to children). Our Figure 5.5 shows adults' genuine reference to thoughts and beliefs for the four primary children we studied. Genuine reference is apparent throughout, with some increase in such references later in the third year, at just about the same time that the children began to talk about thoughts and beliefs themselves. In our data, this increase in adult talk about thoughts and beliefs seems to coincide with or follow, rather than lead, the children's first references to thoughts and beliefs. This pattern also seems apparent in Brown and Dunn's data, because the increase in parental use of belief and thought terms was limited to the very last part of the third year, after the children began to use such terms.

Brown and Dunn (1991) conclude that, "although the results focused on normative developmental changes, large individual differences in the use of inner state language by both mothers and children were noted with even this small sample. This raises questions about the extent of individual differences in the onset and use of inner state language at this age, as well as the importance of these differences as antecedents and consequences of children's social understandings" (p. 252). Such questions about individual differences have been the focus of Dunn's larger current project.

With regard to that project, consider first the question of language facility as measured by MLU. We have reported that in our data children's MLU was linked to the relative frequency of their genuine belief references, but not to when they first made such reference. Dunn et al. (1991b) examined the effects of both mothers' and children's MLU on children's task performances at 40 months for the 50 children in their project. They found that children's abilities on the false-belief tasks administered at 40 months received no independent contribution from MLU measures (of mother or child). Experimental assessments such as false-belief tasks depend on children's understanding of the concept in question but not, of course, on how frequently children mention or use that concept in everyday conversational situations. Those measures thus seem more similar to our measure of the onset of belief reference than to our measure of frequency of belief references. MLU is unrelated to our measure of onset and is unrelated to Dunn et al.'s laboratory measure of belief understanding.

What about the relation between earlier sorts of talk and later understanding of belief? Dunn's current work focuses on two sorts of conversation: feeling-state talk (children's and parents' talk about emotions such as *happy*, *love*, and *hate*); and causal discourse (children's and adults' talk about causal phenomena). In Chapter 8 we will argue that young children's understanding of simple emotions is similar to their early understanding of desires. Both appear in children's natural conversation well before any mention of thoughts and beliefs, and both can be understood in a similar nonrepresentational fashion. In any event, Dunn, et al. (1991b) report that children's early talk about feeling states is significantly correlated to later understanding of belief as measured on false-belief tasks. Specifically, children who talked more about feelings at 33 months, and children whose mothers talked more to them about feelings at 33 months, were significantly more likely to perform correctly on false belief tasks at 40 months. Thus, similar to our own results, early talk about motivational or affective psychological states—feelings in Dunn's work and desires in ours—is related to earlier achievement of an understanding of persons' representational mental states, that is, their thoughts and beliefs.

Finally, we found that two sorts of early conversations might be particularly related to later increased understanding of mental states: causal discourse, in which children note how desires cause human acts; and interactive conversations about conflicting desires between different persons. In her current longitudinal project, Dunn has paid special attention to early talk about causality. Dunn et al. (1991b) report that children's talk about causal phenomena at 33 months was significantly correlated with performance on the affective perspective-taking task at 40 months, and they also report that mothers' talk to their children about causality at 33 months was significantly correlated to children's performance on the false-belief tasks at 40 months. In both cases, frequent early talk about causality related to better later social understanding.

In this first report (Dunn et al., 1991b), the authors' assessment of talk about causality was quite global; it collapsed together causal conversations about physical events, behavior, and internal states. In a later report, Dunn and Brown (1993) have looked in more detail at early causal conversations. In that report, Dunn and Brown examined the same 50 children's talk about causality at 33 and at 40 months, and they differentiated talk about causal phenomena into such categories as talk about physical reality, talk about behavior, talk about social rules, and talk about internal states (feelings, desires, thoughts, and beliefs). At 33 months children's causal explanations referred most often to behavior, but at 40 months causal-explanatory talk referred predominantly to internal states. Consequently, causal explanations appealing to internal states increased significantly from 33 to 40 months. This increase was found both in children's conversations with their mothers and in children's conversations with their siblings.

Dunn and Brown (1993) have also related various categories of causal-explanatory conversation at 33 months to children's performance on the affective perspective-taking task at 40 months. (Unfortunately for our purposes, they do not report similar analyses with regard to the false belief tasks that were also administered at 40 months.) Children's causal talk about internal states was the only category consistently related to performance on the affective perspective-taking task: causal discourse about internal states to both their mothers and siblings at 33 months was positively and significantly correlated with performance at 40 months.

Additionally, in this report Dunn and Brown (1993) report on the pragmatic contexts in which causal-explanatory remarks were made. They differentiate, for example, among contexts in which the children's discourse served to call attention to their own immediate needs or self-interest, children's engagement in disputes about causal phenomena, and children's more reflective discussions and simple or extended commentaries on the nature of causal events or phenomena. Early disputes with others about causal phenomena was the only pragmatic category consistently related to later performance on the affective perspective-taking task. More disputes about causal phenomena between the child and parent at 33 months, and between the child and sibling at 33 months, were both correlated with higher performance on the test of social understanding at 40 months.

Both Dunn's research and our own thus point to early causal-explanatory conversations about internal states and early social conflicts as breeding grounds for later social understanding. In yet another study, Dunn, Brown and Beardsall (1991a) reported on 41 children whose conversations about feeling states were recorded (in two one-hour sessions) at 36 months. At 6 years of age, these children were tested on Rothenberg's (1970) affective perspective-taking task. The authors reported that children's disputes at 36 months about actions, intentions, and feelings significantly correlated with advanced social understanding at 6 years. Additionally, children's discussion of the causes of feelings at 36 months related significantly to social understanding at 6 years. Dunn and her colleagues argued that disputes and causal-explanatory discourse were related in children's conversation, because

"Children were more likely to be engaged in discussion of cause of feelings when they were in dispute with others than when not in dispute—results that support arguments for the significance of social conflict as a setting in which the development of social understanding is likely to be fostered" (p. 453).

In our study, we can only begin to consider some of the many factors that may be related to differences in children's understanding of persons and minds. Research such as Dunn's tackles these issues more directly. It is helpful, therefore, to find some converging findings across these different research projects. At the same time, Dunn's research encompasses factors and findings that we are unable to address. Dunn's research, for example, reminds us that understanding of beliefs and desires exists within a larger array of inner state understandings. More specifically, in her research early talk about emotions surfaces along with talk about desires as a probable predecessor to later conceptions of thoughts and beliefs. Her work also emphasizes the variety of manifestations of a developing psychological understanding of persons; she targets not just children's belief-desire thinking, but a variety of outcomes and correlates. In several of her studies, as noted, she considers how developing social understandings relate to children's role-taking—to their propensity to take account of others' feelings, goals, and points of view. More recently, Dunn has begun to consider how such understandings relate to children's management of conflicts, their moral reasoning, and their jokes and humorous exchanges with others (Dunn, 1994). Dunn's focus on pragmatic contexts of children's talk about internal states seems especially promising. Regarding younger children's talk about feeling states (Brown & Dunn, 1991) and their talk about causality (Dunn & Brown, 1993), Dunn and her colleagues chart a decrease with age in children's discourse employing such terms and concepts simply to express their own immediate self interests. Concomitantly, they chart a significant increase, at about the third birthday, in children's more reflective commentary about internal states and causes. This is true in children's talk to both parents and siblings (Dunn & Brown, 1993). This increase in reflectiveness may well contribute to children's understanding of thoughts and beliefs, which also emerges around the third birthday, in Dunn's data as well as in our own.

Conclusions

Judy Dunn's reports are laced with appropriate cautions about the limits of her samples (the children are always second children with an older sibling), the ambiguity of correlational findings, and a host of unmeasured factors that may influence any obtained findings. These cautions apply even more strongly to our data in this chapter, limited as we are to conversational data for at most 10 children. Nonetheless our findings, together with those of Dunn and her colleagues, suggest that there are important influences on children's talk and conception of mental states that derive from children's conversational interactions with parents, siblings, adults, and peers.

Our data go beyond Dunn's in that they allow us to view these individual differences not just at a few points in time, but in terms of extensive longitudinal trajectories. Most longitudinal studies assess children individually at several ages, by making a few relatively wide-spaced assessments, for example, at yearly intervals or, as Dunn's current research has done, at 33, 40, and 47 months. Our data, however, provide individual developmental functions (e.g., Figures 5.2, 5.4 and 7.1) based on observations taken every one or two or three weeks and totaling 50, 100, or 200 samples per child (for the primary four children). Such data, when available, have many of the unique strengths that Siegler and Crowley (1991) have argued accrue to microgenetic research, but unlike microgenetic studies can also cover broad longitudinal spans of time.

Our own densely sampled longitudinal data make clear that the variations across individuals discussed in this chapter occur within rather modest limits and around a developmental trajectory that is rather consistent across children. At least these limits and consistencies hold across our sample, and as far as we can tell, would characterize Dunn's data as well. Within a relatively narrow developmental window these children uniformly began to refer to thoughts and beliefs and then evidenced similar steady increases in the frequency of such references. Moreover, such references to thoughts and beliefs were regularly preceded by plentiful references to desires and feelings. Individual differences in the onset and frequency of such references, while significant, clustered around this representative developmental path.

Note

1. Because of our very small sample sizes we adopted the .10 level as our minimal criterion for significance in all the analyses in this chapter.

8

Children's Developing Theory of Mind

When and how do children come to understand people as thinkers, knowers, wanters, wishers, fearers, hopers, and intentional actors? In addressing these questions, we are lucky that children quickly learn to talk and that they talk not just about the physical world but about themselves and others. Children's everyday conversations provide an effective window onto their understanding of people and minds, as demonstrated by the 10 children described in the preceding pages.

Overview of Findings

Our findings are not simply empirical; the data are organized around various conceptual distinctions that underpin and frame the research results. Some of these distinctions were outlined at the start—those between subjective and objective construals, connections and representations, beliefs and desires, for example. Other conceptual analyses were required as we proceeded so that we could more comprehensively characterize children's conversations, such as our analysis of arguments, and of advance belief versus false belief contrastives. When this conceptual groundwork is in place, then the children's conversations "speak for themselves."

Amidst our many findings, children's talk about the mind reveals a relatively clear progression of three phases. There is an early phase when children talk about desires, essentially wants and likes, in a wide variety of situations: desires for objects, desires for actions, desires for current or future states of affairs, and their own desires and the desires of others. Very young children draw revealing contrasts between desires and actions or objects, and they appeal to desires in order to explain human action, emotion, and interaction.

This early talk about desires is followed by a second phase, often beginning about the third birthday, in which children begin to talk about beliefs and thoughts as well as desires. When children first talk about these more cognitive topics, they are not constrained to talking of just fictional thoughts (imaginary ideas) or thoughts unconnected to real states of the world (e.g., a thought *of* horses, in some hypothetical sense). They do talk about such thoughts, but at the same time they also talk about beliefs (a thought that something is so) and even false beliefs (a thought that something is so, when in fact it is not). However, in this second phase, from about 3 to 4 years of age in our data, children's conception of thoughts and beliefs does not appear to be central to their larger understanding of human action. In this period, children talk about desires much more often than thoughts and beliefs, and although they are willing to describe people as having beliefs, their explanations for actions appeal to desires.

In a third phase, children grant the constructs of thoughts and beliefs a larger role in their basic understanding of mind and action. They increasingly refer to thoughts and beliefs and, moreover, they appeal to persons' beliefs, true and false, in order to explain their actions. At this point, children seem to realize that people not only have thoughts and beliefs, but also that thoughts and beliefs are crucial to explaining why people do things; that is, actors' pursuits of their desires are inevitably shaped by their beliefs about the world. It is actors' potentially mistaken conceptions of what the world is like, rather than the world directly, that determine their plans and acts. In our data we see signs of this third phase beginning at about 4 years of age.

We will refer to these phases, in succession, as an early desire psychology, an intermediate desire-belief psychology, and a belief-desire psychology. Whatever we call them, it is important to properly describe and acknowledge that there are a series of understandings and transitions in children's developing understanding of persons and minds. Too often researchers have acted as if there were only one transition in children's understanding of mental states: a change between 3 and 4 years, say, or a shift from before to after an understanding of false belief. But young children's developing understanding of persons and minds undergoes an extended conceptual progression. Even our depiction of three phases oversimplifies the needed account; we employ it to emphasize some important and neglected landmarks in the extended development.

This overview of our findings deserves several sorts of additional elaboration. Before going further, however, it is worth noting some of the strengths of our findings that justify granting them extended consideration, and some of their limitations as well.

Methods, Strengths, and Limits

Our natural language data reflect children's everyday reference to persons' mental states. Recent interest in theory of mind has been fueled in part by arguments that children's reasoning about persons via their beliefs and desires represents development of a pervasive world view. The claim is that such a mentalistic construal is basic to our understanding of persons in the first place and, moreover, that children like adults consistently "see" persons, actions, and selves not in terms of manifest behavioral properties but instead in terms of underlying psychological states. However, research on children's understanding of mind has overwhelmingly been conducted by presenting children with contrived laboratory scenarios and then directly asking them such questions as, "What does Joe want?" or "What does Julie think?" With such methods, the suspicion naturally arises that young children may refer to persons' beliefs and desires only when prompted and constrained to do so by special laboratory studies and techniques. The data we report address such suspicions. The children we have studied talk about the mind often and early in their everyday conversations, spontaneously referring to beliefs and desires, thoughts and wishes. In our data at 3 years of age, for example, children refer to persons' mental states via such terms as *want*, *think*, and *know* about once every 25 utterances. Extrapolated, this means that these 3-year-olds talk about people in such terms more than 100 times a day, revealing, as demonstrated in these pages, a pervasive mentalism.

Investigators have been prepared to believe that talking and thinking about the mind is frequent in even young children, because of results from prior analyses of children's early talk. For example, Bretherton and Beeghly (1982) and Ridgeway, Water, and Kuczaj (1985) reported that children first refer to persons' internal states via such terms as *happy*, *sad*, and *mad* at around 20 to 24 months of age, and do so consistently thereafter. However, these studies relied on maternal report of children's use of various terms, assessments that may be erroneous, or at least generous. More recently, therefore, investigators have examined actual child speech samples. For the most part, however, these later studies have relied on rather brief samples of children's language, such as four hours per child (Dunn et al., 1987; Furrow et al., 1992). Such samples give an abbreviated picture of mental-state language at best, and they fail to allow for the analysis of infrequent but especially informative productions such as contrastives. Shatz et al. (1983) provided a more compelling in-depth look at mental-state language. Yet, as noted in our introductory chapters, that study provided extensive data for only one child, and only for cognitive terms such as *think* and *know*. Moreover, while revealing the existence of contrastives in children's talk about the mind, Shatz et al. undertook no further analyses of them. We provide a comprehensive analysis of extended longitudinal corpora from 10 children and for a variety of mental-state terms, including those for desires as well as for thoughts and beliefs.

The sorts of intensive content analyses that we conducted, on the extensive corpora we examined, were only feasible for a relatively small sample of children. While considerably more representative than a study of a single child, or even 2 or 3, nevertheless only 10 children are examined here, and 4 of these children account for the majority of the data. Our sample is restricted in other ways as well, representing essentially white middle-class children, and over-representing children of language investigators. Still, the 4 primary children span a range of subject characteristics, including a working-class and an African-American family, and their data are convincingly corroborated by the other 6 children at many points along the way. At the same time, these are all English-speaking children growing up in the United States in the second half of the twentieth century, which leaves ample room for questions as to how such developments might proceed in children in other cultures or learning other languages.

In the face of these concerns, it is useful to point out that several components of the three-phase progression we have just outlined receive converging support from other samples of children. Furrow et al. (1992) recorded two-hour language samples from 19 children at age 2;0 and again at 3;0. They followed the methods of Shatz et al. (1983) to code genuine reference to thoughts and beliefs. Furrow et al. did not examine reference to desires and, because of their small speech samples, were unable to examine more intensively children's conceptions in such utterances as contrastives. However, they do report that references to thoughts and beliefs were essentially absent at 2;0 but quite apparent in the same children sampled at age 3;0. More recently, Moore, Furrow, Chiasson, and Patriquin (1993) presented tallies of belief and desire terms (simple use of the terms, not coded for psychological reference) for 14 of these same children. They report frequent use of desire terms (206 uses for the 14 children) at age 2;0, when there was very little use of belief or thought terms (35 total uses). In Chapter 7, we also reported where our findings match those emerging from Dunn's research program. These findings help reduce concerns that our sample just represents unusual or precocious children. Our sample includes at least one very advanced and fluent child, Abe. However, compared to other available samples, our children seem neither generally advanced nor delayed with regard to their use of *know*, *think*, and *want*.

Not only have we tackled a small sample of children, but several of our more precise analyses involve relatively small samples of utterances. For example, our analysis of subjective contrastives yielded 109 such contrastives for thoughts and beliefs (Table 3.3) and 160 for desires (Table 4.7). Our analysis of false belief contrastives yielded a sample of 83 utterances. These numbers, albeit small, indicate at least a minimal productivity (for the four focal children) and hence reveal a genuine conception of certain important distinctions. In this vein, we have mentioned before that our findings from broader coding categories were corroborated by more precise analyses of rarer utterances. Our claims about genuine references to thoughts and beliefs, for example, depend not just on our codings termed genuine psychological reference, but also on a deeper analysis of contrastives. Conversely, it is important to note that our more precise, and hence less frequent, codings were always nested within a tier of broader, less restricted analyses. Thus, our precise findings with regard to subjective contrastives for belief, for example, occur within the context of a larger analysis of contrastives more generally, and a still larger analysis of genuine references to belief. Ascending this series of nested analyses yields a substantial sample of utterances, ultimately almost 2,000 genuine references to thoughts and beliefs and more than 5,000 references to desires. This hierarchy of analyses buttresses our findings concerning rarer categories and yields an overall picture of considerable coherence.

Our analyses, however, provide very little insight into questions as to the strength or fluency of children's conceptions. For example, how well do these children, as 3-year-olds, understand false belief, or how accessible and fluent is that concept? Generally, conversational frequency cannot be easily related to conceptual fluency. Adequate mention, properly analyzed, can provide good evidence that a child understands some conceptual notion, but increasing conceptual fluency certainly does not necessarily correspond to increasing mention in natural conversation. We offer no general procedures for assessing conceptual strength via natural language data; however, we have provided data that help illuminate these questions. For example, the increasing importance and accessibility of a conception of thoughts and beliefs in children's social life is apparent not so much in increasing numbers of references to beliefs, but in several collateral analyses showing the impact of such a notion on children's explanations and verbal conflicts.

Several other limitations of our research are worth noting. For one, it is increasingly obvious that children's understanding of beliefs and desires is intimately related to their understanding of other mental phenomena such as emotions and perception (Wellman, 1993); we have only begun to examine children's talk about these related states as well (see Wellman, Harris, Banerjee, & Sinclair, in press). Additionally, our data begin at about 2 years of age. By this time, many children are already talking about mental states such as desires in sufficiently compelling fashions to make clear that certain psychological conceptions have an earlier developmental course. We cannot speak to those initial developments. Likewise, our data run out when the children are about 5½ years of age. Children's understanding of the mind does not stop developing at that point (see, e.g., Fabricius & Schwanenflugel,1994; Wellman & Hickling, in press). Fortunately, our data are richest just where current interest is strongest and current theories most focused: reference to beliefs and desires in the age period from 2 to 5 years.

A major issue deserving discussion concerns the use of age as a benchmark for charting developmental sequences. Age is used in developmental research as a rough timeline on which to organize and compare a series of achievements, assessments, or observations. Some such metric is especially needed in cross-sectional research, in which each child is sampled at a single point in time and developmental trends must be assembled across children of different ages. The conclusions of such studies often read as, "3-year-olds failed to . . . whereas 4-year-olds succeeded in. . . ." No one advances these statements in order to characterize some hypothetical 3-year-old or 4-year-old, but rather to capture a rough sequence of achievements. Our densely sampled longitudinal data more directly penetrate these developmental sequences. Adam first talks about desires and not thoughts and beliefs, then later talks about beliefs. The same is true for Abe, Sarah, Ross, and the others. Our data provide direct evidence of developmental sequences within individual children, not just extrapolations from ages. The primary sequence, of course, is between talk about desires versus talk about thoughts and beliefs, elaborated and defended in Chapter 5. But our data provide evidence about other sequences as well.

A trickier issue concerns possible conclusions that some sequence is not present in our data. It is obvious in the case of beliefs versus desires, when utterances of similar, large frequencies point to delays of six months or more for every child, that there is a clear sequence in talk on these two topics. It is harder to conclude with equal confidence that in some case there is no sequence. On this issue we wish to note that we have advanced conclusions about only two relatively important nonsequences. One nonsequence discussed in Chapter 3, involves all the various types of contrastives for thoughts and beliefs—for example, subjective, advance belief, and false belief contrastives—which seem to appear at just about the same time in children's speech. The other concerns talk about the mental states of self versus others. In the discussions that follow, we will return to the data and arguments that help establish the plausibility of these conclusions.

Given the longitudinal nature of our data, how shall we compare our findings to others in the field, findings that typically come from experimental research with cross-sectional samples of children? For these comparisons, we must resort to age as a benchmark—what 3-year-olds or 4-year-olds do or say—because the experimental data are presented in these terms. Such age group comparisons are crude at best, but even organized in this fashion our data seem roughly comparable at several important points to available experimental findings. For example, experimental data have begun to emerge showing that 2½-year-olds can solve several desire reasoning tasks but fail comparable belief reasoning tasks, which 3-year-olds pass with ease (Wellman & Woolley, 1990). In laboratory explanation tasks, in which children are required to explain actors' actions in their own words, some young 3-year-olds never mention the actors' beliefs, even if probed about them directly, whereas all 3-year-olds routinely and spontaneously mention the actors' desires (Bartsch & Wellman, 1989b; Moses & Flavell, 1990; Wellman & Banerjee, 1991). Or consider our conclusion that at just about 3 years these children begin to evidence a cogent understanding of thoughts and beliefs. When we first began reporting these natural language data (e.g., Bartsch & Wellman, 1989a), the accepted consensus from experimental studies was that 3-year-olds understand little if anything about beliefs, and a genuine understanding of belief begins at around 4 years of age. More recent experimental research, however, has also begun to find convincing evidence of an understanding of beliefs and even false beliefs in 3-year-olds (e.g., Mitchell & Lacohee, 1991; Moses, 1993; Siegal & Beattie, 1991). We will discuss these studies later; our point here is only that it is possible to make crude but informative age-related comparisons between our findings and those of others. Indeed, these comparisons across studies help speak to one final concern about our findings. Perhaps our data represent only very special conversations, especially "scaffolded"and organized by parents to teach children about mental states.

The possibility that our data represent special conversations manifesting largely parental conceptions raises several theoretical and methodological issues. Theoretically, one possibility is that early child–adult conversations about the mind help children to better understand persons and minds on their own. In accord with a Vygotskian perspective, for instance, perhaps childhood understanding of mind is at first interpsychological, that is, available only interactively in collaborative dialogues with parents, and becomes intrapsychological, or established in the child's conception, only later. The instructional function of adult talk about the mind was examined briefly in Chapter 7 and is an important topic for future research. It seems very likely that, in various fashions, parents help scaffold children's conceptions and guide them into increasingly articulate expression. This theoretical possibility raises a more troubling methodological concern, however. Perhaps the conceptual insights (e.g., reflected in genuine belief references) and distinctions (e.g., thoughts vs. reality) we have discussed are mistakenly attributed to children and were essentially provided by the adult conversational partners in our transcripts.

We believe it is extremely unlikely that our findings can be dismissed as revealing mostly adult conceptions. Our methods carefully exclude conversations in which children are merely repeating or paraphrasing adult utterances. Children may well be learning about the mind via such repetition, but our codings exclude this sort of mimicry. Conversely, we have especially identified revealing child utterances such as contrastives. While many contrastives are implicit in the sense explained in Chapter 3, among the earliest contrastives we also find clearly explicit instances. In such explicit contrastives, it is the child him- or herself who is clearly expressing conceptual insights and distinctions. Moreover, as just noted, recent experimental research, when available, tends to corroborate our attributions rather than suggest that they are overestimations. These experimental findings are not the products of parent–child conversation.

At this point, rather than further clarifying the strengths and limits of our data, we are content to claim that they offer extensive new information and to proceed to the task of sorting out their larger implications.

Children's Naive Psychologies

We want to elaborate on the character of our findings and propose a theoretical description that encompasses our results as well as other extant findings. We begin by considering further the phases outlined previously, particularly those two that we contend precede the belief-desire psychology evident in 4-year-olds. We focus on two issues. One concerns our estimation of what 3-year-olds know about beliefs, and even false beliefs, versus what 4-year-olds know: the nature of desire-belief psychology, as we have termed it. The second issue concerns our conclusion that very young children may know quite a bit about desires at a time when they know comparatively much less, or perhaps nothing at all, about beliefs and thoughts: the nature of desire psychology, as we have termed it.

Desire-Belief Psychology

We will assume that the outlines of belief-desire psychology are clear from our summary in Chapter 1 and from such other discussions as D'Andrade (1987) and Wellman (1990, Chapter 4). The basic idea is that people's actions are seen as stemming from their underlying beliefs and desires and, more specifically, that people engage in actions *that they believe will* achieve their desires. This explanatory system places people's beliefs at the center of understanding their actions: people do not engage in actions that will achieve their desires, but in those they believe will do so. Joe takes his umbrella because he wants to stay dry and he thinks it is raining (even though in fact it is not). Because of this central role of belief in our everyday psychology, children's understanding of belief has received primary scrutiny in the research on children's theory of mind.

Even this brief summary raises two distinct but interrelated questions with regard to children's understanding of beliefs: When do children understand that persons can have beliefs, those special mental states that attempt to reflect the world, but may not do so correctly? And when does such a notion becomes a central part of children's explanatory system, their psychology of human actions? Our data reveal that children understand the presence of beliefs in the human mind before they grant belief a central role in organizing and explaining mind and action. Hence, in advance of achieving a belief-desire psychology children utilize a desire-belief psychology. We term it desire-belief psychology in order to describe a phase, prototypic of young 3-year-olds in our data, in which children recognize the existence of beliefs, at least at times, yet reason about and explain action primarily in terms of desires.

To begin, we want to make credible that children might have something like a desire-belief psychology. Consider the adult's understanding of a related mental state, imagination. Adults, we will assume, understand that persons can have imaginings, mental states that represent some state of affairs, in this case fictional states of affairs. Adults can attribute such states to self and other and can even discuss how imaginings relate to the world; for example, most imaginings fail to correspond to the world, but at times they do so. While adults certainly attribute such states to people, they seldom explain their own and others' actions on the basis of imaginings. Explanations of action typically resort instead to consideration of other mental states—essentially beliefs and desires. Sometimes, of course, adults may appeal to imaginings to explain someone's action, for example, to explain why a person is engaging in an act of pretense. But these are rare, peripheral sorts of explanations of peculiar actions. Our ordinary understanding of mind includes the notion of a mental state of imagining and the existence of imaginary mental contents, but it does not grant that state or those mental contents much potency in our everyday explanation of action.

By analogy to an adult understanding of imaginings, we think that children might understand that people at times have certain sorts of mental states that do not figure centrally, and indeed can mostly be ignored, in attempts to understand action. Our proposal is that for young children there is a point where a notion of beliefs functions like imaginings in just this regard, that is, a desire-belief psychology. We do not mean that young children misunderstand beliefs as imaginings (i.e., we do not mean they mistakenly take beliefs to be fictional, imaginary representations rather than serious epistemic representations), but rather that beliefs function in a desire-belief psychology much like imaginings do for adults. Beliefs are mostly "out of the loop," unrecruited for explaining action; the job of explaining actions is left to other mental states, primarily desires. Beliefs only figure into explanations of actions in some rare and constrained instances.

To underwrite such a claim, we need evidence of a time when young children understand beliefs and attribute them to people, but at the same time explain action largely by appeal to a person's desires without recourse to beliefs. Our natural language analyses provide evidence that 3-year-olds understand beliefs—they talk about them often—and even understand false beliefs, as evident in their false belief contrastives (see Chapter 3). Four-year-olds refer to both beliefs and false beliefs more frequently than younger children, but in our data, even 3-year-olds do so. An understanding of false beliefs, among other things, demonstrates an understanding of mental misrepresentations that depict the world in one way when it is actually some other way altogether. At the same time in our data, 3-year-olds continue to explain action much as they did as 2-year-olds, by referring to actors' desires. Only later, at about 4, do children begin to refer systematically to beliefs in their everyday explanations of actions, as we documented in Chapter 6.

We will have more to say about the nature of 3-year-old children's desire-belief psychology, but this first elaboration of our account, and its fit with our findings, offers justification for further consideration of the notion of a desire-belief psychology. The notion of a still earlier desire psychology requires similar initial elaboration.

Desire Psychology

We propose that before children possess a desire-belief psychology, in which they understand belief but often ignore its importance, there is an earlier phase when children operate with no understanding of belief at all, evidencing a desire psychology. Such a proposal encompasses two claims: young children operate without a conception of thoughts and beliefs; and their understanding of desires provides a basis for thinking sensibly about persons' actions, a basis for reasonable, if limited, psychological understanding. Such claims receive initial support from two findings in our data: there is an early time when children talk about desires and not thoughts and beliefs; and children's early talk about desires is often coherent, extended, and sensibly related to other inferences about people, such as how they will act or feel.

However, proposing that young children do, or indeed that anyone could, understand desires without a concomitant understanding of something like beliefs raises some serious questions. Consider again the depiction of simple desires put forth in Chapter 4 and reiterated in Figure 8.1. Figure 8.1Y attributes a simple desire to Figure 8.1X, and in doing so also attributes to Figure 8.1X an internal subjective state of longing, a desire, for an external object. This is not an attribution of mental content, that is, it requires no conception of a represented state of affairs, in the target person's head (Fig. 8.1X) as it were. Whatever contents are involved are out there, in the world, rather than in the person's mind. The mental state being attributed here is intentional in the minimal sense of being about something; it is about the apple. But the object of the desire, what it is about, is a real apple in the world. That is the essence of the proposal: Figure 8.1Y attributes to Figure 8.1X an internal desire for the external object.

This simple understanding of desire is sensibly nonrepresentational, we claim, because it characterizes the child as seeing the contents of a person's desires as real objects in the world. As noted earlier, in such a construal there is only one set of contents to think about—objects in the world—which the target person either

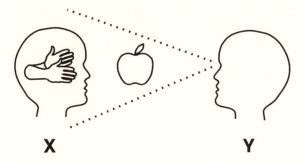

X   **Y**

Figure 8.1. Depiction of one person's (X) simple desire, as construed by a second person (Y).

does or does not desire. In contrast, an ordinary understanding of belief requires consideration of two sets of contents, seen clearly in the case of a false belief, in which we construe the target person as having a set of mental contents (the contents of his belief) and the world as having another set of contents (what's actually so). That is, beliefs properly understood are representational mental states. For beliefs, the person in Figure 8.1Y construes the target person (Fig. 8.1X) as having a representational set of mental contents about the world, beyond mental states simply related to contents in the world.

To be useful, this characterization requires several clarifications. First, as discussed in Chapter 4, the objects of a person's desires are not, even for 2-year-olds, restricted to physical items such as apples, toys, and tools. Objects of desire include actions (e.g., the desire to jump up and down) and states of affairs (e.g., the desire to be asleep). Figure 8.1, and its variations throughout this book, shows only the case of attributing to the target character a desire for a physical object, but it is meant to stand for attribution of desires for actions and states of affairs too.

A related clarification concerns our depiction in Figure 8.1 of the attributor construing the object of the target person's desire as out there, in the world (and the target person as simply wanting those real-world contents). But that is not the extent of what we believe 2-year-olds do, when 2-year-olds are the attributors. In our proposed nonrepresentational understanding of desire, the intentional object of a desire, for the 2-year-old, really exists in the world but is not necessarily visible, immediately available to the target person. The desired object might be deposited in the refrigerator, withheld by a parent, or even somewhere where it cannot be retrieved. Two-year-olds, however, understand that real objects exist even when they are hidden from sight or otherwise unavailable. So even if the desired object is hidden from the 2-year-old or from the target person, the 2-year-old perceives the target person as wanting a real object. Whether the target person's desire is satisfied or not, still the child understands the target person as wanting a real object in a real world that extends beyond the immediate present in space and time (because 2-year-olds understand the world as being extended in this spatiotemporal fashion).

Suppose that a 2-year-old sees the target person as wanting a cup of milk, but the cup is currently empty. The 2-year-old knows that cups can be filled, that they are often full of milk, and so on. So it is a very real cup of milk that the child sees the target person as wanting. Understanding that the world extends to encompass filled cups (even if the relevant cup is empty right now) requires no more cognitive power from the 2-year-old than understanding that the world contains apples (even if all are removed from sight right now). Such an understanding simply grants the 2-year-old a minimal amount of insight into the world of objects and events, an insight that even infants share (Baillargeon, 1993; Spelke, 1991).

How 2-year-olds might construe someone as wanting a future state of affairs (a full cup when the cup is currently empty) leads us to consider what the 2-year-old (a) believes (knows) about objects and events, and (b) attributes to other people (e.g., their desires). In this example, although there is no cup of milk visible in the world to which the target person is connected, a cup of milk is the content of the target person's desire. But since the milk is not visible, where does the child's construal of the target person's desire for it come from? On this proposal, it comes from the 2-year-old's knowledge of the world. The child simply knows (has access to his own cognitive representations that affirm) that there are such things in the world (even if none are currently visible), and he attributes to the target person a simple desire for those real-world contents. The 2-year-old's knowledge of the world fills in certain gaps, but what the 2-year-old attributes to people is a desire for real objects, actions, and events in the world.

Contemplate an alternative account for a moment. A consideration of desires for items or states of affairs not currently available (an apple when none are in sight, a filled cup of milk when the cup is empty) is perhaps what inclines many philosophers to construe our ordinary adult conception of desire as necessarily representational. The alternative account, therefore, would be to grant 2-year-olds something like our adult conception of desire, and to describe our adult conception of a desire as follows: the adult sees the target person as wanting something (a cup of milk), even when all available cups are empty. Therefore, the adult construes the target person as representing some state of affairs (milk in this cup), and wanting that. This construal constitutes a representational understanding of desire because the target person is construed as representing a state of affairs that is quite different from the existing state of the world. The target person desires the represented state of affairs (rather than simply wanting some real-world object). On this alternative, any attribution to persons of desires for future states of affairs thus includes some notion of representation. Moses and Chandler (1992, p. 289) put it this way, on analogy to an understanding of belief:

> Understanding that Maxi believes the chocolate is in the green cupboard, when it is really in the blue cupboard, involves [construing] Maxi as having a mental representation that differs from how things actually stand in the world. In a similar vein, it might be argued, understanding that Maxi wants the chocolate to be in the green cupboard also appears to involve [construing] Maxi as mentally representing things as somehow different from how they really are. If so, a representational theory of mind could be argued to be already in place by the time children begin to give evidence of reflecting on their own and others' desires.

Whether adults ordinarily construe desire in representational terms might itself be arguable (e.g., Perner, 1991, p. 215), but fortunately we need not take a stand as to whether either these accounts accurately captures how adults think about desire. We are concerned for now only with young children. Here, it is quite conceivable that 2-year-olds might work with a nonrepresentational rather than representational conception of desire. Both of the accounts that we are considering agree that in order for the child to consider the target person's desire for an as yet unavailable state of affairs, that state of affairs must first be represented (or conceived of). The issue on which the two accounts diverge is of who does the representing. For the nonrepresentational, or simple desire account, the 2-year-old does the representing. Better put, the 2-year-old's knowledge system simply allows him to know that the world actually encompasses certain objects that are not seen (e.g., hidden cups), certain actions not now being executed (e.g., jumping up and down although one is right now sitting), and various states of affairs (e.g., a filled cup of milk although the cup is empty at present). The 2- year-old conceives of these things and then simply attributes to the target person desires for those objects. He does not attribute to the target person a representation of those states of affairs, merely a desire for them. In the simple desire account, 2-year-olds operate without any conception of representational mental states (such as beliefs or represented objects of desire), only a conception of simple desires (coupled with their own knowledge of the world).

In the representational account, the young child, like the adult, attributes to the target person both a representation and a desire. The target person is seen both as representing a hypothetical state of affairs (a nonactual object, action, or state) and as wanting that state of affairs.

Given that a representational account of desires is the more or less standard one in philosophical and psychological discussion, we want to say more about a nonrepresentational account in order to make it a viable alternative. First, it is worth noting again that a nonrepresentational understanding of desire still allows for the important question of whether one's desires are satisfied. This is clear even in the case of a desire for a real here-and-now apple. I want that visible apple, that one right there. Whether I get it or not is another question, the question of satisfaction of the desire. Indeed, the essence of desire is the wanting of something not currently obtained, and that essence holds true for a nonrepresentational understanding of desire.

A nonrepresentational notion of desire also supports predictions of and explanations for action. That is, such a conception can provide the basis for an extended psychological understanding of persons. As we see it, the essential maxim for a desire psychology is that people do things in order to satisfy or achieve their desires. Thus, if a desire psychologist knows what someone's desire is, he can predict that that person's actions will be attempts (successful or otherwise) to satisfy her desire. If a desire psychologist knows that someone has done something, he can explain that person's action as an attempt (successful or not) to achieve a related desire. This sort of desire-based reasoning is used not only with reference to a person's actions but also a person's emotions. If a desire psychologist knows that someone wants something and discovers that the desire is satisfied (e.g., she gets what she wants), the desire psychologist can predict that the person will be happy (or pleased, etc.). Conversely, if the desire is not satisfied, the desire psychologist can predict that the person will be sad (or mad, etc.) instead.

One further prediction of action is worth considering from the point of view of both accounts. Let's say that a child knows that the target character, Jan, wants an apple and also that the apple is in the cupboard. A child with a conception of desires and beliefs can solve this problem in good belief-desire fashion. He can attribute to Jan something like the knowledge or belief that the apple is in the cupboard and then, in combination with his knowledge of Jan's desire, predict that Jan will go to the cupboard. This is a standard example of belief-desire reasoning: persons act on the basis of their beliefs to achieve their desires. A child with only a nonrepresentational understanding of desire, of the sort that we described previously, can also solve this problem. He predicts that Jan will go to the cupboard, under the maxim that Jan will act so as to fulfill the desire for an apple. In this case, the child knows that the apple is in the cupboard and uses that knowledge to predict where Jan will go. The child with this simple desire psychology sees Jan as having a desire and the world as having certain objects, and predicts Jan will act to achieve the object of desire. Critically, he does not attribute knowledge to Jan, he simply uses his own knowledge of the world to predict how Jan will act.

In this example, as in the earlier discussion of desires for unavailable objects, the chief difference between the two accounts is whether it is claimed that the 2-year-old attributes to the target person knowledge, beliefs, or representations of the world versus whether it is claimed that the 2-year-old merely has such knowledge of the world himself. As Bennett (1991, p. 97) put it in describing an earlier version of this proposal found in Wellman (1991), ''Whereas the five-year-old predicts what *x* will do on the basis of what it thinks *x* wants and *what it (the child) thinks* x *believes about the world*, a two-year-old does it on the basis of what it thinks *x* wants and *what it (the child) believes about the world.*

Not only is a simple desire psychology (bereft of a conception of belief or representation) conceivable, we favor it as an account of 2-year-olds' understanding. In our data, 2-year-olds talk about desires and not beliefs, thoughts, or imaginings. If 2-year-olds are construing people's mental states in representational fashions, why do they not make reference to such representational mental states? It is important to recall here that 2-year-olds have the words and the syntactic wherewithal to talk about such states and that they hear about these states from their parents. It is not that they fail to talk about some one or two representational mental states, say, beliefs alone or dreams; they do not talk of any of them, as far as we can tell from our data—not beliefs, thoughts, imaginings, dreams, knowledge, what have you. If children attribute representations to people, why would that attribution appear in desires alone?

Characterizing 3-year-olds as desire-belief psychologists and 2-year-olds as simple desire psychologists also fits together well. If children at first conceive of persons in terms of desires alone, it makes sense that when they begin to incorporate a notion of beliefs into their understanding that they might not initially recognize how powerful the notion of belief is, and thus might continue to rely primarily on desires to explain action. Along the same lines, it makes sense that if there is a period when children acknowledge beliefs but do not need or rarely use them to explain action, there might well be an even earlier point at which children reason without a notion of beliefs altogether.

In the next sections, we extend our consideration of desire psychology and desire-belief psychology further, in order to articulate how these notions relate to each other and to children's eventual belief-desire psychology.

More about Desire Psychology

Although we use the phrase ''desire psychology'' to refer to 2-year-olds' theory, we envision young children as having an expanded understanding of human behavior, extending beyond a recognition of desires alone. As noted already, for example, we believe that desire reasoning allows children not only to attribute desires to self and others, but also to explain and predict actions (on the basis of desires), and even to explain and predict some other mental states, such as certain emotional reactions. In fact, early desire psychology encompasses an important understanding of three different sorts of experiential states: simple desires, simple emotions, and simple perceptual experience or attention. For each of these states, a simple intentional understanding of subjective experiences characterizes children's initial conceptions; specifically, what is required of the young child is the same sort of understanding of a person's nonrepresentational directedness toward objects that we previously described for simple desires. Simple desires are intentional in the sense of being directed toward or being "about" certain objects, that is, objects, actions, and states of affairs. They are also experiential in the sense of attributing to the target person not just a behavioral directedness to objects (e.g., his hand reaching for that object), but also an internal experiential state, a wanting of that object, a desire for it. This sort of simple intentional conception can also extend to a conception of certain emotions: the target person is seen as feeling something about objects, for example, fearing that thing or being happy or mad about that state of affairs. This simple notion of intentional experience can also encompass a very rudimentary understanding of perception—attributing to the target person a simple experience of seeing objects, attending to them (see also Baron-Cohen, 1993). In this conception of perception, children do more than simply see the target person as directing his or her eyes toward an object; they see the person as experiencing it perceptually, that is, seeing it, noticing it, taking perceptual account of it. The flavor of this sort of a simple intentional understanding of perception is conveyed in Flavell's writings about Level-1 perspective-taking (1978, 1988).

The hypothesis that very young children operate with a simple intentional understanding of these three states is not only conceivable, but it has some empirical support. Wellman (1993) marshalls the evidence that makes such understandings empirically feasible in 1- and 2-year-olds; here we want to concentrate on the sort of interrelated understanding of persons that a simple intentional understanding of these states might allow. If older infants understanding of simple intentional states includes an understanding of attending *and* wanting *and* emotionally reacting to objects, this inclusion has several implications. These three states together, for example, seem to include both mind-to-world and world-to-mind directions of fit (Searle, 1983). As adults, we tend to construe some internal states as directed toward changing the world, making world fit mind. Desires, for example, lead to (and thus underlie) acts such as reaching, searching, and asking for objects. Other states, such as, perception, but also certain emotional reactions such as liking something or not, instead accommodate themselves to objects, that is, mind fits world. The 2-year-old's understanding of intentional states thus would encompass a significant duality: an initial understanding of both intentional action toward the world and intentional experience of it. This understanding foreshadows an aspect of our adult naive psychology, in which internal states occupy an important middle ground, receptive to the world via perception, but also intruding into the world via intentional action.

Perhaps it would be better to call these directions of fit world-to-experience and experience-to-world (rather than mind), so as to emphasize the nonrepresentational character of the mental states involved. But the point remains that a small but cogent package of simple intentional states affords the child considerable power for reasoning about mind and action. Similarly, perhaps this sort of psychology might be better titled desire-perception rather than desire psychology (see, e.g., Gopnik & Wellman, 1992). By calling it desire psychology in this book, we are not claiming that the young child has an understanding of only one mental state. Rather, we are emphasizing the centrality of understanding a person's desires in order to understand their actions, just as belief-desire psychology emphasizes the centrality of beliefs and desires (while still encompassing a wide variety of mental states, as in Figure 1.1).

We believe this larger description of desire psychology—as a simple intentional psychology encompassing an understanding of simple desires, simple emotions, and simple perceptual experiences—will prove itself in further research. For example, Wellman et al. (in press) have just finished a study parallel to the current one, examining the early emotion talk of Abe, Sarah, Adam, Ross, and Naomi. The picture we draw here of an early internal, subjective, experiential but not necessarily representational understanding of desires in 2-year-olds is mirrored in that research by an internal, subjective, experiential conception of emotion. Such a conception is evident in these young children's use of emotion terms (e.g., *happy, sad, mad, like*) and is corroborated by careful analyses of informative contrastive utterances and discourse.

This description of an early similar understanding of desires, emotions, and perceptions is also important for considering a further challenge to the notion that young children first possess something like a simple desire psychology, as we have described it, rather than a belief-desire psychology. As Moses and Chandler (1992) have put it, asynchrony between an early understanding of desires and a later understanding of beliefs confronts the problem of holism:

> According to this widely accepted view, our various mentalistic concepts cannot be treated in a vacuum. Each of these concepts is situated in a network of related concepts, such that their meanings are interdependent. . . . On this view, concepts of desire without attendant concepts of belief, or beliefs denuded of associated desires, would be fundamentally nonsensical. For example, it is not clear what it would mean to say that Joe wanted a drink unless one was also prepared to say that he knew what a drink was. In this holistic view, our concepts of belief and desire come as a "package deal" and necessarily must share a yoked history." (p. 289)

One part of our response to this challenge was explained earlier, namely, our claim that the young desire theorist's own representational system does part of the work here, the child's knowledge of the world replacing any need to attribute to the target person beliefs about the world. A second part of our response is to admit that a system of reasoning encompassing only a single mental-state concept may well be impossible, but that a system encompassing desires, emotions, and perceptions may well be sufficient. Those concepts afford the 2-year-old with an initial, but sensible rather than nonsensical, system for reasoning about human behavior. This system includes a package of related mental-state constructs that underwrite one another and allow for inferences from one state to another and from states to action, and vice versa. Indeed, it is conceivable that young children attain an early facility with this sort of understanding of persons because of the similar nature of these earliest mental-state concepts, in this case uncomplicated by more sophisticated notions of representation.

Another elaboration of our conception of desire psychology concerns the need for consistency and relevance in desire (emotion, perception) reasoning. Desire psychology, as we see it, is similar to adult belief-desire psychology in implying a holism among different types of mental states as acknowledged previously, but also in another related fashion. Namely, children using a desire psychology must, like adults, assume that the specific mental states involved in some focal action, or related to some other focal mental state, are those that are both consistent with and relevant to the focal actions or state (Bartsch, 1991). The intentionality of the various states and acts must converge on the same intentional objects. Adults, for example, attribute to Bill, who is looking for an apple in the refrigerator, a desire for an apple and a belief that an apple is in the refrigerator. We do not explain Bill's action by attributing to him a desire for a Mercedes or a belief that Paris is in France. Similarly, we would not reason that just any desire would account for Bill's happiness on finding an apple; only his desire for an apple accounts for that particular emotional reaction. In making sense of other people in terms of their subjective states, we must select desires, beliefs, actions, and reactions that are relevant to and consistent with each other in terms of content or object.

This assumption of consistency and relevance between actions and mental states is clear for adults with regard to beliefs. Even if Bill can hold contradictory beliefs, in trying to explain or predict his actions or states, we must assume that he does not do so. Harmon (1976, p. 436) refers to this assumption as the demand of joint consistency; the alternative is to simply abandon attempts to predict or explain behavior via a folk (naive) theory of mind and turn to nonrational accounts (e.g., he's insane, or he has a brain tumor). Or, as Davidson (1980, p. 221–22) puts it, "To the extent that we fail to discover a coherent and plausible pattern in the attitudes and actions of others we simply forego the chance of treating them as persons." Without the constraint of focusing only on consistent and relevant mental states and actions, reasoning in terms of subjective states would be quite hopeless; we'd flounder trying to make sense of sequences like the one described by Jerry Fodor (1981, p. 182), "the thought that two is a prime number, causing a desire for tea, causing an intention to recite the alphabet backwards, causing an expectation of rain." Fodor further notes (p. 182) that "though such sequences doubtless actually occur (in dreams, say, and in madness), still if *all* our mental life was like this, it's hard to see what point ascriptions of contents to mental states would have."

Notice that consistency and relevance among the specific psychological states of an individual aid and constrain reasoning about Bill, even if we fail to consider his beliefs at all. If we see Bill heading for his garage, we assume that he wants to go to his garage, that he wants his car or his toolbox. Conversely, if all we know is that Bill wants to mail a letter, we predict that he will act in a manner consistent with his desire: he might go to the post office or go to buy stamps. As adults we may not even consider whether or not Bill believes that letters can be mailed at the post office. And, we claim, young children need not consider beliefs, although they must consider a package of relevant states and actions. In short, even though young children are limited to reasoning only about desires and emotions and perception, and at a nonrepresentational level, we see them as evidencing an important sort of sensible reasoning that considers and honors certain tenets of consistency and relevance within an individual's psychological states and actions.

Two-year-olds' early use of desire terms (and emotion terms in Wellman et al., in press) demonstrates to us that they are for the most part consistent and relevant. They typically attribute desires to themselves or others that sensibly correspond to the situation. In explaining actions in terms of desires, for example, they mention desires that are relevant to and consistent with the action:

> ROSS (2;10): Look, there's a car up in the air.
> ADULT: Oh, Why is it up there?
> ROSS: Man put it up there.
> ADULT: Why did he put it up there?
> ROSS: He want to fix it.

In summary, young children's desire psychology appears to provide a sensible and impressive system for reasoning about an extended variety of states and actions and the relations among them. Such a system seems unmistakably present in these 10 young children's everyday conversations about actions, desires, and emotions; it is a system worthy of considerable further investigation.

Pretense.   While children's simple intentional understanding, their desire psychology, includes an understanding of desires, emotions, and perception, it definitely does not encompass all the sorts of mental states that adults understand. It does not include a conception of some exotic mental states, such as religious conviction, or Freudian repression. More important, desire psychology does not encompass one very basic set of mental states that are essential to adult understanding, namely, beliefs, thoughts, and imaginings. Our natural language data provide no warrant for attributing an understanding of such states to very young children.

In this vein, an important question concerns young children's understanding of pretense. Beginning at about 12 to 18 months, young children engage in pretense (e.g., McCune-Nicolich, 1981). They also begin to engage in shared pretense, which suggests that they have some understanding of others' pretense. Indeed, Leslie (1987) argues that children's early skills at pretense suggest an early understanding of cognitive representations. A child seeing someone pretending a banana is a telephone, in this view, construes the pretender as representing an object as something else. However, this is a hotly contested claim (see, e.g., the review by Lillard, 1993a). Harris (1991), for example, claims that understanding pretense requires no understanding of another's mental state:

> Early shared pretence can operate in a much simpler way. An adult acts out a piece of make-believe. To join in, the child needs to recognize what the other person is pretending to do, and also that what they are pretending is not for real.

> For example, the child needs to recognize that the other person is pretending to pour tea, but that there is no real tea. This may be a lot, but it does not require any insight into the mind of the person pouring the pretend tea. In the same way, a theatre-goer need only respond to the play as if it were real while acknowledging that it is not; he or she can ignore the mental processes by which the actors produce their performance. (p. 302)

In fact, there are several possibilities. A very young child may view someone else's pretense as simply literal action, albeit of some confusing nonunderstood type (acts that are strange, funny, or silly). This possibility seems closest to some of Lillard's (1993b) claims. Another possibility endorsed by Harris (see especially Harris & Kavanaugh, 1993) is that the child understands pretend actions as not-real actions, that is, actions based on stipulated nonliteral object identities rather than real identities (e.g., the pretender pours pretend tea from a literally empty pot). In both these possibilities, the child is seen as having an objective, behavioral construal of pretense. The young child concentrates on the pretend actions and makes no attribution to the pretender of a special mental state involved in producing the acts. An objective-behavioral understanding of pretense certainly contrasts with an adult mental-representational construal. Adults' typical construal of pretense is that the pretend actions stem from the actor's representations of an alternative state of affairs; the actor imagines (mentally represents) some fictional states of affairs and enacts them through pretend actions. Leslie (1987) essentially attributes understanding of pretense to very young children, as they first begin to engage in pretend play at around 18 months.

In short, two starkly different proposals are on offer: children understand pretense as "just action" until 5 years or so of age (Lillard 1993b); or they understand the mental representations behind pretense at about 18 months (Leslie, 1987). We offer yet another hypothesis: at first, children understand persons as mentally connected to pretend not-real scenarios, without yet conceiving of the pretender as representing some fictional scenario in his or her mind (see also Perner, 1991). That is, 2-year-olds understand pretense as more mental and less "just-action" than Lillard or Harris claim, but understanding pretense as enacting mental representations should not possible until age 3 or so. Such a novel prediction follows logically from our proposal that very young children have a nonrepresentational but nonetheless mentalistic-subjective understanding of persons until about age 3.

Current research provides no comprehensive picture of young children's understanding of pretense, hence the current debate. Specifically, no one to our knowledge has provided evidence that 1- and 2-year-old children understand pretenders as mentally representing to themselves the states of affairs that they are overtly enacting. On the other hand, data as to children's understanding of imagination and fantasy—the representational states that would underpin a representational understanding of pretense—are consistent with the claim that children do not understand such states until age 3 or older. In our analyses, children's use and understanding of terms referring to mental states of imagination, for example, *think*, *dream*, and *make-believe* in our data and even *pretend* itself in the Shatz et al. (1983) data, mimics exactly our findings from the larger analysis for terms of thought and belief. As described in Chapter 3, children's genuine reference to fictional representational states, such as fantasy, imagination, and dreams, emerges at the same time as their reference to serious representational states such as beliefs and knowledge, at just at or before the third birthday and not before. In experimental work, 3-year-olds but not 2-year-olds also display an understanding of mental images and imaginings, including the recognition that such images are contentful, yet private and internal in the sense of existing in the imagination and not in the real world (Estes, Wellman & Woolley, 1989; Woolley & Wellman, 1993).

A Theory Transition in the Child's Understanding of Mind

The three phases we have outlined are descriptively useful. In addition, we believe these phases mark a sequence of conceptual developments that represent a transition from an earlier psychological theory to a later one in the years from 2 to 5. That is, the account we favor describes the child's understanding of persons as constituting a naive theory of mind, and describes the developments that we have charted as manifestations of an early theory evolving into a later one.

In this section, we elaborate and apply this larger account for which our natural language data provide support, and it proves useful for organizing the variety of findings we have uncovered. The general argument that children undergo changes in a theory of mind is one that we have advanced before (e.g., Wellman, 1990). More recently, in collaboration with Alison Gopnik, one of us has developed and advanced a detailed version of this account (Gopnik & Wellman, 1992, 1994), terming it "theory theory," the theory that the child's understanding of persons and minds constitutes an everyday theory.[1] Much of the following section is taken from this collaborative work, though we have also expanded and modified the ideas presented there.

Naive Theories

When we say that the child's understanding of mind is a theory, we do not mean it is a scientific theory, we mean a naive theory. There are important differences between science and everyday thinking; the point of a theory-theory is not to claim that scientists and children are identical. Rather, the idea is that analyses of one sort of cognitive development—changes in adult thinking enabled and constrained by scientific theories—can help us understand childhood cognitive development enabled and constrained by naive or everyday theories. This idea both requires and is made tenable by advances in understanding the sort of cognitive structures that guide young children's development of basic knowledge (Carey, 1985; Gopnik, 1988; Karmiloff-Smith, 1988; Wellman & Gelman, 1992), coupled with increasingly adequate analyses of the sort of theories that guide scientific attempts to develop basic knowledge (Kuhn, 1962; Lakatos, 1970; Laudan, 1977).

There is considerable debate in philosophy of science about how to characterize theories, and in many ways the scientist's ability to learn about the world is as mysterious as the child's. However, we need no definitive account of scientific theories; we can begin by focusing on several aspects of theories that seem important in almost all accounts. One such aspect rests on a distinction between specific and framework theories, and another concerns the interplay within theories of three crucial components: constructs, evidence, and explanations.

Even a cursory look at scientific theories shows that it is important to distinguish foundational or framework theories from specific theories. Specific theories are detailed scientific formulations about a delimited set of phenomena. To use psychological examples, theories at this level would include the Rescorla-Wagner theory of classical conditioning, Piaget's theory of object permanence, and Freud's theory of the Oedipal complex. On the other hand, framework theories constrain and guide the development of specific theories. Examples in psychology include behaviorism, psychodynamics, and connectionism.

Philosophers of science have called framework theories paradigms (Kuhn, 1962), research programs (Lakatos, 1970), or research traditions (Laudan, 1977). There are important differences in these writers' characterizations, but for our purposes we can focus on commonalities. Framework theories outline the ontology and the basic causal devices for their specific theories, thereby defining a framework for reasoning about a particular set of phenomena.

> A research tradition provides a set of guidelines for the development of specific theories. Part of those guidelines constitute an ontology which specifies, in a general way, the types of fundamental entities which exist in the domain or domains within which the research tradition is embedded. The function of specific theories within the research tradition is to explain all the empirical problems in the domain by "reducing" them to the ontology of the research tradition. . . . Moreover, the research tradition outlines the different modes by which these entities can interact. Thus, Cartesian particles can only interact by contact, not by action-at-a-distance. Entities within a Marxist research tradition can only interact by virtue of the economic forces influencing them (Laudan, 1977, p. 79).

We believe that research on children's theory of mind, our own included, attempts to describe the overall framework that children use to think about persons and minds—a framework theory—rather than children's detailed analyses of any one person or mental process (see also Wellman, 1990). As a framework theory, everyday understanding of mind must encompass the ontological and causal aspects of mind. For adults, the ontological aspect picks out mental contents, states, and processes as a domain of things to consider and distinguishes that mental world from the real world of physical objects, material states, and mechanical or behavioral processes. The essence of the ontological aspect, therefore, is our ordinary understanding of the difference between thoughts or ideas on the one hand and objects or overt behavior on the other. The contents and states of the mind are internal, mental, and subjective, whereas the contents and states of the world are external, substantial, and objective.

Moreover, according to our everyday adult theory of mind, our thoughts, beliefs, and ideas are not only distinct from the physical world of objects and behavior but also causally related to each other and to that physical-behavioral world. Causal influence goes from mind to world and from world to mind; mental states cause actions in the world and the world causes mental states. A phrase like "belief-desire psychology" as a label for our everyday psychology highlights this causal-explanatory aspect by emphasizing the mental states that are held to be causal to each other and to action.

Characterizing the causal-explanatory aspect of theories also requires a consideration of constructs, evidence, and explanations. Attributing to children (or anyone) a theory means attributing to them a system of theoretical constructs that are distinct from empirical phenomena or evidence. Though distinct from the evidence itself, the constructs are used to explain and to understand those phenomena. Theories provide a separate causal-explanatory level of analysis that accounts for phenomena by reinterpreting and explaining those phenomena in terms of the theory's constructs.

As Gopnik and Wellman (1994) put it:

> The relation between theory and evidence is distinctive. It is not like the relation between experience and other cognitive structures. To capture this, we distinguish between two ways of organizing experience. The first kind we will call "empirical typologies and generalizations," the second "theories." Empirical typologies and generalizations are orderings, partitionings, and glosses of evidence and experience, but they share the same basic vocabulary as the evidence itself. For example, I may look at a collection of plants and divide them into ones with no stems, ones with green stems, and ones with woody stems. Similarly, I may make generalizations about the behavior of objects. If the evening star appears at the same place in the heavens every evening we may make the empirical generalization that it will continue to appear at that place this evening (without any theoretical notions of why this may be the case). . . .
>
> Empirical typologies and generalizations contrast with theoretical structures. Theories propose theoretical constructs: Abstract entities, events, or forces. These theoretical entities do explanatory work—they provide casual explanations that account for evidential phenomena. These theoretical explanations are typically phrased in a vocabulary that is quite different from the evidential vocabulary.
>
> For example, suppose we postulate Darwinian species as a theoretical construct in evolutionary biology (rather than describing birds, mammals, etc., as empirical types). We will define species in terms that are quite removed from their apparent features; a green stemmed plant and a woody stemmed one may both be ferns because of their reproductive lineage. Similarly, Kepler's theory of the planets postulates elliptical movements that are notoriously not visible when we look at the stars' perceived motions in the sky. . . . Theoretical constructs are often called unobservable but they need not be definitively unobservable; rather they are appeals to a set of entities removed from, and underlying, the evidential phenomena themselves. Theoretical constructs are designed to explain (not merely type and generalize) those empirical phenomena. (pp. 259–60)

Notice how the sort of explanations offered by theories versus by empirical generalizations differ. To explain that some plant is green because it belongs to the class of green plants rather than brown ones is to provide only a shallow generalization of the empirical phenomena. But to explain that the plant is green because it has chlorophyl, which is green because it has a certain chemical structure, is to provide a theoretical explanation that appeals to constructs (e.g., cholorophyl) that are at a different level of description.

Theories work by utilizing constructs that do not simply restate the data but actually explain them. To do this work, theoretical constructs must be organized together in a system of relations that allow inferences at the theoretical level, which can then be applied back to the evidential level of phenomena. This process is characteristic of theories: phenomena are reinterpreted via theoretical constructs that, because of their organized system of interrelations, provide predictions for and explanations of the evidence.

This interplay between constructs, evidence, and explanations is crucial not just to a static description of theories, but also to characterizing the process of theory change. Again, philosophers of science differ in their accounts of how to describe theory change, but a critical common element is what is called the defeasibility of theories. Theoretical systems of construct and explanation not only organize and account for evidence but in that process are open to defeat or revision by the evidence. Insofar as theoretical constructs attempt to account for some set of empirical phenomena, they offer both explanations and predictions of new, as yet unobserved phenomena. If the constructs fail to predict correctly, they are subject to revision. However, theory revision is more than simple disconfirmation or even falsification. The transition from one theory to a substantially revised one is a complex and an extended process involving certain characteristic intermediate phases or reactions (Kuhn, 1962; Lakatos, 1970; Laudan, 1977).

Initially, a theory may not even recognize opposing evidence as such. It may treat certain failures as noise or as observationally inaccurate rather than theoretically puzzling. That is, the initial observation of the phenomena through the theoretical framework may result in misinterpretation or blindness to certain aspects of the evidence itself. But theories, especially framework theories, are learning devices as well as interpretational structures; they provide a basis for attending to and searching for new phenomena as well as simply for interpretation of known phenomena. Theories provide a lens for exploration, not just explanation. In this process of expansion and exploration, new evidence and even contrary evidence accumulates. At a second phase, therefore, the theory begins to deal with such evidence. However, at first the theory may develop only ad hoc or auxiliary hypotheses designed to account specifically for the new evidence or new discovery. Such auxiliary hypotheses revise the original theory only minimally, via the addition of a new construct appended to the theory to deal with a circumscribed bit of evidence or a simple rephrasing of that evidence in the accepted vocabulary of the larger theory.

However, such auxiliary hypotheses can prove unsuccessful or inconsistent among themselves, or they can accumulate in ways that undermine the theory's original core. In such cases, a final theory change may be required that leads to a substantially revised new theory. Adoption of a new theory may require the availability of some alternative theory from another domain of thought or group of scientists. However, some types of theory change can also result from reorganizing the current theory. In particular, auxiliary or peripheral aspects of a theory can change to become central. Sometimes, what began as an auxiliary hypothesis can prove increasingly successful or applicable to several phenomena. That is, an ad hoc construct or hypothesis may be formulated to deal with a peripheral phenomenon and hence at first be applied to just a few cases, but then it may become clear that the hypothesis can apply to other cases as well. In the end, the theory may change substantially in character, as what used to be peripheral becomes central and auxiliary constructs become core, and the explanatory structure of the theory shifts accordingly.

The development of the heliocentric theory of planetary movement provides some illustration of these processes. The Ptolemaic theory was thoroughly geocentric. Beginning with an initial conception of the sun, stars, and planets as moving around the earth in spherical orbits, scholars invoked several auxiliary hypotheses to deal with the counter-evidence. Most obviously, epicycles and increasingly complex arrangements of epicycles were added. Note that the notion of epicycles itself encompasses an acceptance of several centers of celestial forces. Copernicus then theorized that the sun was the center of celestial movements in addition to the earth. Tycho Brahe more systematically extended the idea of heliocentrism by proposing that other planets revolve around the sum which revolves around the earth, but even he failed to accept the central idea that the earth itself goes round the sun. Finally, Kepler provided a full heliocentric account.

According to a theory-theory account of children's developing understanding of the mind, these same transitional features of theory change should be apparent in children's transition from one view of the mind to another. Specifically,

> Children should ignore certain kinds of counterevidence initially. Later, they might account for them by auxiliary hypotheses, only invoked to deal with particular kinds of counterevidence. Furthermore, children might first use the new theoretical idea in limited contexts, contexts closely related to the conceptual structure of the earlier theory. Only after the theory change is complete will they finally reorganize their knowledge so that new theoretical entities play a central role. (Gopnik & Wellman, 1994, pp. 263–64)

We believe that the three phases identified in our data (and the elaborated descriptions we have provided for them) are usefully viewed in theory terms and furthermore as manifesting a process of theory change taking place in the years from 2 to 5. In this process, there is an initial framework theory of considerable scope that confronts some inevitable anomalies. We spent a good deal of time in the earlier sections of this chapter describing the nature of early desire psychology, because such a system of concepts and reasoning captures key aspects of the child's early mentalistic construal of persons, which functions for the child like a theory in two fashions. First, desire psychology allows the child to understand a large array of phenomena in a systematic fashion, by appealing to a set of related theoretical constructs; second, it provides a starting point for a set of dynamic processes that result in theory change, from one view of mind to another.

Specifically, by about the third birthday in our data, children's theory of mental states and actions becomes more complicated. At this time, children begin using cognitive terms like *think* and *know* to refer to thoughts, beliefs, and imaginings in a variety of ways. In children's contrastives particularly, we see explicit acknowledgments of distinctions between beliefs and imaginings, between the beliefs of different individuals, between beliefs and states-of-affairs, even explicit acknowledgments of false beliefs. In short, the ontological category of mind has become more extensive by admitting of several new mental states, thoughts, beliefs, and imaginings. Moreover, these states encompass an additional sort of difference between mind and world, namely, the distinction between a world of mental representational contents versus the real world of physical-behavioral contents and states of affairs.

When these constructs first appear, however, they have an interesting character and application. The fact that children do not spontaneously invoke beliefs to explain action until they are older, although referring to beliefs in some fashions, suggests that beliefs do not function in the 3-year-old's theory in the same causal-explanatory manner that they do for older children and adults. We believe that the child's theory at this point is still essentially a desire psychology, in which a construct of belief functions as an auxiliary hypothesis or construct. We call this stage of theory development a desire-belief theory, to capture children's tendency to reason first in terms of the old desire theory, and only refer to beliefs or representations infrequently and in limited circumstances. Thus, the primary theoretical construct for 3-year-olds is the sole one used by 2-year-olds, namely, a notion of simple intentional states whereby persons have subjective experiences directed toward real-world objects, actions, states of affairs, or enactments. Representational mental states, encompassing a set of mental contents that depict or represent the world, are peripheral and auxiliary. By 4 or 5 years of age, however, children have developed a quite different view of mind in which representational mental states and processes are central. In this view, most psychological functioning is mediated by representations, or as Chandler et al. (1989) has stated, ''persons regularly live their life, not with reference to how things actually are, but in accordance with their own sometimes mistaken beliefs'' (p. 1263). In children's everyday talk, this development is reflected by the appearance of explanations of action in terms of beliefs as well as desires, with beliefs playing the determining role when they are false, indicating their central role in the reasoning process.

Transitional Phenomena and Mechanisms

In our analysis, desire-belief psychology represents a transitional, intermediate phase between a relatively consistent desire psychology in younger children and a relatively consistent belief-desire psychology in older children. As might be expected, there seem to be two kinds of transitional phenomena evident in the young 3-year-olds in our data: advance indications of the new theory and retained allegiances to the old. Advance indications concern primarily an initial understanding of representational mental states, including beliefs and false beliefs, which is apparent in only some situations, not consistently, and is peripheral to the causal-explanatory core of the 3-year-olds' theory. The conceptual and explanatory core of the theory, where retained allegiances are evident, reveals that 3-year-olds' psychology remains largely a desire psychology in two ways. First, a person's actions are still thought about largely in terms of this or her desires, emotions and perceptions, not beliefs. Second, children's primary view of the mind, of mental states, remains anchored in the notion of simple intentional states characteristic of simple desires and perceptions, not of thoughts and beliefs related to external real-world contents. This view of mental states as straightforwardly encompassing external real-world objects and states of affairs colors the 3-year-old's reasoning about thoughts and beliefs as well as desires and perceptions. Specifically, 3-year-olds, guided by a simple intentional view of mental states, typically think that a person's beliefs are true, that is, the contents of a person's beliefs are the same as or match the contents of the world.

For 3-year-olds, a person's beliefs (though not necessarily all his or her thoughts, such as imaginings) are directed to the world just as a person's vision is directed toward the world. And to the 3-year-old, what the person sees in the world (such that the person may have failed to see some things but equally may have already seen things now removed from view), is the same as what that person believes is in the world (such as that the person may fail to believe or know some things but equally may believe things not actually seen).

A desire psychology, with its simple intentional emphasis on states of affairs in the world, accounts for the consistent tendency for 3-year-olds to say that people's thoughts about the world are accurate or true—the classic finding in research on children's understanding of belief (Flavell, et al., 1990; Gopnik & Astington, 1988; Perner et al., 1987). It also accounts for young 3-year-olds' overwhelming tendency to explain action by referring to the actor's simple intentional states—his desires, emotions, and perceptions—rather than his thoughts, beliefs, and imaginings. However, a genuine, albeit peripheral representational understanding of thoughts and beliefs accounts for 3-year-olds' ability to refer at times to mental contents rather than world contents, and hence their ability to refer at times to beliefs, false beliefs, and imaginings.

If a theory-theory view of the development of mind is true, then it must pass several tests, the first being consistency with our data. Second, variable, transitional performance is predicted at about 3 years of age for many children; but to simply say that 3-year-olds will sometimes be right and sometimes wrong, or sometimes but not always talk about belief accurately, is unconstrained. Theory-theory should predict situations in which 3-year-olds' thinking will reflect their core theory and others in which it will reflect their auxiliary representational hypothesis. Third, theory-theory should be able to hypothesize children's process of transition from earlier to later theory. However speculative at first, such a hypothesis must be conceivable and plausible. In the next two sections we begin to tackle these tasks.

Variable performances. Two sorts of situations should enhance young children's ability to genuinely consider mental representations: those that disrupt a focus on external contents of the world and allow or force a more separated consideration of mental contents; and those in which desire reasoning forces the child to consider some additional explanation or explanatory construct.

Our natural language data show infrequent but genuine reference to mental contents and even at times false beliefs by 3-year-olds, who refer much more frequently and consistently to desires and emotions, and who refer almost exclusively to such simple intentional states, and not thoughts and beliefs, to explain behavior. Although our data do not permit analyses of the sorts of situations in which 3-year-olds may refer to representational mental states and contents, extant experimental studies provide some extremely suggestive demonstrations. Specifically, recent studies that successfully demonstrate false-belief reasoning in 3-year-olds seem to show the effectiveness of each of the two just outlined.

First consider traditional studies of belief reasoning in preschool children. For example, in change of location tasks first used by Wimmer and Perner (1983), preschoolers are shown a character, Maxi, who hides his chocolate in one of two locations and then departs. Maxi's mother then moves the chocolate to a second location. On Maxi's return, children must predict where Maxi will look for the chocolate or state where Maxi thinks the chocolate is. Similarly, in unexpected-contents tasks, preschoolers are shown a distinctive container, such as a crayon box, that is revealed to have candy in it instead. They are asked what someone else who has not seen the container, will think is in it. Four-year-olds typically answer correctly, reporting the other person's false belief or mistaken action (e.g., Perner et al., 1987). In solving false-belief tasks such as these, 4-year-olds have been taken to manifest an understanding of beliefs, of mental representations in the convincing case of misrepresentations, and a belief-desire understanding of action. In contrast, 3-year-olds do not merely respond randomly on such tasks but typically fail in a particular way. They answer that the character would act successfully (instead of mistakenly) and would think what is true instead of what is false. These data, replicated in many careful and converging studies (e.g., Gopnik & Astington, 1988; Moses & Flavell, 1990; Perner et al., 1987), have been taken as demonstrating that 3-year-olds do not understand beliefs, or at least that beliefs could be false, and therefore do not understand mental representation (Perner, 1991) or, at the least, mental misrepresentation (Wellman, 1990).

Several recent studies, however, have shown 3-year-olds to reason successfully about false mental representations; these studies have downplayed the nature and existence of the real-world states of affairs involved (Fritz, 1991; Zaitchik, 1991), actively directed children to the mental rather than real-world contents at issue (Mitchell & Lacohee, 1991; Woolley & Wellman, 1993), or involved intriguing extensions of desire reasoning (e.g., Bartsch & Wellman, 1989b; Flavell et al., 1990; Moses, 1993; Wellman & Banerjee, 1991). For example, Fritz (1991) tested 3-year-olds on a revised false-belief task. In the revised version, the chocolate that Maxi hides is not visible; rather the child is simply asked to imagine that there is chocolate, but no visible chunk is used. Again, while Maxi is away his mother moves the chocolate. In either the standard or revised version, Maxi should have the false belief that the chocolate is in the original location. In the standard version of the task, however, a set of very present real-world contents (the chocolate seen in the second location) contradicts this belief. In the alternative version, no tangible piece of chocolate offers such an obvious contradiction. Three-year-olds were correct at the revised version of the task, which downplays the real-world contents (see also Zaitchik, 1991).

Mitchell and Lacohee (1991) asked children about their own past false beliefs. In the standard condition, children saw a candy box that turned out to have not candy but pencils in it. They were asked what they had thought when they first saw the box, before it was opened. In a comparison task, children were shown the box and then asked to draw a picture of what they thought it contained and to mail the picture by putting it in a mailbox. They were then shown the real contents of the box and asked about their prior false belief. Three-year-olds were much better in the comparison task when they were strongly directed toward thinking about, and even depicting, their initial mental contents.

Even more intriguingly, several studies have used children's own reasoning about desires and action to confront them with the need to think about some other (consistent and relevant) mental states as well. In such circumstances, 3-year-olds can resort to an appeal to beliefs and false beliefs. We (Bartsch & Wellman, 1989b) provided an early demonstration of this sort. Rather than having children predict what an actor would do on the basis of a false belief, or simply state the contents of a person's belief in a situation where it should be false, we presented children with situations where a person's actions thwarted his or her own desires. For example, Jane wanted a kitty and went to look for it under the piano, when the kitty actually was under a chair. When asked to explain why Jane was looking under the piano, 3-year-olds were at times able to appeal to her beliefs, in this case Jane's false belief that the kitty was under the piano. Three-year-olds were significantly better at this task than at a comparable but standard false-belief task. Wellman and Banerjee (1991) followed up this study, adding several controls, in a task that required desire psychology reasoning about emotions rather than desires.

Flavell et al. (1990) tested 3-year-olds' understanding of what they termed fact beliefs and value beliefs. Fact beliefs are like those typically focal in false belief tasks, for example, Maxi's belief that that the chocolate is in a particular location. Value beliefs are based on opinions or preferences, for example, someone's belief whether a particular drink tastes good or not. Value beliefs are closely related, therefore, to desires and emotions, likes and evaluations of certain states of affairs, although they are expressed in the language of belief, for example, "Ellie thinks that's really yucky." In carefully matched tasks, Flavell et al. found that 3-year-olds were much more able to judge that someone else held a value belief discrepant with the children's own experience (Ellie thinks it's yucky while the child has tasted it and thinks it's sweet and delicious) than they were able to judge that someone else held a comparably discrepant fact belief (Ellie thinks a milk carton is full, although the child has seen it and thinks it is empty).

Moses (1993) extended this analysis further by exploring children's understanding of beliefs that are directly relevant to the actor's desires or intentions. For example, if a person says he is going to do something, then one related inference is that he wants or intends to do it, but another is that he thinks he will do it. Moses found that 3-year-olds were good at attributing false-intention beliefs to a character (Studies 1 and 2) and better at attributing intention beliefs than false beliefs of the more standard sort (Study 2). For example, if Joey says he is going to do *X*, 3-year-olds were significantly correct at judging that he was "trying" to do *X* (the intention question) and that he "thought" he would do *X* (the intention-belief question), even if they had just seen that Joey failed to do *X* (and hence that Joey's thought that he would do it was false).

We believe these findings, and others, can be interpreted as showing that children using a desire-belief theory (just like 2-year-olds with a desire theory) assume the mental states involved in actions are both consistent with and relevant to those actions. In circumstances where desire reasoning alone would not yield a consistent and relevant explanation, 3-year-olds can resort to beliefs. When told Jane wants her kitty but is looking in the wrong place, the 3-year-old recognizes that Jane's desire cannot provide a relevant, consistent mental explanation. Resorting to belief can resolve the puzzle. In the Moses (1993) study, Joey says he is going to do X, but visibly fails and is visibly disappointed. Then the child is asked whether Joey thought he would do X or that he would fail to do X. Saying Joey thought he would fail is consistent with what actually happened, but saying he thought he would do X is consistent with his desire, with his displayed emotional expression of disappointment and dismay, as well as with desire psychology's acknowledgment that we often fail to attain our desires. In contrast, consider the standard false-belief tasks. In change-of-location tasks the child is told Maxi wants his chocolate. Predicting either that Maxi will act so as to get it (go where it is), or that Maxi thinks it is where it really is, is consistent with Maxi's desire. Also consider unexpected-content tasks. Saying that a person who has not seen the unexpected contents (e.g., that the crayon box contains candy) will nonetheless think what is true, is consistent with a desire psychology understanding of simple intentional mental states: mental states encompass real-world contents. Note that in unexpected-content tasks, nothing is said about the target person's desires. Since there is only one container, however, even if the child imagines the person as having a relevant desire, it would most likely be a desire to open the container. In addition, if the child imagines the person as wanting to open the container, the desire consistent with that person's desire for action would be for candy (since that is what is there) accompanied by a belief that the container contains candy.

In short, on standard false-belief tasks 3-year-olds make consistent, relevant (albeit incorrect) predictions and attributions on the basis of desire reasoning alone; but in situations where desire reasoning alone fails to lead to consistent relevant predictions and attributions, 3-year-olds can resort to beliefs as well.

Three-year-olds' seemingly inconsistent performance on false belief tasks and with false belief reasoning has constituted an embarrassment for many current accounts of children's developing theory of mind. For a theory-theory, such variable findings are to be expected. However, the expectation of variable performance is also appropriately constrained. In our account, this sort of performance is characterized as transitional and thus only to be expected at some ages, not others. More important, the sorts of variable performance observed should be related to the operation of some factors, not others, as predicted by the nature of the 3-year-old children's predominant theory, desire psychology.

The transition from desire to desire-belief psychology. Besides predicting specific transitional performances, a theory theory affords hypotheses concerning actual transitional processes from children's earlier to later theory. Here we advance such a transition hypothesis, focusing on the transition at about age 3 from a desire to a desire-belief psychology.

We begin, of course, with desire psychology. Desire psychology as a framework theory provides the child with considerable resources, including a focus on subjective mental states of persons and a system of explanation about persons and actions that recruits mental state concepts in consistent and relevant fashions. Framework theories of this sort do not merely conceptually parse and explain a set of phenomena; the initial conceptual parsing of phenomena also provides the child with a territory for discovery. In the case of desire psychology, the territory is the domain of mental states. Framework theories launch open-ended research programs.

Desire psychology's focus on mental states leads the child to attend to a variety of such states. The child can do this by observation of others but also by attention to his own mental states as experienced. A growing awareness of mental experience as instigated by desire psychology leads to consideration and conception of a different sort of mental state, that is, thoughts. For example, the child's experience of confronting unexpected circumstances, surprising states of affairs that do not accord with his or her desires or expectations about the world, must push for a way to describe that sort of mental state. In such an experience, the child actually briefly experiences mental contents at odds with real-world contents. Likewise, the child may experience situations in which the real-world cause of her emotions is different from the emotion's intentional object. Hearing a noise under her bed, the child may be afraid of a snake. Upon looking, she finds the noise was caused by a heating vent. She was afraid of a represented snake, not a real one. Additionally, it is likely that young children experience such mental representations in mental states such as dreams, images, or imaginings. What is distinctive about these states is that they may have little connection to what occurs in the world, and this fact may aid children in conceiving of an alternate realm of mental contents.

In these ways, certain mental experiences call for more than a simple intentional conception of internal experiences of real-world contents; they present mental contents for consideration as well. However, our hypothesis is that an initial experience-driven awareness of mental contents is constrained by children's framework theory, desire psychology. Mental representations at first are an auxiliary concept used to describe special mental states but are integral to children's explanations of mind and action. Imaginings and dreams, for example, have little causal connection to real-world states of affairs; this quality allows a consideration of their contents separate from real-world contents but also means children can easily ignore such states in their reasoning about how world and mind, mental state and action, relate. At first then, children's understanding of representational mental states remains segregated from their explanatory efforts; representational states are phenomena eventually uncovered by the impetus of desire psychology to scrutinize and conceptualize mental states, but they are not central to it.

However, children's explanatory efforts, framed by desire psychology, are expanding at the same time as their awareness of mental states. In the process of utilizing desire psychology to predict and explain peoples' actions and emotional reactions, children may encounter certain puzzles or explanatory failures. For example, the child may notice that he and another person have similar desires but engage in two different actions. More compelling, people often do things that thwart their own desires. It is not just that they act sensibly and yet fail to achieve their desires, but their actions seem to fly in the face of their own desires. Jane wants to find her kitty but she is searching for it under the piano, when the 3-year-old knows that it is not there at all. Or a child may search fruitlessly for some object in several places before finding it in another place altogether, or before being told by her mom that it is somewhere else. Acting against one's own desires is a commonplace occurrence that is one easily explained by a notion of belief—Jane thought the kitty was under the piano—but such actions are a puzzle, a theoretical anomaly, for a desire psychologist. Indeed, the puzzle is specific to desire psychology. It is thinking of persons in desire psychology terms in the first place that forces children to confront such puzzles. A behaviorist, for example, would not find these examples perplexing; he or she could easily account for such behavior via histories of conditioning.

In short, desire psychology generates puzzles and anomalies that force consideration of a different mental state construct in order to explain acts. Additionally, as just described, 3-year-olds have the peripheral but available concept of mental representational states to appeal to. At first, any appeal to representational states is recruited only when desire psychology breaks down or in order to provide a mental state explanation that is consistent and relevant. Consideration of what the actor wants still drives children's explanatory efforts, but at times a consistent and relevant story about the person's desires and actions and emotions requires, and thus comes to recruit, a notion of beliefs as well, representational mental states that frame one's desires. Consideration of beliefs as framing the actor's desires, not merely existing as auxiliary to desire psychology, is the key notion behind belief-desire reasoning; that is, the person's desire-based actions are perceived as being filtered through his or her representations of the world, rather than working on the world directly.

In this account, children's first-hand experiences of mental states are an important ingredient in the formulation of a belief-desire psychology. Such experiences, in part, sponsor a conception of mental representational contents, but such a conception is much more than simply the experience itself. The experience is conceptualized within a theoretical framework that provides a conceptual base for initially conceiving of and attending to such states, namely, desire psychology. Within desire psychology, however, a notion of mental representations at first remains peripheral, initially excluded from the explanation of action, and typically misunderstood in simple desire terms as necessitating mental contents that match real-world contents. Thus, children at first achieve a desire-belief psychology, which remains at its core a desire psychology and not a belief-desire psychology. Only because desire psychology also fails to explain certain everyday actions and events does the notion of belief and representation become increasingly utilized and central to children's explanatory understanding of persons and actions. What began as an auxiliary hypothesis becomes increasingly typical and finally prototypical of all mental states.

Conclusions

In this chapter, we have summarized our data, elaborated the three phases of development evident in our findings, and then offered an extended account of development of a theory of mind. The theoretical account is consistent with our data (although it goes beyond them as well) and it helps organize and make understandable these new findings. Conversely, the data provide an extensive organized set of findings that can be used to comprehensively describe children's developing understanding in this domain. In addition, the data can be used to evaluate competing accounts of children's development. In the next chapter, we compare several alternative accounts with our findings.

Note

1. We owe the term "theory theory" originally to Morton (1980).

9

Alternatives and Controversies

Children's understanding of mind has been extensively discussed and researched lately. New clarity and consensus have emerged from these efforts; investigators increasingly agree on descriptions and findings that were unknown or controversial just 5 or 10 years ago. At the same time, however, conflicting interpretations and predictions have been inspired by contrasting basic characterizations of everyday understanding of mind and contrasting explanations for developmental change. In the last chapter, we argued that children's talk about the mind can be characterized as reflecting several phases in their development of a theory of mind. In this chapter, we discuss some alternative accounts, compare them to the one we have offered, and examine how they fare when tested against our natural language findings. Some of the alternatives we discuss involve specific points of controversy, but basic questions of general import are at issue: Is knowledge of mental states innate? Is knowledge of the mind largely introspective, a manifestation of first-person awareness of one's own mental experiences? Are the changes apparent in children's talk and judgments about the mind deep or shallow; do they reflect substantial changes in children's basic conceptions or in children's abilities to express or access relatively unchanging conceptions? Are changes in reasoning about the mind specific to children's understanding of this topic—their developing expertise at understanding persons, action, and minds—or do they manifest some larger cognitive change that influences other domains as well?

Role of First-Person Experience: Simulation or Theory

In describing children's understanding of persons as being framed by a theory of mind, we emphasize the child's conceptual knowledge; folk psychological reasoning is organized by and takes place via a distinctive conceptual system that includes constructs such as belief and desire. From this point of view, children acquire understandings of beliefs and desires, among other mental notions, which function for them like theoretical constructs. These understandings allow children to interpret behavior in intentional terms by attributing to themselves and others these mental states. They also allow children to make certain inferences about persons, to predict and explain actions.

Recently, several philosophers (e.g., Goldman, 1992; Gordon, 1992) and developmental psychologists (e.g., Harris, 1989; Johnson, 1988) have argued that theory of mind is a serious misconstrual of our ordinary folk psychological under-standing of persons because reasoning about persons and minds does not proceed through anything like mental-state concepts. When reasoning about minds, we do not resort to concepts but rather more simply to our first-hand experience of mental life. Since we are organisms who have mental states, like beliefs and desires, we certainly come to refer to such states; however, this referral comes about not through acquiring concepts and theories of such states but simply by experiencing and reporting our own mental states. Such a claim has plausibility, especially when the focus is on our knowledge of our own states. If true, then it may be more accurate to say that we experientially discover our own mental states than that we conceptually construct them; we inherently possess mental states, experience them, and learn to refer to them. Such an idea goes back at least as far as Descartes.

The challenge for such accounts is to explain our ability to reason about others' mental states. This is where the idea of simulation comes in. According to simu-lation theory, the same process of discovering, rather than conceptually inferring, also applies to our understanding of others. The theory proposes that we simulate someone else's mental states for ourselves, and by this process discover what he or she must feel and think. That is, we mentally project ourselves into the other person's situation, discover what we would feel or think in that situation, and attribute that (simulated) experience to the other. In this account, people understand others' states not by appeal to constructs such as belief and desire that span self and other, but by simply running a working model of the other's mind and dis-covering its outputs. Fortunately, each of us has our own working model of a mind to use in this process. In using our model, we need know nothing about beliefs and desires conceptually. We simply feed perceptual-situational inputs into our mind, inputs that are appropriate for the other person; mentally run through this contrived, imaginary situation; and then attribute the results that we experience (off-line as it were) to the other.

Paul Harris (1989) has convincingly described how even very young children might employ such a process. He says our understanding of mind is not the work of a theory, it is a "work of the imagination" (Harris, 1991). He notes that even young children are very good at pretending and imagining and says young children (and adults) understand others' minds by simply imagining what the other feels, thinks, and wants. On learning that Billy wants peanuts, the average child (or adult) simply imagines what her own actions would be if she wanted peanuts and predicts that Billy will act the same way. On hearing that Bob spent all day searching through empty boxes in the garage, the child consults her own working model— her own mental-state experience when she pretends to be rummaging through boxes—to find a reason for Bob's behavior. She concludes she would have been thinking that something she wanted was in one of the boxes, and attributes that thought to Bob. It is not necessary, in this view, for the child to have the abstract construct of belief as a representational state in order to accurately predict or ex-plain the behavior of other people; an imaginative simulation and projection of mental states will serve.

Based on several challenges to a simulation account (e.g., Gopnik, 1993; Gop-nik & Wellman, 1992), Harris has increasingly detailed how a simulation theory would apply to the development of children's understanding of mind, how it would explain why children are adept at certain attributions of mental states before others (Harris, 1992, 1994). Both a simulation theory and a theory-theory predict development: children can be predicted to solve simple problems before they are later able to solve complex or difficult ones. But the notions of what constitutes simple and difficult problems differ considerably between the two accounts.

For simulation theory, a critical difference is between states that are directly reported versus those that must be simulated, for example, current states of the self that can be simply experienced and reported versus the states of others that must be simulated. An additional difference is between states that should be easy to simulate versus those that require complex simulations. In contrast, for theory-theory the critical difference concerns states that are easy or difficult to conceive of. If children find some states (e.g., simple nonrepresentational desires) simpler to conceive of than others (e.g., ordinary representational beliefs), then the development of reasoning about mental life will proceed in that order.

Note that in a simulation account there is no reason to expect different mental states, beliefs versus desires, to be easier or harder to simulate. Both beliefs and desires are equally available to the child as states of her own mind. Children, like adults, experience beliefs as well as desires; the basic working model, their own mind, necessarily includes both states. In a parallel way, in a theory-theory account, there is no reason to expect that a basic understanding of mental states should differ for self and other. Theoretical conceptions of the sort we have described are generic, equally applicable to the self and others. If a theory has formulated a particular theoretical construct, such as the concept of belief, it should be able to use this concept to explain the child's behavior and the behavior of others. If the theory does not include this construct, it will not be applicable to either the self or others. Of course, each person might have a privileged position for knowing the content of his mental states over those of another, but the basic constructs, beliefs, and desires, and their importance in organizing an understanding of mental life, should apply uniformly.

We feel our natural language data fit a theory-theory better than the simulation account. In broad strokes, following the reasoning just outlined, our data seem to show that knowledge about thoughts and beliefs, when acquired, is very similar for self and other; similarly, knowledge about desire is very similar for self and other. However, knowledge of simple desires greatly precedes knowledge of representational beliefs. Thus, development seems to order itself much more with regard to mental-state concepts of increasing conceptual complexity, that is, desires versus beliefs, than it does with regard to knowledge of self versus other, a factor of prime importance to a simulation account. This observation requires closer scrutiny, however.

Harris (e.g., 1991) claims that children's simulations operate against a background of two "default settings" and that simulations are more or less difficult depending on how many of these defaults the child must override or adjust. The default settings consist of mental states of the self, or as Harris terms it, the child's own intentional stance; and states of reality, what is true in the world. Some simulations, to be correct, require adjusting just one's own mental stance. To simulate someone else's desire, for instance, one must ignore one's own desires and imagine the intentional stance of the other. Simulations of beliefs about unknown targets have this same character. Suppose a child does not know what is in a box, but thinks it is a doll. To simulate someone else's belief (the belief of someone who thinks it is a ball), the child must override his own intentional stance. A second and more difficult set of problems, however, require that the child override both default settings, including reality. This is necessary for understanding false beliefs. Suppose the child knows that the box contains a doll and now must simulate that the other thinks, mistakenly, that it contains a ball. In this case, the child must override or set aside known reality and then also imagine the other as having a different intentional stance toward that reality.

In this analysis, Harris's position is that children can easily report on all sorts of mental states for self—desires, beliefs, imaginings—and moreover can equally simulate these for others as long as they require equivalent simulations. After all, children experience both beliefs and desires, and when they have the capacity to imaginatively project one such state onto others, that capacity is similarly available for dealing with the other state. Thus, in our language samples we would expect to see a good amount of both belief and desire talk early on, albeit little or no false-belief talk. However, our data, at both the level of genuine psychological reference and contrastives, do not support these predictions. Talk about desires markedly precedes talk about beliefs, and when children begin to talk about beliefs they appear to be able, at least on occasion, to refer to false beliefs as well.

Harris (1992, 1994) clarifies how his account predicts that developments in this domain should proceed. He begins his account with Step 1 in infancy, but the two phases that concern us more are Step 3 for 2- and 3-year-olds and Step 4 for older children (e.g., Harris, 1992, p. 126). In Step 3, "Imagining an Intentional Stance," young children "can anticipate or enact the reactions of people . . . whose current mental stance differs from their own. The other can diverge from the self with respect to [what] he or she sees, wants, likes, expects, knows. For example, whereas the target X is currently . . . wanted by the self, the child can anticipate the fact that someone else currently . . . wants a different target" (p. 126). Harris typically attributes this step to 3-year-olds, but also to 2-year-olds (p. 126), and it is clear from the logic of his account and from his examples that regardless of the exact ages involved, he predicts that with the advent of this step children can deal with thoughts, beliefs, and knowledge, as well as desires and emotions, as long as the simulations only require the one adjustment. All these mental states are included because all are similarly experienced by the child, all are similarly products of the child's own mind and hence can be simulated via that mind for others (and for self if needed). Step 4 is termed "Imagining an Intentional Stance for Counterfactual Targets": "At around 4 years, and quite systematically by 5 years, one of the evident limitations of Step 3 is overcome. Children acknowledge that people can diverge not just with respect to the targets of their mental stance, they can also construe the very same target differently" (p. 126). "The child . . . now incorporates hypothetical situations that run counter to particular existing situations as intentional targets. The child can imagine someone believing . . . a state of affairs that runs directly counter to what they currently take to be the case—as exemplified by the false belief task'' (p. 130). Children can override known reality and attribute a construal that differs from known reality to others, or simulate such a state for themselves to account for past mistakes.

These predictions fail to square with our natural language data. Talk about beliefs and desires, even in comparable "simulations," evidences a marked developmental difference, not similarity. For example, consider Harris's Step 3. A good example of Step 3 thinking concerns what we have called subjective contrastives. In subjective contrastives for desire, the child distinguishes her own intentional stance toward an object (she likes it) from the other's intentional stance (he does not like it), in just the way that Harris describes adjusting one's own intentional stance at Step 3. Similarly, in subjective contrastives for thoughts and beliefs, the child distinguishes her own intentional stance toward a target (she thinks the box contains X) from the other person's stance (he thinks it contains Y). Again, this is just as Harris describes it, because in subjective constrastives about belief (as opposed to thought-reality contrastives) reality is unknown; nobody yet knows what is in the box. In Harris's analysis, the child need not engage in any overriding of reality; she has only to attribute different thoughts and beliefs to two persons, herself and another.

Yet, children produce subjective contrastives describing persons' differing desires consistently and significantly before any such contrastives for beliefs. Why would this happen, from a simulation account? Children have first-person access to both beliefs and desires, and the simulations needed are equivalent. Indeed, as just outlined, Harris predicts there would be no difference between such attributions.

Moreover, consider our data on children's references to their current mental states.

> We have very little understanding of children's ability to report their current mental states. What would such an investigation produce? . . . The simulation model [makes] a prediction. In general, young children should be quite accurate at answering questions about what they currently think, know, pretend, want or see, because privileged access can be used in applying those terms to the self. It can inform them about the current object or target of experience, and their current attitude toward that target. (Harris, 1992, p. 139).

> Simulation theory holds that young children . . . should be relatively accurate in reporting their own current mental states. . . . The theory theory makes no claim to such privileged access, arguing instead that mental states, whether belonging to self or other, must all be filtered through the same theoretical lens. . . . The evidence suggests that 3-year-olds are quite accurate in reporting on a variety of mental states: what they currently think, want, perceive, pretend, and so forth. . . . To the extent that theory-theorists argue that children's accuracy varies only with the nature of the mental state, ignoring their privileged access, they cannot explain children's relative accuracy in reporting their current mental states. (Harris, 1994, p. 300)

These passages again show simulation theory's logic. The child's understanding and reporting of his current mental states should be similar across all types (beliefs, desires, what have you) because the child's own mind produces such states, and the child's access to his mind is equivalent in these cases, unfiltered by any "theoretical lens." However, our data are at odds with this prediction. In our data, young children (i.e., 2-year-olds) refer to and reason about their current desires, emotions, and perceptions (as well as those of others), but never mention or report on thoughts, beliefs, and imaginings. In terms of simulation theory, these data make no sense. Young children clearly experience such states, both beliefs and desires. In simulation theory, they need only report such states: no simulations are required, just reference to two equivalent, experienced states. Why should the child's reports at first involve desires but not beliefs? Indeed, as Harris contends, there is good reason to expect equal and accurate mention of both such important states, whenever the child learns to talk about the mind at all.

With theory-theory, in contrast, there is a good reason why children's talk about themselves (as well as talk about others, and talk about past and future as well as current states) at first ignores beliefs and thoughts. Young children have yet to come to a theoretical conception of such representational mental states. Without such a conception, they do not see themselves (or others) as experiencing such states. Reference to and reasoning about these states requires more than simply experiencing them, it requires some conceptual understanding of such states in the first place. The progress of development in this domain, as shown in our data, indicates a strong influence of conceptual advances, in particular a change from conceiving of nonrepresentational mental states like simple desires to representational states such as beliefs and thoughts.[1]

The arguments thus far all pertain to a simulation theory in which both beliefs and desires are part of the child's cognitive system, his or her own mind. No detailed description of young children's cognition is intended here, just the general characterization that even young children's cognition encompasses internal representations of the world such as memories, expectations, and mental models, that is, states or processes roughly like beliefs, as well as motivational processes and preferences, or states roughly like desires. Of course, if young children's minds did not include representational mental states but only motivational states of some sort, then a version of simulation theory could predict that reference to desires would precede that for belief. Children's simulation of belief, in this account, would appear only at the same time as representational mental states. However, almost all current developmental accounts and descriptions grant representational mental states even to infants (Mandler, 1988, 1992) and certainly to language-speaking 2-year-olds. Accordingly, no simulation theorist has advanced such a proposal.

However, simulation theories rest in part on children's experience of various mental states, not just the existence of such states (e.g., Johnson, 1988). That is, children's phenomenological experience or awareness of the states in question is what allows them to imagine that state in themselves or others. In this sense, it is the phenomenological aspects of children's minds that seem more relevant than cognitive architecture.

Little is known, as yet, about the phenomenology of mental states for young children. What does the mental world seem and feel like to them, how is it experienced, how is it "there"? This is a fascinating question on many grounds (see, e.g., Flavell, 1992). To illustrate, Foulkes (1982) argued that dreams, as phenom-

enologically experienced and reported (in contrast to REM sleep states), were rare
or absent in his 3- to 5-year-old subjects. If so, then their mental world would be
phenomenologically different than it is for older children and adults. The more
general possibility is that various mental states have very different developmental
paths with regard to their phenomenology. Some states might at first be absent in
the child's phenomenological world. Some states might be more memorable, more
vivid, more imaginable than others, and hence more simulable.

One can imagine a version of simulation theory that would, in light of our data,
propose that desires are phenomenologically salient to young children whereas
thoughts and beliefs are not. According to such a position, our data would reflect
a difference in the phenomenological feel of desires versus beliefs, nothing more.
Unless this proposal is simply circular (e.g., the data show understanding of desires
before thoughts and beliefs, hence desires must be more phenomenologically salient
than beliefs), some independent analysis of desires as more experientially vivid or
distinctive is needed.

Desires, it might be argued, are typified by an inner urging, a sense of being
without something that is essential or greatly needed. Moreover, desires have many
physical phenomenological correlates. Hence, desires are rich, memorable, con-
struable, phenomenological experiences. For example, before their fulfillment, desires may be accompanied by a sense of pleasant anticipation. The fulfillment of
desires results in a felt pleasure (and concomitant facial expressions, such as smil-
ing). Unfulfilled desires result in a distinctive experience of disappointment (and
facial expressions, such as frowning). Beliefs, it might be argued, are less embedded
in a cluster of related distinctive signs and experiential associations. It might also
be argued that desires are phenomenologically experienced as more of an internal
state than beliefs. Beliefs describe the external world; desires are the expression of
internal urges.[2]

This proposal may face serious difficulties. Its key assumption is that states of
thought, belief, and knowledge pale phenomenologically in comparison to states
of desire. However, consider, for example, the state of "not knowing." Much of
children's early talk about thoughts and beliefs includes references to knowing and
especially not knowing. Children frequently talk of not knowing so-and-so's name,
or where something is. Not knowing is an arguably rich and salient experience,
involving a recognizable personal lack (which is potentially like that found in
wanting) and often accompanied by feelings of curiosity, annoyance, or perplexity
(and associated facial expression). Among adults, feelings of not knowing (as in,
"His name is on the tip of my tongue"), are related to other urges and inner
feelings (e.g., Brown & McNeil, 1966). When not knowing is overcome, in some
process of finding out, that change of state is associated with an "aha" experience
and cognitive satisfaction. Not knowing seems as individualized and internal an
experience as wanting: it is oneself who doesn't know how to do *X*, or can't
remember *Y*. Also consider the related experience of surprise that occurs when an
expectation or belief is violated, or when a state of not knowing appears that was
unexpected. Surprise has a definite and salient phenomenological feel, at least to
adults. Moreover, surprise reactions are apparent in even young infants.

In short, a priori analyses of the phenomenology of mental life are neither easy nor clear. The experience of mental life in young children is particularly difficult to intuit. It seems difficult at best, and arguably inaccurate, to claim that desires are more present, salient, or frequent in the child's phenomenological experience than thoughts, ignorance, surprises, fantasies, and the like. Moreover, simulation theory, as currently proposed, does not make such an argument.

We want to be clear in this discussion that our claim, that the child's folk psychological understandings represent a theory of mind, does not imply a rejection of an important role for first-person knowledge in the formation and application of that theory. The child's first-person experiences of mind (see also Wellman, 1985, 1990) provide an important body of data that strongly informs his or her concepts. As argued at the end of Chapter 8, although first-hand experiences of surprise and false belief fuel the child's attempts to conceive of representational mental contents, these experiences do not simply constitute the child's knowledge (leaving only the tasks of reporting and attributing). Those experiences are also organized and understood via certain concepts of mind that change with development. (See Gopnik, 1993, for an elaboration of one version of this claim.)

Similarly, we do not claim there is no role for simulation processes in understanding others' mental states. However, such simulations are theory-driven. Why does the child simulate the other's beliefs and desires to begin with? Because these are organizing constructs that allow for an understanding of the other's actions, *if* the child conceives of persons in accord with a mentalistic theory. Simulations are attempts to acquire information, framed by a theory. As such, they will be limited by the child's conception. The child will not accurately simulate someone else's beliefs and false beliefs; indeed, he will not even properly interpret or remember his own beliefs and false beliefs (see, e.g., Gopnik & Slaughter, 1991; Gopnik, 1993; Wimmer & Hartl, 1991), until he develops an initial understanding of, a conception of, such states. First-person experience of mind greatly informs our theory of mind; it does not stand in the place of such a theory.

Self and Other, External and Internal

Harris does not claim that there should be an early age at which children talk only about their own mental states or when children's understanding of others encompasses no more than their external features. In Harris's account, some sort of simulating goes on early in infancy (see his Step 1). Our account, too, assumes that children are developing theoretical constructs of mental states applicable to other people as well as themselves. Huttenlocher and Smiley (Huttenlocher, Smiley, & Charney, 1983; Smiley, 1987; Smiley & Huttenlocher, 1989), however, propose that attribution of internal mental states occurs first for self and only later for others. They make this proposal within a larger account of children's early understanding of persons that draws several important distinctions.

Huttenlocher and Smiley argue that person concepts, properly conceived, require a merging of two sorts of information: information about externals, for instance, what different people look like, or what exact movements they make; and information about internals, for example, people's internal states, their goals and intentions in acting (see also Barresi & Moore, 1992; Gopnik & Meltzoff, 1993). According to Huttenlocher and Smiley, young children's information about the self primarily centers on their own internal states, such as their own desires and goals. Conversely, young children's information about others necessarily includes only externals, because only external aspects of other persons can be directly perceived, not their goals, desires, and thoughts. Huttenlocher and Smiley are especially interested, therefore, in when children attribute internal psychological states to others.

With regard to young children's understanding of the internal states of others, such as their desires, intentions, and emotions, Huttenlocher and Smiley see two similar and related sets of developments. First, they claim that an understanding of internal states is evident for self considerably in advance of any attribution of such states to others. Second, they think that children's understanding of others proceeds in two phases. Initially, children see others as animate movers, organisms who engage in certain movements and who cause changes to occur in the world. For example, they might see someone using his or her hand to make things happen— to open a door or to stack blocks on top of each other. Only later, sometime in the third year, do children see others as intentional actors, that is, as persons with internal states such as desires and goals. At this point, other people not only move and make things happen, but these actions (including emotional reactions and displays) manifest internal states. "Children develop the notion of others as . . . creators of change, before they understand that they possess intentional states. . . . They achieve the latter notion by about 2½ years" (Smiley, 1987, p. 97). Huttenlocher and Smiley thus propose "that person categories in general may follow a developmental course where instances at first involve internal states of the self, then the perceptually available aspects of others' experiences, and finally internal states of other people" (Smiley & Huttenlocher, 1989, p. 44). They argue that by noting first the physical similarities across their own and others' movements, and then the similarities across the changes in the world that they and others initiate, children finally become able to infer that others' acts are the products of internal states, such as desires, intentions, emotions, and beliefs, as are their own.

There are many intriguing aspects of Huttenlocher and Smiley's proposals, some concerning children younger than the ages we focus on. According to these authors, however, the change from seeing others in terms of external features to attributing to them internal states occurs in the third year and is therefore evident in young children's talk about people, their comprehension and production of action verbs (Huttenlocher et al., 1983), emotion terms (Smiley & Huttenlocher, 1989), and desire terms (Smiley, 1987). This focus on early mental-state talk overlaps with our own.

To be clear, we interpret our data as demonstrating that the children we studied have a cogent concept of others' internal states, especially their desires, evident in their use of terms like *want*, from about 2 years on. Huttenlocher and Smiley's apparent claim that such an understanding of persons is lacking until 2½ years of age seems to us to underestimate young children's person conceptions. Such age estimates are only rough markers, however, to Huttenlocher and Smiley's central thesis concerning the external-to-internal sequence in young children's understanding of others.

Huttenlocher and Smiley see this shift as occurring in the third year, after children begin to talk about emotions, desires, and so on. Thus, this shift should be evident in children's early talk. Huttenlocher and Smiley predict that genuine reference to internal mental states appears first for self and only later for others, and requires a substantial conceptual advance. After all, in their analysis, children's references to their own internal states are straightforward, based on internal experience. Reference to such states in others, however, requires much more conceptual work, that is, noting sufficient external similarities between self and others to warrant the inference that others' external characteristics are in fact the products of analogous internal states. Huttenlocher and Smiley's account therefore seems to predict that children's references to their own mental states should precede references to others' mental states by sizable periods. In summarizing their own and others' data on children's use of emotion words, these researchers claim that "children's word meanings at first cover internal states of the self and some observable aspects of others' experiences. By six months to a year later, children begin to use words, not just for observable aspects of others' experiences, but apparently for their internal states as well'' (Smiley & Huttenlocher, 1989, p. 39).

In Chapter 4 we analyzed our data for children's genuine references to the desires of self and others. Children's first references were typically to their own desires, but they quickly thereafter referred to others' desires as well. Reference to others' desires often followed first genuine reference to self desires by two to three months; for only three children were the delays as long as six months, and one child made reference to others' desires six months before referring to his own (see Table 4.13). We stated in Chapter 4 that these data reflected the fact that children preponderantly talked about themselves, their desires, no matter what age they were. Probability alone, therefore, would dictate that reference to desire would first occur for self. A deeper conceptual inability to conceive of others in internal-state terms, of the sort that Smiley and Huttenlocher posit, should result in a much more substantial delay between reference to self and others.

Our data are far from conclusive about this issue. As mentioned in Chapter 8, there is no clear way to conclude from our findings that some observable delay is so small or variable as to be insignificant. However, informative comparisons can be made within the data. One such comparison concerns the delay between reference to desires versus beliefs. In our data for genuine psychological reference, this delay is six months to a year (e.g., Table 5.1). Such a substantial delay reflects, as noted in Chapter 5, a substantial conceptual transition for children. In comparison, the delay between references to self versus others for desire is considerably smaller in our data. Moreover, it is quite clear in Chapter 3 that our data for thoughts and beliefs mimic our data for desires. Young children's first genuine references to thoughts and beliefs also typically refer to the self's thoughts and beliefs, but references to others' thoughts and beliefs follow quickly, rather than tardily, thereafter; the typical delay is one or two months (see Table 3.11). Again this finding seems due to the fact that children preponderantly talk about their own mental states. A similar interpretation holds for the earlier references to desire, and the similarities for belief and desire help support such a conclusion.

When it comes to data rather than interpretation, our natural language data seem reasonably consistent with those offered by Huttenlocher and Smiley. For example, Huttenlocher et al. (1983) report results from a cross-sectional study of 16 children aged 23 to 28 months. Transcripts were collected for each child for four hours. These data included 222 total child uses of *want*, 207 of which were references to self and 15 to others. Huttenlocher et al. do not report the sort of content analyses we describe in Chapter 4, but given the childhood propensity to talk about one's own states, the data could certainly reflect a preponderance of references to self mixed with infrequent but genuine references to others.

In short, our data provide no convincing evidence of a deep schism between attribution of mental states to others versus self in these time periods. Our data are silent about even earlier developments, and here Huttenlocher and Smiley's proposed sequence of conception, displaced downward, could prove correct. Such a proposal remains controversial, however, and is balanced by several competing claims.

In general, there are two options with regard to infants' and toddlers' earlier conceptions of persons and minds. On the one hand, concepts of mental states may apply to self and others generically, from the start. Such concepts might thus fuse first-person and third-person perspectives, as Barresi and Moore (1992) put it, from a very early age. On the other hand, early person and/or mental concepts might apply at first only to self (or to others), as Huttenlocher and Smiley conclude, and leave the young child with the task of merging first- and third-person perspectives. That is, two different developmental sequences can be hypothesized. In one account, infants would start out with, and theory of mind begin with, a behavioral understanding of others; in other words, when infants show an initial understanding that others can see things, at about 9 to 14 months (e.g., Butterworth, 1991; Lempers, Flavell, & Flavell, 1977), they are evidencing only an understanding that another person's eyes are open and directed toward a certain object. When they show an understanding of others' goal-directed actions, they understand at first, simply and literally, that the person is reaching for, grasping, taking, or chasing after an object. When they seem to understand that the other is experiencing emotion about something, at about 9 to 12 months of age (e.g., Hornick, Risenhoover, & Gunnar, 1987), they understand nothing more than that the person is displaying distinctive facial expressions toward certain objects. If infants' initial understandings are strictly behavioral in nature, then a needed and genuine developmental advance occurs when they later come to see people as not just behaviorally oriented toward objects, but as having inner experiences of those objects; not just orienting their sense organs toward an object, but in some sense perceptually experiencing it; not just reaching for or grasping after some object, but wanting it; not just displaying certain expressions toward objects, but liking or fearing them, or at least experiencing some sort of affect.

Another account can be hypothesized, in which by 9 to 12 months of age infants' interpretation of others' orientation toward and interaction with objects includes both behavioral and experiential data. In this account, infants achieve early on an understanding that other people actually experience objects, not just orient themselves toward objects. We interpret the arguments for secondary intersubjectivity (Stern, 1985; Trevarthen & Hubley, 1978), social imitation (Gopnik &

Meltzoff, 1994), intentional communication (Bretherton et al., 1981), and social referencing in 9- to 12-month-olds (Feinman, 1985) as being more in line with a hypothesis that attributes to infants a very early understanding of others that encompasses both external acts and internal experiences. In fact, we lean toward an account that sees infants achieving an understanding of others' capacity for internal states by about a year of age, but the data are as yet inconclusive (e.g., Wellman, 1993).

To reiterate, our present findings are silent about these earlier developments. What the current data do show is that by about 2 years, children readily refer to the internal states of others as well as themselves. Whatever account about earlier development proves true, those early developments must culminate at some point in an ability to view others as possessing internal states. Our data suggest that this development had already taken place in the youngest ages we surveyed.

Changing Heuristics, Not Conceptions

Huttenlocher and Smiley's account and ours share the general premise that childhood conceptions of mind change in substantial fashions in the period from 2 to 5 years. Variations of this assumption have become incorporated into many extant accounts (e.g., Flavell, 1988; Gopnik, 1993; Perner, 1991). The alternative is that such changes are only apparent, not real. In fact, Fodor (1992) has recently offered such an alternative account of young children's theory of mind.

Not surprisingly, perhaps, Fodor endorses the general nativist position that theory of mind represents a specialized module or faculty for reasoning about mental states, evolved in humans to explain self and others in intentional terms. This faculty encompasses something like basic belief-desire reasoning and, Fodor claims, includes as part of its basic equipment an appreciation of both desires and beliefs. In short, there is no developmental change wherein children must add to their folk psychology a notion of beliefs and an ability to reason about beliefs or representational states of mind.

> The experimental data offer *no* reason to believe that the 3-year-old's theory of mind differs in any fundamental way from adult folk psychology. In particular, there is no reason to suppose that the 3-year-old's theory of mind suffers from an absent or defective notion of belief. . . . According to this account, the child's theory of mind, as such, undergoes no alteration; what changes is only his ability to exploit what he knows to make behavioral predictions. So what I have on offer is a ''performance'' theory of metacognitive development rather than a ''competence theory.'' . . . This account is intended to be compatible with, though not to demand, an extreme Cartesianism, according to which intentional folk psychology is, essentially, an innate, modularized database. (Fodor, 1992, p. 284)

Fodor proposes that very young children understand that persons have beliefs and that ''people act in a way that will satisfy their desires *if their beliefs are true*'' (p. 286, emphasis added). That is, even very young children understand that a person's actions are attempts to satisfy his or her desires, given the person's representations of the world. If so, how does Fodor account for the data from false belief experiments, for example, that seem to show no understanding of beliefs in young children? Here, Fodor claims both younger and older children solve such reasoning problems by applying two heuristics:

> H1 Predict that the agent will act in a way that will satisfy his desires.
> H2 Predict that the agent will act in a way that would satisfy his desires if his beliefs were true.

> The difference between 3-year-olds and 4-year-olds is this: 3-year-olds use H1 *whenever it affords a unique behavioral prediction*; they use H2 only when this uniqueness condition is *not* satisfied. By contrast, 4-year-olds (and adults) use H1 whenever they think the beliefs that the agent is acting on are true. If they think that the beliefs the agent is acting on are false, they use H2. (pp. 286–87)

There is much to discuss in Fodor's thought-provoking proposals. He advances an account of belief-desire reasoning, with special emphasis on false belief understanding in 3- and 4-year-olds. He argues that such reasoning undergoes no fundamental developments; all the needed conceptions are possessed by very young children, and apparent changes can be explained by "assuming that the child's access to the computational resources required for problem solving increases with age" (Fodor, 1992, p. 284). Fodor extends his account from beliefs and desires and begins to sketch an analysis of children's understanding of representations of all sorts: beliefs, pictures, utterances.

As may be clear by now, our account and Fodor's proposal have much in common for 3- and 4-year-olds. Both propose that 3-year-olds understand beliefs, but predict action first on the basis of desire reasoning (H1) and only resort to consideration of beliefs (H2) in rare circumstances. Fodor's proposal encompasses some interesting details that could be easily tested (e.g., 1992, pp. 295–96), but at a more general level his account, like ours, claims that 3-year-olds understand beliefs and false beliefs but simply do not yet apply that understanding in the same fashion as 4-year-olds and adults do in reasoning about action and mind. As Fodor states, a virtue of such an account is that " it thus accommodates the experimental findings that there are situations in which even young children do invoke the concept of false belief" (p. 291). It also accommodates our natural language finding that 3-year-olds talk about beliefs and even false beliefs.

Fodor downplays the magnitude of the shift in heuristic use between ages 3 and 4, but it is worth pointing out that this change seems substantial. Three-year-olds, in Fodor's account, only consider beliefs if H1 fails, where "fails" means fails to yield a unique solution, which happens infrequently. Four-year-olds, in contrast, always consider beliefs, even in their use of H1: "4-year-olds (and adults) use H1 whenever they think the beliefs that the agent is acting on are true." The fact that four-year-olds always first consider beliefs and then reason (employ H1 or H2) accordingly, constitutes a considerable reorientation of the child's understanding of persons. We describe this reorientation by saying that children go from being desire-belief psychologists to being belief-desire psychologists.

The difference in our accounts comes when considering children younger than 3 and 4. Fodor applies his analysis of 3-year-olds to 2-year-olds as well, specifically in footnote 4 (1992, p. 287). More generally, he says that "the child's theory of mind, as such, undergoes no alteration" (p. 284), and humans are "the species that is born knowing its own mind" (Fodor, 1987, p. 133). Fodor's more precise claim is that the infants' innate folk psychology includes an understanding of beliefs as well as desires. In contrast, we claim that in an early phase, which we call desire psychology, children operate without an understanding of beliefs. Although we agree with Fodor that such a description cannot characterize 3-year-olds, who are typically beyond this phase, younger children are a different matter.

Our critical finding here concerns an early phase when young children never talk about thoughts and beliefs at all. In this regard, Fodor explicitly predicts that young children will invoke the concept of belief (and false belief) when desire-based reasoning fails—"the child will invoke the concept of false belief when he knows that predictions based on H1 (viz., purely desire-based predictions) are disconfirmed"(1992, p. 291)—and that in such cases, belief reasoning should be easy rather than difficult to employ. If children younger than 3 years of age have recourse to belief reasoning along with desire reasoning, then why do they talk about desires but not about thoughts or beliefs? Why don't these very young children make at least some infrequent references to beliefs and thoughts, as 3-year-olds do? Talk about beliefs might be relatively infrequent, of course, based on the occurrence of situations where desire-based reasoning fails, but in Fodor's account the belief talk of younger children and 3-year-olds should nevertheless be quite similar. For 3-year-olds, we know from our data that although talk about beliefs and false beliefs is infrequent, nonetheless it does occur. Why do 2-year-olds not similarly refer to persons' beliefs?

It is also worth noting that in our published (Wellman & Woolley, 1990) and unpublished research, 2-year-olds consistently failed belief reasoning tasks that 3-year-olds passed with ease. The belief reasoning tasks used were not tasks (such as false-belief tasks) that only 4-year-olds could pass, but those in which 3-year-olds easily and correctly reason about beliefs. By Fodor's account, 2- and 3-year-olds should be similar in their talk about beliefs and in their performance on such simplified belief reasoning tasks; differences should occur only between those children and 4-year-olds. In contrast, by our account, 2-year-olds should differ from 3-year-olds even more profoundly than 3- and 4-year-olds differ. Accordingly, our natural language data reveal profound differences between 2- and 3-year-olds in their reference to (or lack of reference to) thoughts and beliefs. Young 2-year-olds provide no evidence of recognizing, referring to, or reasoning about thoughts and beliefs, yet they talk voluminously about desires. Fodor's position is at least in need of an additional component that would account for these observed differences between 2- and 3-year-olds.

Our description of an extended sequence of developments in children's theory of mind also helps in evaluating another aspect of Fodor's general position: Fodor reasons that children's rapid acquisition of a theory of mind argues against its undergoing major conceptual changes:

> It is surely plausible that the child's rapid and spontaneous transition from stage
> to stage reflects the increasing availability of computational resources rather than

a practically instantaneous mastery of a concept with the logical complexity of the notion of misrepresentation. Paradigm shift, conceptual revolutions, and the like are not generally supposed to be swift.'' (1992, p. 290)

Such an argument is part of a larger nativist argument that Fodor employs: apparent changes in early cognition are either manifestations of innate cognitive structure or mere performance adjustments, rather than fundamental reorganizations of concepts.

We have deep sympathies with certain nativist assumptions and accounts, as will be explained shortly, but the course of early development of theory of mind evidences a sufficiently extended progression, from 1 to 5 years or so, to also allow room for true conceptual reworkings: ''naturalistic language data, for example, suggest that the three-year-old child may be working on theory of mind virtually all his waking hours. And quite possibly many of his sleeping ones as well. Who knows what adults could accomplish in three years of similarly concentrated intellectual labor?'' (Gopnik & Wellman, 1992, p. 167). We continue this discussion in our ensuing consideration of another modular innatist account, advanced by Alan Leslie.

An Innate Theory of Mind Module

Leslie (1987, 1988, 1991, 1994) terms his modular innatist account of folk psychology ToMM, or theory of mind module. Our comments about his proposals reiterate and extend those made recently in Gopnik and Wellman (1994).

An important focus for an innate modular account of our ordinary understanding of mind concerns the developmental nature of core mental constructs, such as those for beliefs and desires. According to an innate modular account, such concepts are not constructed from evidence in the course of childhood development; instead, an innate structure dedicated to interpreting behavior in terms of beliefs and desires has been forged phylogenetically through evolution. Ontogenetically, that structure may need to be triggered by certain sorts of inputs, but once triggered it creates mandatory interpretations of human behavior in mentalistic terms.

As Gopnik points out (Astington & Gopnik, 1991; Gopnik, 1993; Gopnik & Wellman, 1994), descriptions of a theory of mind module seem to encompass two separable claims. The first is the claim of innate knowledge of the mind. The second is that this knowledge is modular. With regard to the first point, claims as to the existence of innate conceptions of the mind are compatible with at least two very different versions of theory-theory.

A naive theory probably begins from an innately specified mapping of inputs onto representations. However, from the theory-theory account advocated in Chapter 8 and first described in Gopnik and Wellman (1992, 1994), any starting conceptions would then be revised and reorganized as a result of encountering countervailing evidence. In this theory-theory view, the initial structures, while innate, would be in philosophical terminology defeasible; any part of them could be modified or altered with new evidence, analogous to theory development in science. We think it highly likely that infants or young children possess innate conceptions of, representations of, or proclivities to learn about, persons. Such initial products, however, do begin a process of theory development. In theory development, experience can substantially alter the nature of the theoretical concepts.

Talk of a theory of mind module, on the other hand, stakes out a different claim. In Fodor's (1983) analysis, for example, modules are not only initially innately specified, but their processing is mandatory, encapsulated, perceptual, and very fast. Moreover, the basic modular representations do not change. In Fodor's account no conceptual revisions are countenanced, only performance changes such as an increase in computational resources. The basic conceptual primitives of the module, such as the notions of belief and desire, are not revisable vis-à-vis the evidence. Along these lines, Leslie (1987, 1991), for example, suggests that there is an innately specified, privileged system of representations of psychological knowledge—what he calls meta-representations. These representations are analogous to the proposed specialized representational systems of the visual (Marr, 1982) or syntactic (Chomsky, 1975, 1980) systems. This theory of mind module automatically maps given perceptual inputs (say, a person's behavior) onto a more abstract set of representations (representations of the actor's mental states). It automatically mandates certain outputs and not others.

Leslie believes that this modular account is compatible with "the theory-theory view in general terms," because "the vital question for any developmental theory-theory is where the theory and its concepts come from in the first place" (Leslie, German, & Happe, 1993, p. 56). However, the mandatory, nonrevisable character of core modular representations distinguishes Leslie's account from the theory-theory one advanced here or in Gopnik and Wellman (1994). This feature means that the basic representations of the module are indefeasible. Given a normal brain, once the module is developmentally triggered, certain representations of the mind will result. Conversely, other representations could not be formulated, no matter how much evidence supported them. The crucial differences between Leslie's account and our own or Gopnik's therefore concern the interplay of experience and conceptual structure and the possibility of theory development.

In fact, in modular accounts the acquisition of representational systems is developmental in only a limited sense. Apparent changes in core representations occurring over time can only be accounted for by processes outside the representational system. Apparent changes in core concepts might only manifest performance changes, as in Fodor's proposals, or they could reflect the maturation of another representational system, a later model coming on-line.

In his latest writings Leslie (1991, 1994) posits two transitions in children's representations of the mind, accounted for by a series of mental modules coming on-line. First, there is activation of an initial theory of mind module at about 9 months, what Leslie terms ToMM system1. Then another modular system is triggered at about 18 months, ToMM system2, that stimulates engagement in pretense and an understanding of desires and perceptions. Similarly, in modular linguistic theories it is sometimes proposed that early language, up until about 3 or 4 years of age, when complex syntax appears, is not really language at all (Chomsky, 1980). It instead reflects the operation of a quite different representational system that is supplanted by the maturation of a "real" language acquisition device at about three.

We prefer our theory-theory account over a modular account because of the developmental data. As described in Chapter 8, the developmental data chart a succession of conceptions, each progressively related to earlier conceptions and revealing several intermediate transitional phenomena and partial conceptions (see also Gopnik & Wellman, 1994). These theory developments, in our account, come from within the conceptual system; the theory's concepts change as a result of the accumulation of new evidence and also as a result of internal reworkings of the theory itself. According to this version of theory-theory, therefore, we would expect to see not a single privileged representation of the input, but rather a series of developmentally related concepts. Moreover, as an earlier conceptual system is replaced by the next, we would expect to see intermediate theory-formation stages and processes. For example, as discussed in the preceding chapter, auxiliary hypotheses and the limited application of ideas would be invoked in the new theory, before it became completely dominant. Just such a sequence is detectable in children's developing theory of mind.

Such a sequence of dependent, successor theories, with characteristic transitions among them, is difficult to explain in any principled way by an innate-module maturational account. Following Leslie's latest account, a succession of two modules, one triggered later than and replacing the first, could possibly be made to do the job, but this explanation seems decidedly ad hoc in comparison to the theory development account. It is logically possible that a maturational sequence of successive modules might just by accident parallel a theory-formation process, and that the triggering inputs just happen to bear the same relation to the privileged representations that evidence bears to theory. Such a view, however, seems unmotivated.

Perhaps for this reason no one has made such a proposal. Leslie's (1994) system1-system2 proposal covers a different and earlier development. The change from system1 to system2 that Leslie describes is meant to explain the infant's shift from considering actions to considering mental states at all. "This emerges between 18 and 24 months" (p. 141). System2 thus allows the child the ability to consider mental states, such as wanting, thinking, perceiving that, pretending, and so on, according to Leslie. Note that this proposal provides no basis for why understanding of desires, for example, systematically precedes understanding of beliefs. In fact, it seems to predict a different result: with the emergence of system2, the young child should be able to represent people as having beliefs as well as desires. Our data, of course, suggest that young children understand desires before beliefs, unlike the system2 proposal.

More generally, our data describe a sequence of conceptual changes and revisions whereby children's early conception of nonrepresentational mental states, such as simple desires, changes to admit a conception of representational mental states as well, and then changes again to encompass a more representational understanding of mind and action in general. It would be possible to invoke still further mental modules coming into play to account for these developments as well, but again this possibility seems ad hoc. The process of theory development makes a proliferation of modules unnecessary; later conceptions are the products of earlier ones revised in order to better fit the data. Another way to put it is that later conceptions result from changes that result from the failures and anomalies children encounter in applying their earlier defeasible conceptions to the data.

We think the interplay between data and (innate or achieved) cognitive structures is critical for the early development of a theory of mind. Understanding this interplay is an important issue in the larger task of understanding the acquisition of core concepts in general (e.g., Carey & Gelman, 1991; Hirschfeld & Gelman, 1994a; Wellman & Gelman, 1992). We have no comprehensive analyses of this interplay to offer. It seems to us that theory of mind benefits from a healthy dose of innate structure. Human theory of mind represents, in part, an evolved primate social intelligence. Human infants come prepared to see persons in certain ways and to work in certain ways, on some problems and not others. But indefeasible modules seem to provide an implausible account of this development. What seems plausible, instead, is that evolution has selected for a social cognitive capacity to revise initial concepts on the basis of evidence. Put differently, it seems plausible that evolution equips the child with certain initial conceptions that are open to evidence, revisable in the face of the child's attempts to apply them to the world. Innate structure can play several roles in the development of a theory of mind without constituting a mental-modules theory of mind.

Larger Cognitive Changes

Our account not only proposes that children's conceptions and reasoning change substantially in the years from 2 to 5, it characterizes those changes as taking place in children's understanding of persons and actions. An alternative possibility is that the cognitive changes we focus on reflect a broader change in children's thinking and reasoning that influences their theory of mind but is not specific to those conceptions, and thus influences children's reasoning in other domains as well.

Several cognitive abilities are developing in the period from 2 to 5 years (see e.g., Flavell, Miller & Miller, 1993; Siegler, 1991) such as attending to various aspects of the world systematically, talking and listening, overcoming a here-and-now focus on the child's own immediate world, playing with peers, and so on. These developments also affect children's developing understanding of mind, although the way in which these developments work together is not currently understood. A stronger possibility exists, however, that some underlying change in children's general reasoning accounts for the developments we have charted here, specifically change in forms of systematic or logical reasoning that would apply to many sets of information—numbers, objects, relations, spatial arrays—as well as intentional actions and mental states. Proposals of this sort have been advanced (e.g., Case, 1989; Frye, Zelazo, & Palfai, 1992; Russell, Maunther, Sharpe, & Tidswell, 1991). Several of these proposals focus, in one form or other, on the idea that young children have general difficulties in juggling, coordinating, or reasoning about two or more different perspectives, representations, or sets of information. We use Frye et al.'s recent proposals to illustrate these sorts of accounts.

Frye et al. (1992) concern themselves with the theory of mind tasks that have been used in the experimental literature. These tasks generally tackle children's understanding of beliefs and mental representations, and show younger children, such as 3-year-olds, performing poorly, and 4- and 5-year-olds performing considerably better. Frye et al. argue that these tasks are inferentially complex, and that their solution thus requires certain general reasoning skills that children must develop. Frye et al. go on to describe a "cognitive complexity" hypothesis; specifically, the tasks young children fail require reasoning about "embedded conditionals" that "require one if-then statement to be nested in another" (p. 5).

Consider a traditional false belief task, such as the unexpected-contents task described in Chapter 8. The child sees a candy box and opens it, then discovers it is actually full of pencils, and must answer questions about his or her own and others' thoughts about the box. Frye et al. argue that the child must reason as follows: (1) if the question is about me, and (2) if the question is about what is thought, then (3) the answer is pencils. However, (1) if the question is about the other person, and (2) if the question is about what is thought, then (3) the answer is candy. In each case the answer, (3), requires consideration of a nested set of conditionals, (1) and (2). According to Frye et al., such reasoning is very difficult for 3-year-olds but develops in the years from 3 to 5. It is this larger cognitive development that accounts for children's better performance on theory of mind tasks at 4 years or so.

In support of this contention, Frye et al. (1992) constructed several tasks that require the same sort of conditional reasoning, but that have nothing to do with mental states. Instead, these tasks required children to reason about card sorting and about physical causality. For example, in the card-sorting task children saw cards containing colored shapes such as red circles and blue triangles. They were taught several complex card-sorting rules that involved embedded conditionals. For example: if the sort is about color, and the card is a blue triangle, put it here; but if the sort is about shape, and the card is a blue triangle, put it there. In a series of three experiments, Frye et al. report that children's performance on these comparison tasks changed in the years from 3 to 5. Furthermore, scores on these alternative comparison tasks were significantly correlated with children's scores on parallel theory of mind tasks.

Children's ability to reason systematically about complex sets of information certainly develops in the period from 3 to 5. However, the developments we have charted cannot be reduced to just the operation of a general trend, because substantial developmental differences remain between tasks that seem extremely equivalent in terms of their logical structures or cognitive complexity. The most obvious difference in our data concerns reasoning about beliefs versus desires. Children talk and reason successfully about desires in advance of beliefs, even when the complexity of the reasoning tasks and forms of expression otherwise seem quite comparable. This difference suggests that there is an important conceptual issue, specific to an understanding of internal mental states, that requires its own explanation.

To illustrate, Gopnik and Slaughter (1991) experimentally compared children's reasoning about their past and now-changed beliefs and desires. In the case of past beliefs, Gopnik and Slaughter used the unexpected-contents task described earlier. Children were questioned about what they believed was in the candy box before they discovered it contained pencils. In the case of desires, children were questioned about something they had earlier desired, before that desire was satisfied and replaced by a new one. If we apply Frye et al.'s (1992) analysis, in one case the reasoning required was (1) if the question is about the earlier time, and (2) if the question is about what was thought, then (3) the answer is candy. In parallel, (1) if the question is about an earlier time, and (2) if the question is about what was desired, then (3) the answer is [crackers]. These two tasks with equivalent reasoning and questioning demands were answered differently by 3-year-olds, who were largely correct on the desire task and largely incorrect on the belief task. (For other such demonstrations, see Flavell et al., 1990; Lillard and Flavell, 1992; Woolley & Wellman, 1990).

In our natural language data, the equivalent finding is that children make certain complex statements about desire well in advance of making the equivalent statements about belief. For example, subjective contrastives for belief have a sentence structure reminiscent of Frye et al.'s analysis. Consider, "You think that was smoke, but I think it was clouds." Arguably, this statement involves reasoning such as, (1) if the subject is you, and (2) if the question is what something is thought to be, then (3) the answer is smoke; but if (1) the subject is me, and (2) if the question is what something is thought to be, then (3) the answer is clouds. Significantly, subjective contrastives for desire seem to have the very same underlying form. Consider, "You like sour-tasting stuff, but I hate it." Here the paraphrase runs, (1) if the subject is you, and (2) if the question concerns preferences, then (3) the answer is that you like sour-tasting stuff; but (1) if the subject is me, and (2) if the question is about preferences, then (3) the answer is that I hate sour-tasting stuff. In spite of this apparent similarity of underlying form, children express subjective contrastives for desire well in advance of subjective contrastives for belief. Similarly, as noted in Chapter 5, sentence complexity, as an index of cognitive complexity, does not seem to account for children's earlier talk about desires in contrast to later talk about beliefs.

In short, these analyses based on the cognitive complexity of the reasoning behind children's judgments and statements fail to predict or account for certain sizable developmental differences that we observe. Children who make certain statements and judgments about desires fail to make equivalent judgments and statements about beliefs. This problem applies not just to Frye et al.'s analyses but to this sort of analysis more generally. In a related way, data from autistic children seem incompatible with the claim that developments in children's theory of mind are simply the result of the development of general reasoning strategies or capacities. High-functioning autistics can reason impressively about physical causation tasks but fail formally similar tasks when the topic is about mental states instead (Baron-Cohen et al., 1986; Leekam & Perner, 1991; Leslie & Thaiss, 1992).

To reiterate, several cognitive developments occur and interweave in the period from 2 to 5 years. Theory of mind is certainly not immune from these other changes. Tasks used to assess children's understanding of mind also require the development of other related skills—logical reasoning, memory, language-comprehension, and information integration. The changes we have charted do not reflect just changes in these other skills; something more conceptually specific is at issue, children's ability to understand certain mental-state concepts and not others. In particular, representational mental states such as thoughts and beliefs pose conceptual problems for children whose initial conceptions of mental states are more simplistic, as is apparent in their understanding of simple desires.

Developing Representations

The proposal that children have difficulty conceiving of representational mental states and achieving a representational theory of mind now figures prominently in several descriptions of children's developing theories of mind (Flavell, 1988; Forguson & Gopnik, 1988; Perner, 1991), including our own. In our proposal, the change to understanding representational states of mind is viewed as a development within children's theory of mind. Conceiving of the distinctive representational nature of some mental states comes about for children via their struggles to understand mental states at all (e.g., desires, emotions, and so on) and their emerging conception of an internal world of mental contents separate from the real world of occurrences or states of affairs. An alternative proposal would shift the focus from children's understanding of mind to their understanding of representations. Perhaps in the years from 2 to 5 children go from misunderstanding of representations in general—including pictures, drawings, and words—to achieving an understanding of representations and representational relations generally. Perhaps children's theory of mind changes to become representational in nature only as a result of acquiring a larger understanding of representation that then affects their understanding of mind. Perner (1991) has advanced an account of cognitive development and theory of mind along these lines.

Perner advances the view that children's changing talk and reasoning about the mind are the result of even broader and more dramatic cognitive changes, specifically, the result of changes in the child's ability to represent phenomena. This progression culminates in an ability to represent representation itself, or to meta-represent. Representation of representations requires two major steps. First, a change in the child's basic cognitive capacity must progress to the point where he or she can entertain multiple representations (multiple models) at the same time. This development occurs roughly in the second year of life. The second step is more a conceptual change than a change in basic cognitive structure, but nonetheless it has broad implications. This step involves acquiring a conception of representations themselves. Based on the achieved capacity to represent multiple models, the child goes on to form a conception of representations such as pictures and drawings. Specifically, the child becomes able to conceive of these representations as representations rather than misunderstanding them in other terms. The achievement of a conception of representation also allows the child to conceive of representational mental states, such as beliefs, and hence to acquire a representational theory of mind. Achievement of an adequate conception of representations—metarepresentation—and initial emergence of a representational theory of mind occurs roughly at 4 years of age according to this view. Thus, it is Perner's last two stages and the conceptual transition between them that are relevant to our findings concerning to children aged 2 to 5 years or so.

In advancing his account, Perner takes on several tasks: he provides an extended discussion of the nature of representations and how they might be conceived; he explains how young children, 2- and 3-year-olds, might function rather well without a concept of representation; and he marshalls other evidence suggesting that 3-year-olds, but not 4-year-olds, have problems with representation in general.

In describing young children's conceptions before metarepresentation, Perner pays special attention to how they might interpret people's actions and states with a simpler nonrepresentational understanding. He proposes that 2- and 3-year-old children are "situation theorists." They see others as being merely related to various situations that are not understood as represented in the minds of the actors, but that are simply understood and envisioned by the young children.

According to Perner, as a situation theorist the young child has a substantial capacity for successful reasoning about people and their actions:

> I have characterized the young child as a situation theorist who is not yet capable of metarepresentation. That is, young children can represent different situations, real and imagined, but have no conception of something representing these situations. It is important to realize that even without such a conception the young situation theorist can go far in understanding goal-directed action and desirability, because adult commonsense rarely takes a representational view of these matters. . . . The situation theorist views people as actors in a landscape of possible situations that can be reached by different possible actions. . . . Among these one situation is the real one . . . Then there are different possible future situations into which the real situation can develop depending on what action is taken. (1991, p. 215)

Perner's situation theorist and our desire psychologist proceed similarly in their thinking and reasoning about people. In both cases, it is the child's representational system, his or her own knowledge of objects and events, that allows the child to conceive of some object or situation; then the young child simply sees the target person as being related to those objects or situations. The child does not see the target person as representing these states of affairs merely (as we describe it) desiring them or acting so as to achieve them.

Earlier we noted that our account agrees substantially with Fodor's in its depiction of 3-year-olds; our disagreements were about 2-year-olds. Conversely, we agree in several ways with Perner about 2-year-olds, but disagree about 3-year-olds. Specifically, we and Perner disagree about when and how the child first conceives of representational mental states. In Perner's view, this task is not accomplished until the child is 4 or 5 years old, as indicated by performance on false belief prediction tasks, among other things. In our view, 3-year-olds understand that people have representational mental states including representational beliefs. These disagreements about ages reflect underlying differences in our descriptions of certain sequences of conceptions. Perner emphasizes a single transition, at about age 4, from situation theory to a representational theory of mind. However, we view that developmental description as wrongly collapsing two separate achievements: first, the child's recognition of the existence and basic representational character of mental states such as beliefs and thoughts, and second, the child's incorporation of such states into his or her comprehensive causal-explanatory theory of mind. Perner's description runs together these separate conceptual achievements of 2- and 3-year-olds. We posit an intermediate stage of reasoning, between the nonrepresentational desire theory and a full-blown belief-desire theory, namely, the period in which the child has a desire-belief theory.

First consider Perner's and our estimation of 3-year-olds. According to Perner, 3-year-olds are essentially like 2-year-olds; both are situation theorists who cannot understand representations as representations. More specifically, they fail to understand that beliefs represent the world and can also *misrepresent* the world, that is, they can be false. Both we and Perner accept that understanding false belief provides reasonable evidence of understanding belief as representational. In Perner's terms, understanding representation requires understanding that the sense of a representation may differ from its referent. The sense of Maxi's belief to Maxi is that the chocolate is in the cupboard, but the referent of the belief is the chocolate in the refrigerator. In the terms we have used throughout this book, understanding representation requires children to appreciate that the contents of a representation (e.g., the mental contents of a mental representation such as a belief) can differ from the contents of the world, even though the representation is supposed to capture or depict the world. In short, representational understanding is apparent in an understanding of misrepresentation, which occurs when representational contents depict the world (their sense) in a way that deviates from how the world actually is (the referent).

In Perner's account, 3-year-old situation theorists, although they talk about "thinking" and "knowing," fail to understand false beliefs. In Chapter 3, however, we report that the children in our study produced false belief contrastives at just after the third birthday, close to when they began talking of thinking and knowing at all. Perner, appropriately enough, regards reports of early talk about false beliefs with suspicion. For example, although he acknowledges that several explicit comments about false beliefs, attributed to Abe as a 3-year-old in the Shatz et al. (1983) study, would be made only by someone with a representational understanding of belief (Perner, 1991, p. 307), he supposes that Abe must be precocious. Here, our larger set of data seem at odds with Perner's supposition. As described in detail in Chapter 3, Abe was precocious in some regards, but other young 3-year-old children also talked about false beliefs. Of the four primary children, three talked about false beliefs early on. In our data it seems not so much that Abe was precocious with respect to false beliefs as that Sarah lagged behind the others, and even Sarah made reference to false belief by age 4;0.

Our data are not conclusive, to be sure. False-belief utterances were infrequent, and the children varied in the ages at which they expressed them. Fortunately, there are other related findings. In Chapter 3 we argued that children's advance belief contrastives sometimes evidenced a false-belief-like understanding as well. Perhaps these instances could be called "falsifiable beliefs." At times children talked of thinking that something would occur while seeming to admit that they might be wrong; the outcome is as yet unknown, but the belief may prove false: "I think it's so and so, but I don't know." Moreover, these children's talk about knowledge included consistent early references to sources of knowledge (e.g., Table 3.10). Perner (1991, Chapter 7) argues that reference to knowledge sources is also indicative of a representational understanding of mind and thus should appear at about age 4 along with false belief. In our data, it appeared at about age 3, along with early references to thoughts and beliefs.

Of course, in our data all these utterances—false belief contrastives, advance belief contrastives, and references to knowledge sources—come from the same small unrepresentative sample of children. Perhaps these children were all precocious. However, our data seem largely consistent rather than inconsistent with other natural language samples. Strikingly, our report of early, albeit rare, references to false belief now seems corroborated by experimental evidence as well. As described in Chapter 8, an increasing number of studies have documented impressive false-belief reasoning among a wide range of young 3-year-olds in several countries and laboratories (Fritz, 1991; Mitchell & Lacohee, 1991; Moses, 1993; Siegal & Beattie, 1991; Wellman & Banerjee, 1991). It is increasingly difficult to contend that false-belief statements and false-belief judgments begin at 4 years, with only rare precocious exceptions.

Comparing Perner's predictions and our own in terms of some age group, say 3-year-olds, is only a proxy for understanding sequences and concurrences in development. In this regard, Perner's account attributes to 2- and 3-year-olds an early situationist understanding of and reference to desire. Similarly, Perner attributes an early situationist understanding of thoughts and beliefs to young children of this age, followed by a representational understanding of these states at age 4. In explaining how a young situationist theorist could nonetheless have a conception of a person's thoughts, Perner distinguishes between an understanding of thinking-of versus thinking-that. Thinking of Marilyn Monroe as the queen of England is clearly different from thinking that Marilyn Monroe is the queen of England, in that only thinking-that claims to represent the real world. Perner claims that young children understand statements about thinking to be statements about thinking-of, such that the target person is merely thinking of a situation. In essence, the 3-year-old imagines Marilyn Monroe as queen, that is, she cognitively envisions a (not real) situation with that content, and understands the target person as merely being related to that situation.

In short, Perner's sequence characterizes 2- and 3-year-olds as situation theorists who much later shift to an understanding of representations. Young children can "situationally" understand not only desire (and emotion) but thoughts and beliefs as well. Our sequence, in contrast, has young children understanding desires, perception, and emotions, then only later understanding thoughts and beliefs; but even this initial understanding of thoughts and beliefs construes them representationally. Understanding of and reference to thoughts and beliefs awaits the child's recognition, at about age 3, that such representational mental states exist, that people have representational mental contents as well as desires and feelings. In regard to Perner's account, if the young child has a situation-theory understanding of thoughts as well as desires, we wonder why reference to thoughts and beliefs would lag significantly behind reference to desires (and emotions). At the least, this phenomenon needs some sort of explanation in Perner's terms.

It also seems that Perner's account should predict a sizeable delay between first reference to thoughts, beliefs, and knowledge, and later reference to false beliefs and sources of knowledge. Achieving a representational understanding, in his account, requires a considerable advance over the concept of thinking available to young situation theorists. In our data, however, it seems that reference to knowledge sources and false beliefs follows very quickly after children's first genuine reference to thinking and knowing. Shortly after children make genuine reference to thoughts and beliefs, they are making more explicit, albeit less frequent, references to knowledge sources, to advance belief, and even to false belief.

Again, our data provide some insight into various sequences but are not unambiguous or definitive. In particular, it is difficult to conclude that some sequence is *not* apparent in the data, that the delays observed are so small and variable as to be insignificant. These interpretive difficulties become especially problematic if the two sorts of utterances to be compared differ greatly in explicitness or frequency, as do genuine references to belief versus specific sorts of contrastives, such as false belief contrastives. Still, informative comparisons can be made. In particular, initial reference to thoughts and beliefs lags behind reference to desire in our data by six months to a year. In comparison to that delay, children's contrastives for thoughts and beliefs emerge very quickly after their initial references to thoughts and beliefs. Within contrastives, false belief contrastives for the most part appear at the same time as other contrastives for thinking and believing, such as subjective contrastives and ignorance–fact contrastives. A long delay between referring to beliefs versus desires, compared to a short delay between reference to thoughts and beliefs versus belief contrastives (including false belief contrastives), seems more in line with our proposed sequence than Perner's.

In total, we favor a sequence in which a nonrepresentational understanding is apparent in and confined to certain nonrepresentional states, such as simple desires, emotions, and perceptions. A representational understanding comes later, but still reasonably early, and entails an understanding of mental states such as thinking, dreaming, imagining, and believing.

Some of the difference between our account and Perner's may be due to how we define what an understanding of mental representation entails. Our view emphasizes a difference between the real world and a mental realm of representational contents such as one's thoughts, dreams, and images. These mental contents are representational in the sense that they depict or describe—represent—certain happenings or objects. For example, the content of a mental image or thought about a dog is not literally a dog; but the thought-content represents a dog, in the mind. Similarly, a picture of a dog is not literally a dog, it represents or depicts a dog. Conceiving of a separate realm of representational mental contents, in one's own mind and that of others, is not part of an early understanding of desires (or emotions or perceptions), but it is central to even 3-year-olds' understanding of thoughts and beliefs.

Perner's view of representation emphasizes instead what he calls the representational relation. Understanding representations as such means "modeling the representational relationship" between mental state and reality. This process encompasses several difficulties in understanding that representations have both a sense (e.g., what they depict) and a referent (e.g., what they aim to truthfully represent). Understanding the complexities of the representational relationship is complicated, as Perner's discussions amply reveal. Hence, he may well be right that a full or more insightful understanding of the representational relationship is achieved only at 4 years or later. Still, we claim that a genuine appreciation of the existence of mental representations—dreams, thoughts, images, beliefs— emerges earlier and constitutes a momentous addition to children's understanding of mind.

What about developments beyond 3 years of age? Here, our account and Perner's begin to parallel one another again. As we see it, children must not only recognize the existence and representational character of mental states such as thoughts and beliefs, they must come to view such representational states as having a larger and more central role in their understanding of action and mind. Mental representations must become more than peculiar adjuncts to children's basic understanding of persons, they must come to be seen as necessary cogs in the system manifesting a basic property of mind. Older preschool children, beginning at age 4 or so, recognize not only the existence of representational entities such as thoughts and beliefs, but also begin to appreciate something of the ever-present processes of representation that characterize mental life. Hence, Perner's emphasis on 4-year-old children's understanding of representational processes and a larger understanding of the representational mind seems apt, and we are indebted to some of his discussions and demonstrations.

According to Perner, mental representation is understood by children because they are achieving a larger understanding of representation itself. Hence, it remains critical to Perner's account that children fail to understand beliefs and false beliefs until age 4 or later. Again, specific ages are not the issue but rather sequences and concurrences; Perner argues for a concurrence between children's understanding of mental representation and their understanding of other representations such as pictures or drawings. He claims that age 4 is a watershed for understanding all sorts of representational devices and systems, because what children acquire at about this time is a general conception of representation, rather than an understanding of specific mental states as representational. To support this claim, Perner offers interpretations of extant research showing that 3-year-olds, but not 4-year-olds, fail to understand representation in other areas of reasoning too (e.g., Perner & Leekam, 1990; Zaitchik, 1990). Research indicating understanding of mental representations at age 3 instead of 4 is thus problematic for Perner's larger account. We believe that it is more likely that children come to understand representation within specific domains more independently. In this case, children's understanding of mental representation need not be connected developmentally to understanding of other representations such as pictures (see, e.g., Leslie & Thaiss, 1992).

Our Own Prior Accounts

The account we have outlined in this book about young children's developing
theory of mind can also be compared to our own previous views (e.g., Bartsch &
Wellman, 1989b; Wellman, 1990). While the current account is similar to our
earlier positions, those views have evolved considerably. On the one hand, many
of our earlier suppositions gain support from the current investigation: these include
the hypothesis that a desire psychology (likely involving only simple or nonrepresentational desires) precedes belief-desire psychology, the claim that there is an
extended period of transition between these theories, and the assertion that 3-year-
olds are beginning to have some grasp of belief (or put better, that an intermediate
phase exists between desire psychology and belief-desire psychology, a transitional
phase we now label desire-belief psychology). On the other hand, the current account includes some substantial revisions and clarifications of earlier hypotheses
that deserve mention.

Desire Psychology

The idea that 2-year-olds operate with a simple desire theory was forwarded in
previous work (Wellman, 1990; Wellman & Woolley, 1990) but is considerably
elaborated in Chapter 8 and by our current findings. Our earlier statements were
directed primarily at describing how a simple (i.e., nonrepresentational) notion of
desire might work, something along the lines of Figure 1.3. As explained in Chapter
8, that figure encompasses only the easily depicted case of construing a desire for
a here-and-now physical object. It has caused the misperception of our position
that an understanding of simple desires includes only a notion of persons wanting
physical items (and not actions or states of affairs), and only wanting visibly present
ones at that. Several investigators have commented that such a limited notion of
desire offers little explanation of behavior or indeed is self-contradictory. For example, Leslie (1994) comments:

> Wellman depicts the child as imagining a pair of hands in the other person's head
> stretched out to an apple, "wanting" the apple. . . . His formulation has the un-
> fortunate effect of making the child's putative drive notion almost useless for
> predicting behavior. When Wellman's child thinks of Mary as wanting an apple,
> he is incapable of representing what Mary wants to do with the apple or what
> state she wants the apple to be in. Somehow Mary just "wants" an apple. . . .
> When Wellman's child thinks that Billy wants a swing, he cannot represent
> whether Billy wants to sit on the swing, swing on the swing, just sidle up and be
> close to the swing, or anything else specific. To do so would be to represent Billy
> as desiring a state of affairs rather than just an object. Billy simply "wants" the
> swing, full stop. Unfortunately, such a notion is pretty useless for predicting be-
> havior. (pp. 138–39)

Similarly, Perner (1991) says,

> a simple conception of desire as proposed by Wellman . . . limits children's un-
> derstanding of what Sam wants to being an "attitude about an actual object or

state of affairs." This means that children could only understand "Sam wants the rabbit [which exists]." They could not have encoded "Sam wants to take the rabbit to school" because "taking the rabbit to school" is a nonexistent state of affairs. (p. 279).

As we hope is now clear from Chapter 8, our conception of a simple desire psychology is not limited in these ways. Desire psychologists construe others as wanting not only physical objects but also specific actions and states of affairs. To do this, the desire psychologist must be able to represent such states of affairs, and does so. But what the desire psychologist does not do is construe the other person as representing such states of affairs; the other person is viewed more simply as merely wanting those objects, actions, or states of affairs. This conception of desire psychology, as presented in Chapter 8, proves very useful in supporting consistent and relevant prediction of behavior.

Our current account of desire psychology, in contrast to a more limited interpretation of that view, is well supported in 2-year-olds' talk about desires and behaviors. Indeed, children's talk about desires shows their early conception of desire to be quite rich and useful. The young children in our study, as described in Chapter 4, talked about their desires and those of others; they talked about desires for visible physical objects and for objects not currently visible (as, for example, in their advance desire contrastives); they talked about desires for physical objects but also for actions, events, and states of affairs; and they usefully employed their conception of desire to predict and explain actions.

Note that children's subjective desire contrastives make clear that they know that different people have different desires, that objects vary in desirability across individuals.[3] Thus we can go beyond claiming that children's earliest concept of desire is nonrepresentational and suggest that it nevertheless respects the subjectivity of mental states, a fundamental property of both beliefs and desires even in their most advanced conceptions. In understanding the subjective nature of desires if not their representational capacities, young children show a respect for persons as the psychological unit—obviously a touchstone for any theory of mind. Judging from their conversation, 2-year-olds appear to view people's desires as experiential, subjective states directed toward specific objects, events, or states of affairs known (by the 2-year-old) to be real-world possibilities. In short, in their talk about desires 2-year-olds show an understanding of many properties of mental states that will be retained in an adult understanding. Our elaborated notion of a nonrepresentational desire psychology captures this rich early understanding.

Desire-Belief Psychology

We contend that our characterization of 3-year-olds as having a desire-belief psychology explains their variable performance on tasks that require an understanding of beliefs. Our explanation here replaces and revises several earlier proposals. For example, in an early study we uncovered one variable understanding of belief in 3-year-olds, namely, an inability of many 3-year-olds in standard false-belief tasks to correctly predict action on the basis of a person's false belief, coupled with an ability to appeal to beliefs and false beliefs in order to explain some sorts of behavior (Bartsch & Wellman, 1989b). For example, children looked inside two boxes, one a Band-Aid box empty of Band-Aids and the other a plain unmarked box full of Band-Aids. When the children were asked to explain why Jane (who wanted a Band-Aid) was looking for one in the Band-Aid box when they were all really in the other box, many 3-year-olds invoked false beliefs in their explanations. For example, they said "because she thinks they're in there." However, if asked to predict where Jane (who had never seen inside the boxes) would go to look for Band-Aids, the same 3-year-olds predicted she would go to the plain unmarked box.

To explain these findings, we initially hypothesized that belief and desire concepts were co-equal parts of 3-year-olds' naive psychology, as for adults, and were equally employable in causal-explanatory thinking, with only one exception. The exception was that in cases where belief reasoning and desire reasoning conflicted, children chose to reason in accord with the actor's desires.

> According to our hypothesis, for 3-year-olds at any rate, the false belief prediction task presents a conflict between reasoning that would satisfy the actor's desire [Jane wants a Band-Aid and it is in the unmarked box, therefore looking in that box will satisfy Jane's desire] and reasoning in terms of the actor's beliefs [Jane thinks the Band-Aid box has Band-Aids so looking in that box will satisfy Jane's belief]. Faced with this conflict 3-year-olds predict according to what would satisfy the actor's desire. (Bartsch & Wellman, 1989b, p. 963)

Children's spontaneous talk about beliefs and desires, among other things, suggests that this hypothesis is too simple. For 3-year-olds, conceiving of and reasoning about a person's beliefs is not co-equal with conceiving of and reasoning about desires (save only in cases of direct conflicts). Early understanding and reasoning about beliefs is more profoundly overshadowed by desire psychology than our original hypothesis suggested. Three-year-olds have a genuinely representational understanding of beliefs, but such a conception remains for them peripheral rather than central to their larger understanding of mental states and functions only as an auxiliary hypothesis within their causal-explanatory understanding of mind and action. The role of belief as an auxiliary hypothesis accounts for 3-year-olds' general tendency to misconstrue belief information in causal-reasoning situations. In short, we now contend that it is not conflict between belief—and desire-based predictions, or its absence, that solely determines children's early performances on belief-desire reasoning tasks; rather, 3-year-olds' conception is constrained by their predominating desire theory. As our current account of desire-belief psychology is described in detail in Chapter 8, we will not say more here except to note that this is a serious revision of our earliest hypothesis.

More does need to be said, however, about our current view of 3-year-olds' concept of belief. We now claim that 3-year-olds have the concept of representational mental states such as thoughts and beliefs, but that they invoke it in reasoning about people only in rare constrained circumstances. Where does this leave children's typical thinking and reasoning about beliefs? In the last chapter, we suggested that given the simple intentional understanding of mental states that lies at the core of desire psychology, then 3-year-olds generally suppose that people's beliefs reflect the real world much as their vision must reflect the world directly. More precisely, for 3-year-olds the contents of a person's beliefs are often (with certain important exceptions) thought of as real-world states of affairs (and not merely representational mental contents), just as the contents of a person's desires, emotions, and perceptions are real-world states of affairs. Hence beliefs are, by default, thought to be true or correct.

In earlier work, one of us (Wellman, 1990) attempted to capture this tendency for 3-year-olds to say that beliefs are true, or to cite only known states of affairs as the contents of persons' beliefs, by attributing to 3-year-olds a "copy" understanding of belief. This attribution was an attempt to resolve the apparent contradiction in saying both that (a) 3-year-olds understand beliefs to be representational mental states, and (b) they systematically take beliefs to be true. The notion was that 3-year-olds understand beliefs to be only true representations, that is, they have a concept of belief that is akin to a simplified understanding of photographs or photocopies. For 3-year-olds, beliefs faithfully copy whatever is so in the world and hence are always true representations. Three-year-olds can conceive that people either have a belief about the world or they don't; if they have one, however, it reflects the world veridically, like a good photograph would.

Older children and adults, of course, understand beliefs as more interpretive, as allowing for misrepresentation. That is, we understand that all beliefs about the world are vulnerable to interpretive mishap, such that one can have a belief that the cup is brown when in fact the cup is white. In this view, in contrast to the "copy" view, just having a belief does not mean that the belief is correct. As Wellman (1990) noted, much of the variable performance of 3-year-olds on belief tasks might be explained by their possession of a "copy" theory that sees beliefs as representational but not as encompassing misrepresentation.

In our current account we offer a different resolution to the apparent contradiction between claiming that 3-year-olds know beliefs (and thoughts and imaginings) are representational mental states and claiming that the same children tend to think that belief and real-world contents are the same. It still seems to us that young children often do take beliefs to be true, and that they take serious thoughts, since they are representational, to represent some real state of affairs. However, we offer a revised view of how this might obtain. Our new view is required by, and also helps to account for, the fact that 3-year-olds at times clearly understand that beliefs (and other mental representations) can misrepresent reality. Our language data, as well as current experimental work, indicate that 3-year-olds at times appreciate full-blown representational—and thereby interpretive, misrepresentational—notions of belief and false belief. A "copy" view, which limits children to a consideration of only true beliefs, for some period of time, cannot encompass this finding. At the same time, however, 3-year-olds largely and insistently talk about true beliefs rather than false ones, and they fail to normally use beliefs in explanations. Our current account handles this apparent contradiction not by trying to forge for 3-year-olds a comprehensive, precise, but erroneous understanding of belief (a full blown copy notion), but rather by attributing to 3-year-olds a sensibly representational understanding of belief but one that is typically overshadowed by a larger and earlier established desire psychology. To reiterate, our current thinking is that 3-year-olds' representational understanding of thoughts and beliefs exists as an auxiliary hypothesis, peripheral to their comprehensive causal-explanatory framework that remains largely a desire rather than belief-desire psychology.

Summary

This chapter has mapped out some of the debates within which our account and our data take their place. Our data have strong implications for several of these debates; for others, they may be informative. Our account shares certain assumptions with several alternative positions but contrasts sharply with others. The data and our account are independent; the findings exist regardless of our interpretation and no doubt will be subject to other interpretations. Still, the two go hand in hand. Our account is inspired in part by our findings and is consistent with several findings that pose challenges for other accounts.

Notes

1. In his claims, Harris, (1992, 1994) emphasizes a different prediction. He clearly says that first-person reports for desires and beliefs should be equally easy and accurate for children, which is what we have emphasized. But he also claims that simulation theory predicts more accurate reports of children's current states (whether beliefs of desires) than past states. Current self-reports should be easier than past reports because the former require merely reporting one's own privileged access whereas the latter require a simulation of a past state. Experimental data suggest that reporting current desires, for example, is more accurate than reporting past ones. Theory-theory is consistent with this prediction. Theory-theory does not claim that conceptual developments are the only influence on children's development or performance. Other information-processing factors also have their roles. Certain reports and inferences, for example, require not only conception of mental states but memory for target information as well. Children's report of current states may well be more accurate than those for past states; children may simply misremember their past mental states. Analyses must therefore concern tasks with similar memory- and information-processing demands but based on different mental states and hence, according to theory-theory, recruiting different conceptual understandings, such as either reports of current states or reports of past states. Here, simulation theory predicts similar reports for such states as beliefs and desires (unless different simulations are required), but theory-theory predicts different reports, at least in children developing the relevant conceptions of mind. The data are clearly consistent with theory-theory, indicating different performances for conceptually different mental states rather than similar performance across such states.

2. We are indebted to Lou Moses and to John Flavell for several suggestions in these paragraphs.

3. This is one of the ways in which our notion of an early desire psychology differs from Perner's notion of young children as situation theorists. Perner's emphasis on young

children's understanding of situations, in contrast to our emphasis on their understanding of certain specified mental states and experiences, leads him to predict that young children have only an objective notion of desire (e.g., Perner, 1991, pp. 213–15). Our position predicts, and our data on subjective contrastives for desire demonstrate, that young children's desire psychology encompasses a subjective understanding of desires.

10

Ordinary Talk about Persons and Minds: Questions and Conclusions

Adam at 3;3

ADAM: "It's a bus; I thought a taxi."

Adam's simple observation reflects a remarkable but common insight. In this utterance, as in others, Adam reveals an intriguing understanding of mental states as distinct from reality. He is in good company; all 10 children in our study comment regularly on mental states and make distinctions between mental states and actions, between mental states and reality, between one sort of state and another, and between the states of different persons. They do so first in their talk about desires and then later in their talk about thoughts and beliefs, and they do so at an early age. In three or four short years, children who began life as speechless infants become able to conceive of and comment on mental life.

When and how does this talk about the mind develop? What does it tell us about children's understanding of people, about children's naive psychology? These are the questions with which we began. Through our examination of children's early talk, we offer some partial answers. In this endeavor, we have immersed ourselves in children's early conversations and wrestled with extant theories about how an understanding of mental life develops. We have presented an account suggesting that children's understanding progresses through at least three phases: an early desire psychology, based on nonrepresentational mental-state constructs such as simple desires; a transitional desire-belief psychology, in which desires continue to dominate causal-explanatory reasoning despite the existence of an auxilary concept of belief; and a belief-desire psychology akin to adult understanding. We argue that children's developing understanding of mind is aptly termed a developing theory of mind. Perhaps our stance is not surprising; we began our research initially favoring a theory-theory. Nevertheless, it has proven possible to separate theory and data; we believe our data add support to a theory-theory and pose difficulties for several other alternatives. Indeed, although it is only one theory that they develop, children's theory of mind provides evidence supporting the more general view that conceptual development may be fruitfully characterized as occurring within commonsense theories of specific domains.

Our study, like any systematic investigation, brings into focus areas of ignorance as well as of knowledge, questions as much as answers. Many intriguing issues surface or resurface in light of our findings. In particular, our investigation spawns questions about language and mind and culture, hypotheses relevant to anthropology, philosophy, cognitive science, and development. We conclude with some thoughts about these far-reaching issues.

Language and Mind

Several unanswered questions concern the rather regular patterns of development we observed in children's talk about the mind. As noted in Chapter 7, variation in children's talk about thoughts, beliefs, and desires occurs in both a fairly circum-scribed manner and period of time. One question, of course, is empirical: How widespread and consistent is the developmental trajectory that we have charted? Apparently, it does not extend to autistic individuals (see, e.g., Baron-Cohen et al., 1993). Basic understandings of mind do seem to be acquired early and rapidly in normal and in mentally retarded individuals (e.g., Baron-Cohen, Leslie, & Frith, 1985). For the most part, however, variation in the nature and timing of children's understanding of mind has not been widely studied.

Suppose we were to find that most children do proceed through a regular series of conceptions of mind in the ages from 2 to 5. From our perspective, this finding would raise the question of whether such consistency could be reconciled with a view of children as acquiring a naive theory. Consider scientific theories. At first glance, at any rate, scientific discovery and theory change do not seem to adhere to a predictable timetable. Insight can be achieved by one investigator but not another; conceptual advances are made in one lab but not another. In contrast, the children in our study seem to keep to a fairly regular schedule of "discoveries."

Here it is important to reiterate that in our view, naive theories and theory formation processes are not individual, asocial enterprises, contingent purely on the efforts of the individual theorist. Even scientific theorizing takes place in a collaborative social context. Communities of investigators share findings, critique each others' ideas, and forge collaborative research programs based on common conceptual frameworks and language. Scientific advances thus often emerge in similar fashions across individual scientists, within relatively narrow time periods. A better analogy to the young child might be the fledgling science student. Students learning the accepted framework theory of a scientific discipline engage in con-ceptual discoveries or "rediscoveries," but are guided and encouraged by others who already hold the theory. Science students assimilating accepted theories often proceed through a regular series of partial understandings, just as do children ac-quiring a naive theory.

Indeed, children acquiring a theory of mind are immersed in a complex and instructive social life that guides and informs their conceptual development and in itself also manifests psychological phenomena. Within their social environments, children encounter languages containing interrelated sets of terms and expressions referring to mental phenomena, and they encounter others who have vested interests in raising them to become competent social actors and who therefore implicitly and explicitly direct them to attend to various psychological phenomena and distinctions. The following dialogue between Sarah and her mother illustrates a common sort of interchange that may well influence conceptual development:

> MOTHER: What's the kitty and the dog's name?
> SARAH: Tippy.
> MOTHER: No, that's the dog's name. The dog's name is Tippy. What's the kitty's name?
> SARAH: Uhmmm.
> MOTHER: You know.
> SARAH: What?
> MOTHER: Think.
> SARAH: I don't wanna know.
> MOTHER: Yes ya do, you're foolin' me.
> SARAH: What?
> MOTHER: Tammy.
> SARAH: Tammy.

Sarah may be learning not only the name of the dog, but something about the meanings of *know* and *think* and her capacity to do both.

It is probably no accident that children acquire a theory of mind just when they acquire language. The relationships between language and thought are deep and mysterious. Some argue that language is fundamentally a device employed to make public private thoughts and experiences. Bloom (1993) claims that language acquisition is driven by children's needs to share personal experiences.

> Our intentional states—the beliefs, desires, and feelings that we have—are themselves unobservable, but they determine how we relate to one another in everyday events. Children learn language for acts of expression in the effort to make known to others what their own thoughts and feelings are about, and for acts of interpretation in the effort to share the thoughts and feelings of other persons. Intentional states underlying acts of expression and interpretation provide the mental meanings for which knowledge of language—its vocabulary, semantics, syntax, and discourse procedures—is acquired. (p. 4)

Such a description represents one account about how language and thought relate: the child acquires a device to express his or her thoughts. In our own findings, we noted that children's first genuine references to belief tended to be simply expressions of subjective experience rather than, say, explanations of behavior; this observation is consistent with Bloom's position. A different account, however, would emphasize how language in general, as well as the specific language learned, shapes concepts. Languages parse, organize, and create information about the structure of the world—a linguistically constituted world. Children, in this view, acquire the categories and concepts of their language.

These differing positions are part of a reemerging concern about the relationships between language and thought, how one shapes and constitutes the other (Lucy, 1992; Hill & Mannheim, 1992). In particular, as researchers increasingly adopt a focus on conceptual development within specific domains, questions about the acquisition of concepts and concept labels, and the relationship between them, take center stage (e.g., Gelman & Coley, 1991). We will make little progress in understanding how theory of mind is acquired unless we investigate more closely how development of a theory of mind relates to development of language. Our investigation does not answer these questions, but it does show how language and concepts of mind can be investigated together. Children's talk about the mind may be especially likely to hold answers to these complex questions.

Mind and Culture

Not surprisingly, in view of the preceding discussion, developmental psychologists who study early understanding of the mind are increasingly tempted to conclude that a mentalistic construal of persons, indeed a belief-desire psychology, may be a universal human conception. Plausibly related to a primate heritage of sophisticated social intelligence (e.g., Cheney & Seyfarth, 1990; Povinelli, 1993), such a mentalistic construal does seem to be acquired early and rapidly in many children. An early childhood understanding of internal states such as beliefs, desires, and emotions has been empirically demonstrated in North America (e.g., Gopnik & Astington, 1988; Moses & Flavell, 1990; Wellman & Bartsch, 1988), Europe (e.g., Brown & Dunn, 1991; Perner et al., 1987; Sodian, 1991; Wimmer & Perner, 1983), Australia (e.g., Siegal & Beattie, 1991), and Asia (Flavell, Zhang, Zou, Dong, & Qi, 1983; Gardner, Harris, Ohmoto, & Hamazaki, 1988), as well as in at least one nonliterate, hunter-gatherer African society (Avis & Harris, 1991).

However, a widespread childhood recognition of beliefs, desires, and emotions suggests a universality that is at odds with the reports of many cultural anthropologists. Researchers who study cultural conceptions of persons report widely differing views of personhood, human action, and self in different cultures (e.g., Heelas & Lock, 1981). What counts as persons or selves (humans, animals, ghosts, dead ancestors) differs widely among different people (Fogelson, 1982), as do conceptions of actions, emotions, morality, gender roles, and the like (Markus & Kitayama, 1991; Shweder, Mahapatra, & Miller, 1987). Moreover, belief-desire psychology, as investigated in the studies cited in the previous paragraph, focuses on the private internal states of individuals and with the motives and conditions that lead to individual actions and reactions. This focus is consistent with a larger Western European concern with individualism and may be argued to be indelibly stamped by that cultural perspective. In contrast, other cultures could conceivably adopt a different emphasis, for example, one in which social groups and social relations are more constitutive of persons and selves (e.g., Markus & Kitayama, 1991). There are even claims of cultures that are essentially without folk psychologies:

> The most challenging and interesting thing about the Baining (of New Britain, Papua New Guinea) from the point of view of ethnopsychological studies is that they appear not to have a folk psychology. The Baining exhibit a pervasive avoidance of modes of discourse about psychology. If we understand the latter to be a domain of culture which includes a concern with affect and emotions, concepts of

person and self, theories of deviance, interpretations of behavior, and ideas about cognition and personality development, the Baining manifest very little interest in these areas. They are reluctant to speculate about the personal motivations, actions, and feelings either of themselves or others. They do not offer interpretations of the meanings of the behavior and events around them in these terms. (Fajans, 1985, p. 367)

At the very least, it is safe to say that in anthropological studies something like belief-desire psychology has often gone unreported (but see D'Andrade, 1987), perhaps because in many nonwestern cultures people simply do not think about each other that way.

However, we suspect that belief-desire reasoning, as opposed to more elaborate and specific ethnotheories, may be so basic to all human understanding of action that it goes unreported just because ethnologists are more concerned with cultural differences than with similarities in how people think about each other. The false-belief task that developmental psychologists have often used to investigate children's conception of beliefs is suggestive: a person puts a desired object, such as food, in a particular place, intending to retrieve it later. During that person's absence, someone removes the food. On returning, what does the original person do? Some scenario such as this must occur in every culture in the world. People everywhere live in an environment of objects; things are inevitably misplaced, moved, hidden. While some cultures may focus more than others on the individual's actions and feelings in such a situation, it seems to us that in all cultures adults surely could and would assume that the person would search at the food's original location; and surely this assumption has to do with attributes specific to the person: he hid the food and carried that knowledge with him until it was time to retrieve the food, and he was the one who did not witness the transfer. There is a simple but profound sense in which many actions take place at the level of the person, not at a sublevel, say at the level of hands or legs, or at the level of multiple people. Cultures may make every attempt to thwart this biological and physical brute fact, but perhaps the attempts are necessarily limited, and especially so in childhood. Indeed, it seems to us that it could easily be the case that divergent, adult world views about persons, actions, and mind develop from an early acquired universal infrastructure for reasoning about human action and persons that is only consistently apparent in childhood. Quite different ethnopsychologies could develop from the same initial fundamental framework theory.

Unfortunately, experimental methods for exploring this possibility are notoriously difficult and underdeveloped. Natural language investigations, however, of the sort we report in this book, offer an alternative and promising methodology. Adults and children in all cultures talk. In this regard, we find it intriguing that Wierzbicka (e.g., 1994), a linguist who studies cross-linguistic aspects of the lexicon, claims that *think, know,* and *want* are three of the "universal semantic indefinables," that is, "universal human concepts, lexically embodied (as far as we know) in all languages of the world" (Wierzbicka, in press). If so, then our analyses of English-speaking children's talk about thoughts and desires may be relevant to issues of universality in lexical and conceptual development. In any case, children's talk about persons and action should offer important insights in other cultures and languages.

Philosophy of Mind

The questions that motivate our research take their shape from issues in the philosophy of mind as well as from a curiosity about children's minds. Philosophical arguments about mind typically proceed without reference to children's concepts of mental states, but analyses of ordinary conceptions of mental states and terms do play significant roles in such arguments (e.g., Bratman, 1987; Davidson, 1980). The development of such ordinary conceptions in childhood may provide crucial insights: developmental analyses can reveal fault lines in conceptual systems, and developmental trajectories may suggest that certain distinctions are more deeply entrenched in, and fundamental to, everyday understanding than others. Quite recently, the writings of several philosophers indicate that they have found children's conceptions of mind, as revealed in experimental studies, fertile ground for theorizing (e.g., Fodor, 1992; Goldman, 1992; Gordon, 1992; Stich & Nicholls, 1992). They may find children's everyday talk about the mind to be equally intriguing.

What implications, specifically, might our research have for philosophical debate about the nature of mind? One example concerns the evidence suggesting that 2-year-olds possess a simple desire psychology. The typical philosophical perspective is that both beliefs and desires are mental states, intentional and propositional, and necessary for rational reasoning about action. From the perspective of development, in contrast, we perceive some very deep divisions. For example, for the 2-year-old desire psychologist, we have argued that the holistic world of mental constructs need not include both beliefs and desires. As Fodor (1992) recently put it, "though you can predict behavior on the basis of desires alone (viz., by assuming that agents will do what is objectively conducive to satisfying their desires) there is no analogous principle that allows you to predict behaviors from beliefs alone" (p. 294).

Similarly, our characterization of an early simple intentional conception of states like desires and emotions suggests it is possible to conceive of intentionality, a notion of subjective mental experience "of," "toward," or "about" some state of affairs, without having an understanding of intentional inexistence. Specifically, we claim that 2-year-olds' conception of desire is such that they can imagine persons wanting things that 2-years-olds know to exist in the real world; but they cannot conceive of persons wanting things that 2-year-olds know to be nonexistant. Such a conception may fall prey to certain logical difficulties, but it also seems to highlight something basic about our everyday conception of how mind and world interrelate. Mental states such as beliefs and desires bridge mind and world; they describe a person's mental state about some real-world state of affairs.

Indeed, it intrigues us, when we consider philosophical discussion of mental states, to note just how far 2-year-olds seem to get with a "deficient" notion of mental life that fails to include representation or nonexistent mental objects. Even without any apparent understanding of the representational aspects of mental states, 2-year-olds reason quite sensibly about desires, perceptions, emotions, and actions. Critically, they appear to appreciate the subjective qualities of mental states, treating the person as the psychological unit, as an individual with potentially unique desires. They do not equate mental states with observable or objective states, but instead evidence an appreciation for the internal, mental quality of experiences that is further reflected in their expressions of their own states. Moreover, the consistency and relevance requirements of an adult theory of mind are evident in even the earliest desire psychology. That is, even 2-year-olds realize that a desire for a puppy will be satisfied by a puppy (not a kitten) and that a wish for a kitten will culminate in happiness only if a kitten is obtained. Not just any desire will lead to just any action or reaction; these elements must be semantically consistent and relevant. As we see it, such an appreciation of consistency and relevance is a requirement unique to a system that involves intentional elements, intentional in the broad sense of being about certain objects and not others. Two-year-olds are already capable of appreciating these many aspects of mental state reasoning, although they are without any apparent understanding of intentional inexistence or representation and misrepresentation.

Theories and Domain Specificity

Throughout this book we have focused exclusively on how children understand and talk about persons and minds. A complete understanding of these issues, however, requires that we place such conception and language in a larger context, for example, contrasting it with children's understanding and talk about the physical world of objects or the biological world of plants and animals. One possibility is that children's developing understanding proceeds quite similarly in these various domains of thought. As discussed in Chapter 9, however, this is unlikely. High-functioning autistic individuals, for example, fail tasks that require understanding of mind while simultaneously passing parallel tasks that require comparable reasoning about physical objects (e.g., Baron-Cohen et al, 1986; Leekam & Perner, 1991; Leslie & Thaiss, 1992). In addition, children reason about and explain mental phenomena differently from physical phenomena. Even 3-year-olds know that physical objects (e.g., a cookie) can be touched and seen by themselves and others, whereas corresponding mental entities (e.g., a thought about a cookie) are neither tangible nor public, but rather are immaterial, private, and "mental" (Estes et al., 1989; Wellman & Estes, 1986).

Another possibility, then, is that children's understanding reflects specific reasoning abilities and explanatory constructs tailored for specialized domains of understanding, such as mental states versus physical events. That is, human knowledge and cognition may well be domain-specific (e.g., Carey, 1985; Hirschfeld & Gelman, 1994a; Wellman & Gelman, 1992). The notion that human cognition is composed in part of specialized devices to deal with specific sorts of information is an old one, revived more recently by Chomsky (1980) and Fodor (1983), and now encompassing quite a few theoretical possibilities (see Hirschfeld

& Gelman, 1994b). For example, sensory modalities (e.g., vision versus audition), specialized areas of expertise (e.g., chess versus dinosaurs), or naive theories (e.g., naive psychology versus naive physical understanding) might all stand as models for different cognitive domains. Among these possibilities, one cogent proposal is that children rapidly develop a limited number of broad foundational theories of the world and that the domains of naive physical, biological, and psychological reasoning serve not only to illustrate these broad naive theories, but quite probably constitute the three earliest developing cognitive domains of this sort (e.g., Carey, 1985; Wellman & Gelman, 1992). Both the objects that they target (physical objects versus plants and animals versus mental states and intentional actions) and the causal-explanatory devices they appeal to (mechanical force transmissions, versus biological processes such as growth, inheritance, and illness, versus belief-desire intentional causation) serve to distinguish these domains.

It would be not be surprising if these three areas of psychological, biological, and physical understanding were to constitute children's earliest foundational theories. Given that humans are a distinctly social species evolved to use objects as tools and to hunt and forage for animals and plants, it is hard to imagine more important domains of knowledge. In addition, children themselves are psychological, biological, and physical beings. Each theory, according to the theory view, is fundamentally a framework for explaining things. As physical beings, children, even infants, experience first-hand being the force that causes movement, as when their hand accidentally bumps against a ball. Children's experience of internal agency, of voluntarily reaching for the desired food or drink, must also be salient. In each of these domains, children may be said to experience being the cause of events. On this basis too, it would be sensible if these domains were to constitute children's initial fundamental frameworks for comprehending and accounting for events in the world.

Delineating the basic domains of human thinking, and especially the emerging domains of childhood thinking (e.g., Gopnik & Wellman, 1994; Hirschfeld & Gelman, 1994a) is done empirically via data about childhood thought. In this regard, we suggest that children's everyday conversations are especially fruitful for generally exploring children's developing domains of conception. Our data, for instance, suggest that young children use specifically psychological constructs, especially the notion of a person's desires, to explain and predict human behavior (see Chapter 6). Hood and Bloom (1979) examined children's everyday causal discourse more broadly. They identified both explicit and implicit causal expressions in 2-year-olds' language. Explicit expressions included causal connectors such as "because," "so," or "and then" (e.g., "Bend her like that and then she sits down") as well as production of and response to causal questions, such as "Why?" and "How come?" Implicit expressions intimated causal connections, for example, "I won't"; "I don't want to." When Hood and Bloom undertook this investigation, the plausible a priori hypothesis predicted that young children would be confused and ignorant about causal relations, and hence their causal-explanatory talk would be largely unsystematic and inappropriate. However, Hood and Bloom discovered systematic, appropriate causal understanding: "There was no evidence that children in the study either merely juxtaposed causal events or interpreted them as only temporal'' (p. 29). Moreover, they reported that children's first causal explanations were psychological rather than physical: "the children in this study simply did not talk about causal events that occurred between physical objects in the world . . . the children did talk about intentions and motivations" (pp. 29–30).

Hood and Bloom provided several insightful analyses, but there are compelling reasons to examine children's everyday causal expressions further. For example, although Hood and Bloom's (1979) work is invaluable for its focus on very young children (language data were examined for eight children studied from 24 to 36 months of age) a longitudinal examination of older children's explanations seems equally desirable. Current theorizing identifies the years from 2 to 5 as encompassing rapid changes in children's understanding of the psychological, physical, and biological domains. A natural language investigation covering this more comprehensive time period would be easy to achieve. With regard to domain-specific reasoning, a crucial question concerns Hood and Bloom's claim that young children's causal-explanatory language exclusively focuses on psychological rather than physical (or biological) topics. If true for 2-year-olds, then we would certainly want to examine how physical, biological, and psychological explanations emerge and interrelate in older children. However, it seems unlikely that Hood and Bloom's description will prove true even for 2-year-olds. We know from research with infants that even 6- and 9-month-olds are sensitive to physically caused events (Baillargeon, 1993; Leslie & Keeble, 1987; Spelke, 1991). Why would 2-year-olds not provide such causal explanations as well? Indeed, on closer inspection, 2-year-olds seem to talk about physical as well as psychological causalities, even in Hood and Bloom's data. Consider the example quoted above: "Bend her like that and then she sits down," said about a doll. This child's utterance certainly seems to describe a physical-causal sequence, application of a physical force resulting in a physical outcome. Our knowledge of children's understanding of mind, and of how this understanding relates to other domains of cognition, would be advanced by systematic examination of the entire range of children's everyday language topics and explanations.

Conclusion

Chapter 9 examined attempts by a number of researchers to characterize the child's developing understanding of mind. In this chapter we have briefly alluded to the interest of philosophers and anthropologists in this topic. Why are scholars so interested in children's conceptions of beliefs and desires? Why have we ourselves spent more than four years "listening" to 2-, 3-, 4-, and 5-year-olds talk about these matters?

One reason is the topic itself. Mind is fascinating, encompassing a world remarkably different from our everyday one of physical objects and external events, but ordinary in its own fashion. Mind intrigues philosophers, anthropologists, psychologists, laypeople, and even 2-year-olds. Perhaps the intrigue for adults stems from an interest in mental phenomena in childhood, a fascination inherited from ourselves as children. If so, as we hope to have demonstrated in this book, young children can help adults to see the mind, or at least to see our everyday conceptions of mind, more clearly. When children talk about the mind, they are worth listening to.

Another reason for the attraction of this topic, as we stated in the introduction to this book, is that understanding the mind, for humans, is part of understanding the larger social world. Infants are born into, and adults live within, a complex social world of adults and children, friends and strangers, a world of social interaction, communication, cooperation, and collusion. It is essential for children to come to understand this world, and doing so requires that they, and we, understand the intentions, feelings, beliefs, desires, and actions of those persons who share the world with us. It might be supposed, if we were to look at their books and toys, for example, that very young children's interests concern mostly animals (especially baby animals), blocks, vehicles, food, dolls, colors and sounds (especially stylized animal sounds). However, people are more compelling; interest in people begins in infancy and strengthens in early childhood. This interest manifests itself in children's conversations; in the transcripts from our 10 children, talk is dominated by a focus on parents, siblings, friends, babies, adults, and television and book characters, and, of course, themselves. It is worth noting that this talk arises in family interactions. Children grow up in a family world filled with discourse about each other, as has been emphasized by other investigators such as Dunn (1988). Our data are subsets of such family conversations and confirm the centrality of talk about the mind in children's everyday discourse. Children do not talk about the mind or think about the mind academically. A conception of mental states underpins social understanding, and social understanding is not only manifest in children's talk but shapes their actions and interactions.

In sum, our examination of 10 children's everyday talk about the mind has confirmed that from their early speech, children are engaged in talking about themselves and others, attempting to make sense of people and talking about those attempts. In these endeavors, very young children refer to the mental, subjective lives of people, not merely their physical bodies or their manifest behaviors. Viewed carefully, this talk illuminates children's thinking and provides important insights into their reasoning. Specifically, the pattern of talk that emerges in our analyses points to a rather definite pattern of concept development and use, consistent with the notion that children move from a simple desire theory to a desire-belief theory and finally' to a belief-desire theory. Such a developmental progression, whatever the proper theoretical account of it turns out to be, has implications for children's communications, explanations, and disputes, if nothing more. But, in fact, we believe that theory of mind touches almost every aspect of our understanding of and commerce with people, including our social interactions and our notions of ourselves. Regardless of whether such claims fully pan out or prove in the final analysis to be overblown, the developmental story of theory of mind is engrossing. It is a story both familiar and exotic. Listening to children talk about the mind offers the chance to eavesdrop on our own past, a good dose of nostalgia, a sense of having been there before. Besides the familiar, however, there is suspense and strangeness, a sense of being able to peek at something forever lost, our own childhood thoughts.

REFERENCES

Astington, J. W., & Gopnik, A. (1991). Developing understanding of desire and intention. In A. Whiten (Ed.), *Natural theories of mind* (pp. 39–50). Oxford, England: Basil Blackwell.

Astington, J. W., Harris, P. L., & Olson, D. R. (1988). *Developing theories of mind*. New York: Cambridge University Press.

Avis, J., & Harris, P. L. (1991). Belief-desire reasoning among Baka children. *Child Development, 62*, 460–67.

Baillargeon, R. (1993). The object concept revisited: New directions in the investigation of infants' physical knowledge. In C. E. Granrud (Ed.), *Visual perception and cognition in infancy* (pp. 265–315). Hillsdale, NJ: Erlbaum.

Baron-Cohen, S. (1990). Autism: A specific cognitive disorder of ''mind-blindness.'' *International Review of Psychiatry, 2*, 81–90.

Baron-Cohen, S. (1993). From attention-goal psychology to belief-desire psychology. In S. Baron-Cohen, H. Tager-Flusberg, & D. J. Cohen (Eds.), *Understanding other minds: Perspectives from autism* (pp. 59–82). Oxford: Oxford University Press.

Baron-Cohen, S., Leslie, A. M., & Frith, U. (1985). Does the autistic child have a theory of mind? *Cognition, 21*, 37–46.

Baron-Cohen, S., Leslie, A. M., & Frith, U. (1986). Mechanical behavioral, intentional understanding of picture stories in autistic children. *British Journal of Developmental Psychology, 4*, 113–25.

Baron-Cohen, S., Tager-Flusberg, H., & Cohen, D. J. (1993). *Understanding other minds: Perspectives from autism*. Oxford: Oxford University Press.

Barresi, J., & Moore, C. (1992). Intentionality and social understanding. Unpublished ms.

Bartsch, K. (1990). Everyday talk about beliefs and desires: Evidence of children's developing theory of mind. Paper presented at the meeting of the Piaget Society, Philadelphia, PA.

Bartsch, K. (1991). Children's reasoning about beliefs in the context of desires. Paper presented at the meeting of the Society for Research in Child Development, Seattle, WA.

Bartsch, K., & Wellman, H. M. (1989a). From desires to beliefs: First acquisition of a theory of mind. Paper presented at the biennial meeting of the Society for Research in Child Development, Kansas City, MO.

Bartsch, K., & Wellman, H. M. (1989b). Young children's attribution of action to beliefs and desires. *Child Development, 60*, 946–64.

Bartsch, K., & Wellman, H. M. (1993). Before belief: Children's early psychological theory. Paper presented at the meeting of the Society for Research in Child Development, New Orleans, LA.

Bennet, J. (1991). How to read minds in behaviour: A suggestion from a philosopher. In A. Whiten (Ed.), *Natural theories of mind* (pp. 97–108). Oxford, England: Basil Blackwell.

Bloom, L. (1970). *Language development: Form and function in emerging grammars*. Cambridge, MA: MIT Press.

Bloom, L. (1973). *One word at a time: The use of single word utterances before syntax.* The Hague, Netherlands: Mouton.

Bloom, L. (1991). *Language development from two to three.* New York: Cambridge University Press.

Bloom, L. (1993). *The transition from infancy to language: Acquiring the power of expression.* New York: Cambridge University Press.

Bloom, L., Rispoli, M., Gartner, B., & Hafitz, J. (1989). Acquisition of complementation. *Journal of Child Language, 16,* 101–20.

Bloom, L., Tackeff, J., & Lahey, M. (1984). Learning *to* in complement constructions. *Journal of Child Language, 10,* 391–406.

Bowerman, M. (1978). The acquisition of word meaning: An investigation into some current conflicts. In N. Waterson & C. Snow (Eds.), *Development of communication* (pp. 263–87). New York: Wiley.

Bratman, M. (1984). Two faces of intention. *Philosophical Review, XCIII,* 375–405.

Bratman, M. (1987). *Intention, plans and practical reason.* Cambridge, MA: Harvard University Press.

Bretherton, I., & Beeghly, M. (1982). Talking about internal states: The acquisition of an explicit theory of mind. *Developmental Psychology, 18,* 906–21.

Bretherton, I., McNew, S., & Beeghly-Smith, M. (1981). Early person knowledge as expressed in gestural and verbal communication: When do infants acquire a "theory of mind?" In M. Lamb & L. Sherrod (Eds.), *Social cognition in infancy* (pp. 333–373). Hillsdale, NJ: Erlbaum.

Brown, J. R., & Dunn, J. (1991). "You can cry, mum": The social and developmental implications of talk about internal states. *British Journal of Developmental Psychology, 9,* 237–56.

Brown, J. R., & Dunn, J. (1992). Talk with your mother or your sibling? Developmental changes in early family conversations about feelings. *Child Development, 63,* 336–49.

Brown, R. (1973). *A first language: The early stages.* Cambridge, MA: Harvard University Press.

Brown, R., & McNeil, D. (1966). The "tip of the tongue" phenomenon. *Journal of Verbal Learning and Verbal Behavior, 5,* 325–37.

Butterworth, G. E. (1991). The ontogeny and phylogeny of joint visual attention. In A. Whiten (Ed.), *Natural theories of mind* (pp. 223–32). Oxford, England: Basil Blackwell.

Butterworth, G. E., Harris, P. L., Leslie, A. M., & Wellman, H. M. (Ed.). (1991). *Perspectives on the child's theory of mind.* Oxford: Oxford University Press.

Carey, S. (1985). *Conceptual change in childhood.* Cambridge, MA: MIT Press.

Carey, S., & Gelman, R. (1991). *The epigenesis of mind: Essays on biology and cognition.* Hillsdale, NJ: Erlbaum.

Case, R. (1989) A neo-Piagetian analysis of the child's understanding of other people, and the internal conditions which motivate their behavior. Paper presented at the biennial meeting of the Society for Research in Child Development, Kansas City, MO.

Chandler, M., Fritz, A. S., & Hala, S. (1989). Small-scale deceit: Deception as a marker of 2-, 3-, and 4-year-olds' early theories of mind. *Child Development, 60,* 1263–77.

Chandler, M., Lalonde, C., Fritz, A., & Hala, S. (1991). Children's theories of mental life and social practices. Paper presented at the meeting of the Society for Research in Child Development, Seattle, WA.

Cheney, D. L., & Seyfarth, R. M. (1990). *How monkeys see the world.* Chicago: University of Chicago Press.

Chomsky, N. (1975). *Reflections on language*. New York: Random House.

Chomsky, N. (1980). *Rules and representations*. New York: Random House.

D'Andrade, R. (1987). A folk model of the mind. In D. Holland & N. Quinn (Eds.), *Cultural models in language and thought* (pp. 112–48). Cambridge, England: Cambridge University Press.

Davidson, D. (1963). Actions, reasons, and causes. *Journal of Philosophy, 60,* 685–700.

Davidson, D. (1980). *Essays on actions and events*. Oxford: Oxford University Press.

Denham, S. A. (1986). Social cognition, prosocial behavior and emotion in preschoolers. *Child Development, 57,* 194–201.

Donaldson, M. (1978). *Children's minds*. Glasgow: William Collins.

Dunn, J. (1988). *The beginnings of social understanding*. Cambridge, MA: Harvard University Press.

Dunn, J. (1994). Changing minds and changing relationships. In C. Lewis & P. Mitchell (Eds.), *Origins of an understanding of mind* (pp. 297–310). Hove, England: Erlbaum.

Dunn, J., Bretherton, I., & Munn, P. (1987). Conversations about feeling states between mothers and their young children. *Developmental Psychology, 23,* 132–39.

Dunn, J., & Brown, J. (1993). Early conversations about causality: Content, pragmatics and developmental change. *British Journal of Developmental Psychology, 11,* 107–23.

Dunn, J., Brown, J., & Beardsall, L. (1991a). Family talk about feeling states and children's later understanding of others' emotions. *Child Development, 27,* 448–55.

Dunn, J., Brown, J., Slomkowski, C., Tesla, C., & Youngblade, L. (1991b). Young children's understanding of other people's feelings and beliefs: Individual differences and their antecedents. *Child Development, 62,* 1352–66.

Estes, D., Wellman, H. M., & Woolley, J. D. (1989). Children's understanding of mental phenomena. In H. Reese (Ed.), *Advances in child development and behavior* (pp. 41–87). New York: Academic Press.

Fabricius, W. V., & Schwanenflugel, P. J. (1994). The older child's theory of mind. In A. Efklides (Ed.), *Intelligence, mind and reasoning: Structure and development* (pp. 111–32). Amsterdam: Elsevier.

Fajans, J. (1985). The person in social context: The social character of Baining "psychology." In G. White & J. Kirkpatrick (Ed.), *Person, self, and experience: Exploring pacific ethnopsychologies* (pp. 367–97). Los Angeles: University of California Press.

Feinman, S. (1985). Emotional expression, social referencing and preparedness for learning in infancy. In G. Zivin (Ed.), *The development of expressive behavior: Biology-environment interactions* (pp. 291–318). New York: Academic Press.

Flavell, J. H. (1978). The development of knowledge about visual perception. In C. B. Keasey (Ed.), *Nebraska symposium on motivation 1977* (pp. 43–76). Lincoln, NE: University of Nebraska Press.

Flavell, J. H. (1988). The development of children's knowledge about the mind: From cognitive connections to mental representations. In J. Astington, P. Harris, & D. Olson (Eds.), *Developing theories of mind* (pp. 244–67). New York: Cambridge University Press.

Flavell, J. H. (1992). Cognitive development: Past, present, and future. *Developmental Psychology, 28,* 998–1005.

Flavell, J. H., Flavell, E. R., Green, F. L., & Moses, L. J. (1990). Young children's understanding of fact beliefs versus value beliefs. *Child Development, 61,* 915–28.

Flavell, J. H., Miller, P. & Miller, S. (1993). *Cognitive development*. Englewood Cliffs, NJ: Prentice-Hall.

Flavell, J. H., Zhang, X.-D., Zou, H., Dong, Q., & Qi, S. (1983). A comparison between the development of the appearance–reality distinction in the People's Republic of China and the United States. *Cognitive Psychology, 15*, 459–66.

Fodor, J. (1981). *Representations*. Cambridge, MA: MIT Press.

Fodor, J. A. (1983). *Modularity of mind*. Cambridge, MA: MIT Press.

Fodor, J. A. (1987). *Psychosemantics: The problem of meaning in the philosophy of mind*. Cambridge, MA: Bradford Books/MIT Press.

Fodor, J. A. (1992). A theory of the child's theory of mind. *Cognition, 44*, 283–96.

Fogelson, R. (1982). Person, self, and identity: Some anthropological retrospects, circumspects, and prospects. In B. Lee (Ed.), *Psychological theories of the self* (pp. 67–109). New York: Plenum.

Forguson, L., & Gopnik, A. (1988). The ontogeny of common sense. In J. Astington, P. Harris, & D. Olson (Eds.), *Developing theories of mind* (pp. 226–43). New York: Cambridge University Press.

Foulkes, W. D. (1982). *Children's dreams*. New York: Wiley.

Fritz, A. S. (1991). Salience bias as a constraint on a developing theory of mind. Paper presented at the meeting of the Society for Research in Child Development, Seattle, WA.

Frye, D., & Moore, C. (1991). *Children's theories of mind: Mental states and social understanding*. Hillsdale, NJ: Erlbaum.

Frye, D., Zelazo, P. D., & Palfai, T. (1992). The cognitive basis of theory of mind. Unpublished ms.

Furrow, D., Moore, C., Davidge, J., & Chiasson, L. (1992). Mental terms in mothers' and children's speech: Similarities and relationships. *Journal of Child Language, 19*, 617–31.

Gardner, D., Harris, P. L., Ohmoto, M., & Hamazaki, T. (1988). Japanese children's understanding of the distinction between real and apparent emotion. *International Journal of Behavioral Development, 11*, 203–18.

Gelman, R., Spelke, E. S., & Meck, E. (1983). What preschoolers know about animate and inanimate objects. In D. Rogers & J. A. Sloboda (Eds.), *The acquisition of symbolic skills* (pp. 297–324). New York: Plenum.

Gelman, S. A., & Coley, J. (1991). Language and categorization: The acquisition of natural kind terms. In J. Byrnes & S. Gelman (Ed.), *Perspectives on language and thought: Interrelations in development* (pp. 146–96). New York: Cambridge University Press.

Gerhardt, J. (1991). The meaning and use of the models HAFTA, NEEDTA, and WANNA in children's speech. *Journal of Pragmatics, 16*, 531–90.

Goldman, A. I. (1992). In defense of simulation theory. *Mind and Language, 7*, 104–19.

Gopnik, A. (1988). Conceptual and semantic development as theory change. *Mind and Language, 3*, 197–217.

Gopnik, A. (1993). How we know our minds: The illusions of first-person knowledge of intentionality. *Behavioral and Brain Sciences, 16*, 1–14.

Gopnik, A., & Astington, J. W. (1988). Children's understanding of representational change and its relation to the understanding of false belief and the appearance–reality distinction. *Child Development, 59*, 26–37.

Gopnik, A., & Graf, P. (1988). Knowing how you know: Young children's ability to identify and remember the sources of their beliefs. *Child Development, 59*, 1366–71.

Gopnik, A., & Meltzoff, A. (1994). Minds, bodies, and persons. In S. Parker, M. Boccia, & R. Mitchell (Eds.), *Self-awareness in animals and humans* (pp. 166–87). New York: Cambridge University Press.

Gopnik, A., & Slaughter, V. (1991). Young children's understanding of changes in their mental states. *Child Development, 62*, 98–110.

Gopnik, A., & Wellman, H. M. (1992). Why the child's theory of mind really is a theory. *Mind and Language, 7,* 145–71.

Gopnik, A., & Wellman, H. M. (1994). The theory-theory. In L. A. Hirschfeld & S. Gelman (Eds.), *Mapping the mind: Domain specificity in cognition and culture* (pp. 257–93). New York: Cambridge University Press.

Gordon, R. M. (1992). The simulation theory: Objections and misconceptions. *Mind and Language, 7,* 11–34.

Harmon, G. (1976). Practical reasoning. *Review of Metaphysics, 29,* 431–63.

Harris, P. L. (1989). *Children and emotion.* Oxford, England: Basil Blackwell.

Harris, P. L. (1991). The work of the imagination. In A. Whiten (Edws.), *Natural theories of mind* (pp. 283–304). Oxford, England: Basil Blackwell.

Harris, P. L. (1992). From simulation to folk psychology: The case for development. *Mind and Language, 7,* 120–44.

Harris, P. L. (1994). Thinking by children and scientists: False analogies and neglected similarities. In L. A. Hirschfeld & S. Gelman (Eds.), *Mapping the mind: Domain specificity in cognition and culture* (pp. 294–315). New York: Cambridge University Press.

Harris, P. L., & Kavanaugh, R. D. (1993). Young children's understanding of pretense. *Monographs of the Society for Research in Child Development, 58,* No. 231 (entire serial).

Heelas, P., & Lock, A. (1981). *Indigenous psychologies: The anthropology of the self.* London: Academic Press.

Hill, J. H., & Mannheim, B. (1992). Language and world view. *Annual Review of Anthropology, 21,* 381–401.

Hirschfeld, L. A., & Gelman, S. (1994a). *Mapping the mind: Domain specificity in cognition and culture.* New York: Cambridge University Press.

Hirschfeld, L. A., & Gelman, S. (1994b). Toward a topography of mind: An introduction to domain specificity. In L. A. Hirschfeld & S. A. Gelman (Eds.), *Mapping the mind: Domain specificity in cognition and culture* (pp. 3–36). New York: Cambridge University Press.

Hood, L., & Bloom, L. (1979). What, when, and how about why: A longitudinal study of early expressions of causality. *Monographs of the Society for Research in Child Development, 44,* No. 181 (entire serial).

Hornick, R., Risenhoover, N., & Gunnar, M. (1987). The effects of maternal positive, neutral, and negative affective communications and infant responses to new toys. *Child Development, 58,* 937–44.

Huttenlocher, J., Smiley, P., & Charney, R. (1983). Emergence of action categories in the child: Evidence from verb meanings. *Psychological Review, 90,* 72–93.

Johnson, C. N. (1988). Theory of mind and the structure of conscious experience. In J. Astington, P. Harris, & D. Olson (Eds.), *Developing theories of mind* (pp. 47–63). New York: Cambridge University Press.

Karmiloff-Smith, A. (1988). The child is a theoretician, not an inductivist. *Mind and Language, 3,* 183–95.

Kuczaj, S. A., & Maratsos, M. P. (1975). What children *can* say before they *will. Merrill-Palmer Quarterly, 21,* 87–111.

Kuhn, T. (1962). *The structure of scientific revolutions.* Chicago: University of Chicago Press.

Lakatos, I. (1970). Falsification and the methodology of scientific research programmes. In I. Lakatos & A. Musgrave (Eds.), *Criticism and the growth of knowledge* (pp. 91–196). Cambridge, England: Cambridge University Press.

Laudan, L. (1977). *Progress and its problems: Towards a theory of scientific growth.* Berkeley: University of California Press.

Leekam, S., & Perner, J. (1991). Does the autistic child have a "metarepresentational" deficit? *Cognition, 40,* 203–18.

Lempers, J. D., Flavell, E. R., & Flavell, J. H. (1977). The development in very young children of tacit knowledge concerning visual perception. *Genetic Psychology Monographs, 95,* 3–53.

Leopold, W. F. (1949). *Speech development of a bilingual child: A linguist's record,* Vol. 2. Evanston, IL: Northwestern University Press.

Leslie, A. M. (1987). Pretense and representation: The origins of "theory of mind." *Psychological Review, 94,* 412–26.

Leslie, A. M. (1988). Some implications for mechanisms underlying the child's theory of mind. In J. Astington, P. Harris, & D. Olson (Eds.), *Developing theories of mind* (pp. 19–46). New York: Cambridge University Press.

Leslie, A. M. (1991). Information processing and conceptual knowledge: The theory of TOMM. Paper presented at the meeting of the Society for Research in Child Development, Seattle.

Leslie, A. M. (1994). ToMM, ToBy, and agency: Core architecture and domain specificity in cognition and culture. In L. Hirschfeld & S. Gelman (Eds.), *Mapping the mind: Domain specificity in cognition and culture* (pp. 119–48). New York: Cambridge University Press.

Leslie, A. M., German, T. P., & Happe, F. G. (1993). Even a theory-theory needs information processing. *Behavioral and Brain Sciences, 16,* 56–57.

Leslie, A. M., & Keeble, S. (1987). Do six-month-old infants perceive causality? *Cognition, 25,* 265–88.

Leslie, A. M., & Thaiss, L. (1992). Domain specificity in conceptual development: Neuropsychological evidence from autism. *Cognition, 43,* 225–51.

Lewis, C., & Mitchell, P. (1994). *Origins of an understanding of mind.* Hove, England: Erlbaum.

Lillard, A. S. (1993a). Pretend play skills and the child's theory of mind. *Cognitive Development, 64,* 348–71.

Lillard, A. S. (1993b). Young children's conceptualization of pretense: Action or mental representational state? *Child Development, 64,* 372–86.

Lillard, A. S., & Flavell, J. H. (1992). Young children's understanding of different mental states. *Developmental Psychology, 28,* 626–34.

Limber, J. (1973). The genesis of complex sentences. In T. E. Moore (Ed.), *Cognitive development and the acquisition of language* (pp. 169–85). New York: Academic Press.

Lucy, J. (1992). *Language diversity and thought: A reformulation of the linguistic relativity hypothesis.* New York: Cambridge University Press.

MacWhinney, B., & Snow, C. (1985). The child language data exchange system. *Journal of Child Language, 12,* 271–96.

MacWhinney, B., & Snow, C. (1990). The child language data exchange system: An update. *Journal of Child Language, 17,* 457–72.

Mandler, J. (1988). How to build a baby: On the development of an accessible representational system. *Cognitive Development, 3,* 113–36.

Mandler, J. M. (1992). How to build a baby. II: Conceptual primitives. *Psychological Review, 99,* 587–604.

Markus, H. R., & Kitayama, S. (1991). Culture and the self: Implications for cognition, emotion, and motivation. *Psychological Review, 98,* 224–53.

Marquez, G. G. (1988). *Love in the Time of Cholera.* New York: Knopf.

Marr, D. (1982). *Vision.* New York: W. H. Freeman.

McCarthy, D. (1930). The language development of the preschool child. In *Institute of Child Welfare Monograph Series*, No. 4. Minneapolis: University of Minnesota Press.

McCarthy, D. (1954). Language development in children. In L. Carmichael (Ed.), *Manual of Child Psychology, 2nd Ed.* (pp. 492–630). New York: Wiley.

McCune-Nicolich, L. M. (1981). Toward symbolic functioning: Structure of early use of pretend games and potential parallels with language. *Child Development, 52*, 785–97.

Miller, J. F., & Chapman, R. S. (1991). The relation between age and mean length of utterance in morphemes. *Journal of Speech and Hearing Research, 24*, 154–61.

Mitchell, P., & Lacohee, H. (1991). Children's early understanding of false belief. *Cognition, 39*, 107–127.

Moore, C., Furrow, D., Chiasson, L., & Patriquin, M. (1993). Developmental relationships between production and comprehension of mental terms. Unpublished ms.

Morton, A. (1980). *Frames of mind.* Oxford, England: Clarendon Press.

Moses, L. J. (1993). Young children's understanding of belief constraints on intention. *Cognitive Development, 8*, 1–25.

Moses, L. J., & Chandler, M. J. (1992). Traveler's guide to children's theories of mind. *Psychological Inquiry, 3*, 286–301.

Moses, L. J., & Flavell, J. H. (1990). Inferring false beliefs from actions and reactions. *Child Development, 61*, 929–45.

Nelson, K. (1973). Structure and strategy in learning to talk. *Monographs of the Society for Research in Child Development, 38*, No. 149 (entire serial).

Olson, P. R., Astington, J. W., & Harris, P. L. (1988). Introduction. In J. Astington, P. Harris, & D. Olson (Eds.), *Developing theories of mind* (pp. 1–15). New York: Cambridge University Press.

O'Neill, D. K., Astington, J. W., & Flavell, J. H. (1992). Young children's understanding of the role that sensory experiences play in knowledge acquisition. *Child Development, 63*, 474–90.

Perner, J. (1988). Developing semantics for theories of mind: From propositional attitudes to mental representations. In J. Astington, P. Harris, & D. Olson (Eds.), *Developing theories of mind* (pp. 141–72). New York: Cambridge University Press.

Perner, J. (1991). *Understanding the representational mind.* Cambridge, MA: MIT Press.

Perner, J., & Leekam, S. (1990). Photography versus color transmission: Zooming in on children's problem with "representation." Unpublished ms.

Perner, J., Leekam, S. R., & Wimmer, H. (1987). Three-year-olds' difficulty with false belief. *British Journal of Developmental Psychology, 5*, 125–37.

Piaget, J. (1929). *The child's conception of the world.* London: Routledge & Kegan Paul.

Piaget, J. (1932). *The moral judgement of the child.* London: Routledge & Kegan Paul.

Pillow, B. H. (1989). Early understanding of perception as a source of knowledge. *Journal of Experimental Child Psychology, 47*, 116–29.

Povinelli, D. J. (1993). Reconstructing the evolution of mind. *American Psychologist, 48*, 493–509.

Pratt, C., & Bryant, P. E. (1990). Young children understand that looking leads to knowing (so long as they are looking into a single barrel). *Child Development, 61*, 973–82.

Richards, M. M. (1982). Empiricism and learning to mean. In S. A. Kuczaj (Ed.), *Language development,* Vol. 1 (pp. 365–95). Hillsdale, NJ: Erlbaum.

Ridgeway, D., Waters, E., & Kuczaj, S. (1985). Acquisition of emotion-descriptive language: Receptive and productive vocabulary norms for ages 18 months to 6 years. *Developmental Psychology, 21*, 901–8.

Rothenberg, B. (1970). Children's social sensitivity and the relationship to interpersonal competence, intrapersonal comfort and intellectual level. *Developmental Psychology*, 2, 335–50.

Russell, J., Maunther, N., Sharpe, S., & Tidswell, T. (1991). The 'windows task' as a measure of strategic deception in preschoolers and autistic subjects. *British Journal of Developmental Psychology*, 9, 331–49.

Sachs, J. (1983). Talking about there and then: The emergence of displaced reference in parent–child discourse. In K. E. Nelson (Ed.), *Children's language*, Vol. 4 (pp. 1–28). Hillsdale, NJ: Earlbaum.

Searle, J. R. (1983). *Intentionality*. Cambridge, England: Cambridge University Press.

Shatz, M., Wellman, H. M., & Silber, S. (1983). The acquisition of mental verbs: A systematic investigation of first references to mental state. *Cognition*, 14, 301–21.

Shweder, R. A., Mahapatra, M., & Miller, J. G. (1987). Culture and moral development. In J. Kagan & S. Lamb (Eds.), *The emergence of morality in young children*, (pp. 1–83). Chicago, IL: University of Chicago Press.

Siegal, M. (1991). *Knowing children: Experiments in conversation and cognition*. Hove, England: Earlbaum.

Siegal, M., & Beattie, K. (1991). Where to look first for children's understanding of false beliefs. *Cognition*, 38, 1–12.

Siegal, R. S. (1991). *Children's thinking*. Englewood Cliffs, NJ: Prentice-Hall.

Siegler, R. S., & Crowley, K. (1991). The microgenetic method: A direct means of studying cognitive development. *American Psychologist*, 46, 606–20.

Smiley, P. A. (1987). The development of the concept of person: The young child's view of the other in action and in interaction. Unpublished Ph.D. dissertation, University of Chicago.

Smiley, P. A., & Huttenlocher, J. (1989). Young children's acquisition of emotion concepts. In C. Saarni & P. Harris (Eds.), *Children's understanding of emotion* (pp. 27–49). New York: Cambridge University Press.

Sodian, B. (1991). The development of deception in young children. *British Journal of Developmental Psychology*, 9, 173–88.

Sodian, B., Taylor, C., Harris, P. L., & Perner, J. (1991). Early deception and the child's theory of mind. *Child Development*, 62, 468–83.

Spelke, E. S. (1991). Physical knowledge in infancy. In S. Carey & R. Gelman (Eds.), *The epigenesis of mind: Essays on biology and cognition* (pp. 133–69). Hillsdale, NJ: Erlbaum.

Stern, C., & Stern, W. (1931). *Errinerung, Aussage, und Luge in der fruhen kindheit*, 4th ed. Leipzig, Germany: Barth.

Stern, D. N. (1985). *The interpersonal world of the infant*. New York: Basic Books.

Stich, S., & Nicholls, S. (1992). Folk psychology: Simulation or tacit theory? *Mind and Language*, 7, 35–71.

Trevarthen, C., & Hubley, P. (1978). Secondary intersubjectivity: Confidence, confiding and acts of meaning in the first year. In A. Lock (Ed.), *Action, gesture and symbol: The emergence of language* (pp. 183–229). New York: Academic Press.

Wellman, H. M. (1985). *Children's searching*. Hillsdale, NJ: Erlbaum.

Wellman, H. M. (1990). *The child's theory of mind*. Cambridge, MA: Bradford Books/MIT Press.

Wellman, H. M. (1991). From desires to beliefs: Acquisition of a theory of mind. In A. Whiten (Ed.), *Natural theories of mind: The evolution, development, and simulation of everyday mindreading* (pp. 19–38). Oxford, England: Basil Blackwell.

Wellman, H. M. (1993). Early understanding of mind: The normal case. In S. Baron-Cohen,

H. Tager-Flusberg , & D. J. Cohen (Eds.), *Understanding other minds: Perspectives from autism* (pp. 10–39). Oxford, England: Oxford University Press.

Wellman, H. M., & Banerjee, M. (1991). Mind and emotion: Children's understanding of the emotional consequences of beliefs and desires. *British Journal of Developmental Psychology, 9*, 191–224.

Wellman, H. M., & Bartsch, K. (1988). Young children's reasoning about beliefs. *Cognition, 30*, 239–77.

Wellman, H. M., & Estes, D. (1986). Early understanding of mental entities: A reexamination of childhood realism. *Child Development, 57*, 910–23.

Wellman, H. M., & Gelman, S. A. (1992). Cognitive development: Foundational theories of core domains. *Annual Review of Psychology, 43*, 337–75.

Wellman, H. M., Harris, P. L., Banerjee, M., & Sinclair, A. (in press). Early understanding of emotion: Evidence from natural language. *Cognition and Emotion.*

Wellman, H. M., & Hickling, A. K. (in press). The minds ''I'': Children's conception of the mind as an active agent. *Child Development.*

Wellman, H. M., & Kalish, C. (1991). Early understanding of intentional states. Paper presented at the meeting of the Society for Research in Child Development, Seattle, WA.

Wellman, H. M., & Woolley, J. D. (1990). From simple desires to ordinary beliefs: The early development of everyday psychology. *Cognition, 35*, 245–75.

Wierzbicka, A. (1994). Cognitive domains and the structure of the lexicon: The case of emotions. In L. A. Hirschfeld & S. Gelman (Eds.), *Mapping the mind: Domain specificity in cognition and culture* (pp. 431–52). New York: Cambridge University Press.

Wierzbicka A. (in press). Conceptual issues in the study of emotions (a semantic perspective). In J. A. Russell (Ed.), *Everyday conceptions of emotion.* Dordecht, The Netherlands: Kluwer.

Wimmer, H., & Hartl, M. (1991). Against the Cartesian view on mind: Young children's difficulty with own false beliefs. *British Journal of Developmental Psychology, 9*, 125–28.

Wimmer, H., Hogrefe, J., & Perner, J. (1988). Children's understanding of informational access as a source of knowledge. *Child Development, 59*, 386–96.

Wimmer, H., & Perner, J. (1983). Beliefs about beliefs: Representation and constraining function of wrong beliefs in young children's understanding of deception. *Cognition, 13*, 103–28.

Woolley, J. D., & Wellman, H. M. (1990). Young children's understanding of realities, nonrealities and appearances. *Child Development, 61*, 946–61.

Woolley, J. D., & Wellman, H. M. (1993). Origin and truth: Young children's understanding of imaginary mental representations. *Child Development, 64*, 1–17.

Zaitchik, D. (1990). When representations conflict with reality: The preschooler's problem with false beliefs and ''false'' photographs. *Cognition, 35*, 41–68.

Zaitchik, D. (1991). Is only seeing really believing? Sources of true belief in the false belief task. *Cognitive Development, 6*, 91–103.

INDEX

Actions
  belief-desire reasoning and, 6
  beliefs and, 9
  desires and, 10, 65, 66, 68, 87–88
  explanations, 112–22
    beliefs/desires and, 149–50
    explicit, 116–18
    that go against own desires, 171–72
  goal-directed, expressed by desire
      terms, 75–77
  intentional, desires and, 89, 91
  predicting
    based on belief, 201–2
    based on desire, 154–55, 157–59
    first-person experience and, 175–81
    Fodor's theory, 185–86
  successful, use of *know* to describe, 59,
      60
  understanding, 13
    culture and, 210
Adults. *See also* Parent-child talk
  imaginings and, 150
Advance-belief contrastives, 51, 54, 56–
    57, 100, 196–97
Advance-desire contrastives, 89–91
Affective role-taking tasks, 137, 140
Afraid (that), uses of, 65, 72
Age, use for charting developmental
    sequences, 147–48
Arguments, 122–26. *See also* Conflicts
Arousal, desires *vs.*, 65–66
Autistic children, 125–26
  belief-desire reasoning in, 193

Behavior. *See* Actions
Behavioral references
  to desires, 67, 68
  expressed by desire terms, 75
  using *care*, 72
Belief-desire psychology, culture and,
    209–11
Belief-desire reasoning, 5–7, 154

development in children, 8
Fodor's theory and, 185, 186
3-year-olds and, 200–204
universality of, 210
Beliefs. *See also* Beliefs, talk about
  child's language and, 17
  children's understanding of, 9–10
  "copy" understanding of, 203
  definition, 5
  "direction of fit," 15
  as distinguished from desires, 15
  explaining actions and, 149
  "falsifiable," 196–97
  false, 37, 55, 56, *See also* False beliefs
    expressed by contrastives, 50
  genuine references to, 31–32, 34, 38–
      44
  as intentional states, 37
  past, 193
  predicting, first-person experience and,
      175–81
  as reflections of real world, 14, 37
  as representational, 13–14, 152
  research on the mind and, 9
  thinking-of *vs.* thinking-that, 197
  value *vs.* fact, 101–2
    3-year olds' understanding of, 169
  verbs that express, 25–30
Beliefs, talk about, 10–11, 37–64
  children's verbal ability and, 132–33,
      136
  complexity of, 103–4
  contrastives, 44–49. *See also*
      Contrastives
  conversational *vs.* psychological uses,
      103
  Dunn's research, 138
  emergence, 96
  to explain actions, 112–22
    thought-reality contrastives and,
        119–20
  expressing conflicts, 122–26

About the Authors

KAREN BARTSCH is Assistant Professor of Psychology at the University of Wyoming.

HENRY M. WELLMAN is Professor of Psychology and Research Scientist at the University of Michigan.